Data Governance

How to Design, Deploy, and Sustain an Effective Data Governance Program

Data Governance
How to Design, Deploy, and Sustain an Effective Data Governance Program

John Ladley

AMSTERDAM • BOSTON • HEIDELBERG • LONDON
NEW YORK • OXFORD • PARIS • SAN DIEGO
SAN FRANCISCO • SINGAPORE • SYDNEY • TOKYO

Morgan Kaufmann Publishers is an imprint of Elsevier

Acquiring Editor: Andrea Dierna
Development Editor: Robin Day
Project Manager: André A. Cuello
Designer: Kristen Davis

Morgan Kaufmann is an imprint of Elsevier
225 Wyman Street, Waltham, MA 02451, USA

Library of Congress Cataloging-in-Publication Data
Application submitted

British Library Cataloguing-in-Publication Data
A catalogue record for this book is available from the British Library.

ISBN: 978-0-12-415829-0

For information on all MK publications
visit our website at http://store.elsevier.com

Printed in the United States of America
12 13 14 15 16 17   10 9 8 7 6 5 4 3 2 1

Dedication

To Pam
…..more today than yesterday, but not as much as tomorrow
Tum tee tum tum, tum tee tummmmmm …………..

Contents

Foreword

It takes a special kind of person to really LIKE data governance. After all, this discipline exists at the epicenter of data-related conflict. Day after day, we see how seemingly small actions and decisions create data-related problems that ripple out through an organization, creating bigger problems in reports and other information products, which create even bigger problems in the form of bad decisions, inefficiencies, ineffective practices, noncompliance with laws and regulations, and even security breaches. We stand our ground, watching these problems as they are created, as they grow, and as they impact our organizations' abilities to meet their missions. We engage the people around us, trying to educate them about how to avoid creating those problems, how to find them, and how to fix them. We work with C-suite executives, individual data workers, and everyone in between, preaching the same message over and over: *"You don't have to live with the consequences of bad data. Let us show you a different way."*

But, frankly, most people don't want to hear it.

Most don't love data for its own sake, just for what it does for them. Most people hear the word "governance" and have a negative—even visceral—reaction. Their rational mind might be promoting the idea that "Big G" governance mechanisms (policies, mandates, standards, control objectives, and other types of rules) are necessary. They might rationally agree that "little g" governance mechanisms (controls) are essential. Still, their nonrational, emotional, primal brains will be reacting predictably to any constraints, calling for the listener to fight, flee, or play opossum.

So imagine how delighted I was to meet John Ladley, someone who addresses the human aspects of governance adoption from an anthropologist's perspective, its strategic aspects from an executive's perspective, and its operational aspects from a practitioner's perspective.

I think I heard John laugh before I ever heard him speak. It was at a conference, and someone had just said, "No, they don't want the responsibility [of data governance], but they don't want anyone else to have it either!" John's laugh was contagious, and his face lit up at this example of human nature. He followed up with some words of wisdom regarding organizational change management, and we got into an extended discussion about details concerning some information management strategy that I don't remember now. Later, I discovered that his thought leadership came from a vendor-neutral perspective and a strong sense of intellectual integrity. John has been a part of my personal "Kitchen Cabinet"—as well as a personal friend—ever since.

The funny thing about data governance is that it is both old and new. When I was working in publishing in the 1980s, we didn't have automated workflows. We had hundreds of chunks of information that had to go through multiple iterations and alterations before finally being compiled into a magazine with a specific number of pages. If our content chunks weren't well governed, we couldn't deliver our product. Our mailing lists and other structured data had to be well governed, or we couldn't operate. Oh yes—ask anyone who was working in publishing (or working with mainframes) 30 years ago, and they'll tell you: Data governance was just a part of doing your job back then.

It was the rapid explosion of IT that changed things. In the rush to move to client-server, web-based, and other game-changing technologies, many organizations lost both "Big G" and "little g" capabilities. The focus of IT became the "T" (technology). In rapidly evolving organizations, it seemed like no one group was responsible for the "I" (information). Things got messy, and then they got messier. Somehow, the problem got labeled as poor collaboration between "Business" and "IT." It took the Sarbanes–Oxley Act of 2002 and an ever-increasing number of data breaches to direct attention back to data and the need to properly govern it.

While John and I (and others on the same conference circuit) had many enjoyable discussions about this "new emerging field" of data governance, I have to confess that I really didn't get why John was also devoting his time to writing his previous book on EIM (enterprise information management). After all, I said, the fields of data management and document/content management are pretty well defined. Do we really need this new acronym? Do we need a new book on the topic?

As it turns out, we did. John brought to that book an important new perspective. This work was not merely instruction for data geeks who loved their little slice of data heaven and were happy to learn about other slices. No, his book also looked at this broad field from the perspective of someone who is used to managing large and important resources for the betterment of an enterprise. This was "Business meets Information Management," with a lot of detail. Yes, it needed to be written. And I was glad John did.

The visits to the Data Governance Institute's website told the story of the ever-growing number of people who were getting engaged in governance. And even though more and more of my consulting time turned to helping organizations with strategies, I wanted to talk about data governance practices. Selfishly, I was glad when John wasn't working on his EIM book any more so we could have DG discussions. In a world where governance has so many focus points, and so many different "flavors," I would ask him, what is universal? What is situational? What is need-to-have, and what is nice-to-have?

John is a man of action, so he often countered my topics with ones about specific activities and action plans: the HOW of data governance.

In the past several years, much has been written about why organizations need data governance, and who should do what, and how to sell the concept to those with the budget to fund projects and programs. Much has also been written from tool vendors' perspectives, and much has been written from a motivational perspective. But not much has been written about the details of WHAT to do, and WHEN, and HOW. The world needed a big detailed instruction manual—one that would be relevant in many situations, for the many "flavors" of data governance.

I'm glad John Ladley has written it.

Gwen Thomas
Founder and President
The Data Governance Institute
www.datagovernance.com

Preface

There are two reasons I wrote this book. First, when my previous book came out I realized that data governance as a topic had taken a back seat. This was due to limitations on the size of the book. The data governance chapter was comprehensive enough to get a sense of what was needed in the context of enterprise information management, but it was not enough to really help someone launch their own governance program. Close, but not quite. My firm is very fortunate to have done data governance deployment many times, so we have plenty of material to share.

Second, the blind rage that motivated me to write book one—*Making EIM Work for Business*—continues unabated. This is a bit tongue in cheek, but only to a point. My company is doing a significant amount of EIM and data governance work. Companies are beginning to see that data and information require more than just tools to move and cast data about the company. However, realizing you need to do something, and then sucking it up and actually doing it are two different things. I find many organizations are very good at saying, "We are going to do better with data," and they present myriad reasons and justifications for this. But their follow-through is abysmal. Then they go out and buy front-end tools for delivering and presenting the information. At the time this was being written, vendors were spending gobs of marketing dollars on the value of analytics and "big data." Companies are drinking the Kool-Aid™ deeply, but very few reap the anticipated benefits.

There is also a huge wave of master data management projects underway. CIOs identify the need to create the "single source of truth" and buy tools and collect data, and then ask the business to change over. About 20% of them show some success at this time.

To be candid, the disappointing results from both of these types of projects are entirely due to the lack of management of the data going into these products. It is unsuited for its purpose (in other words, it's junk).

The aforementioned lack of follow-through is the root cause. We know that the vendors are doing what they do—selling stuff and moving on. We see IT shops buy tools before having any business connection or alignment. We know CIOs have to work in environments where they are not permitted to communicate with their business peers, do not get any support when business habits need to change to be successful, and are incented by delivering on time regardless of quality. Yet they are also told to get the data in shape anyway.

The required follow-through sounds simple—start to treat information as an asset. But when we look into the details of information asset management, we see that organizations need to do data governance. Period.

Even a modicum of discipline will reap benefits. When you examine successful master data efforts, you see business alignment and data quality in place, all sustained by data governance. When you examine an almost identical effort where data governance was not applied or was implemented poorly, you see the failures. So deploying data governance is a no-brainer, right?

Sadly, no. As you will discover in the pages ahead, data governance is not setting up some processes and policies and enforcing some rules. These are certainly critical components of data governance, and you can enjoy some success by doing the mechanics of data governance, but data governance will not stick unless you take a much more personal and intimate approach.

This book is for those who need to "do data governance." It is not for IT, it is not for business. It is for anyone who has to make sure information management is happening. To be clear, this is a "how to" book. I tried very hard to eliminate the bromides you can easily hear from a tool vendor or big-name consultant. If you are reading this book, you have heard the platitudes, embraced them, and now want to do something about it instead of talking.

Pundits of all types will talk about the twenty-first century being the era of information and the use of data, and cite its huge dependence on analytics. However, if we continue to treat data as the ugly lubricant of departmental business processes instead of the precious asset it is, we will come nowhere near to fulfilling these forecasts. None of it is possible without this significant change in mindset where day-to-day habits in the treatment of data and information change. Here are some real scenarios you should consider:

- Running a business on 40,000 Access™ databases and consolidated statements from spreadsheets is not considered acceptable by Wall Street. (This is true. A leading financial services company had us do an assessment and we stopped counting at 40,000 Access databases.)
- Expediting a business process or completing a departmental project is no longer measured by completion time or cycle time. They are also measured by data quality metrics and adherence to asset management policy.
- Rather than throw up your hands and start building departmental databases in Access or Excel due to perceived delays, business leaders work with IT and information managers to get the data right. In other words, take the time to be right the first time versus doing it over—again and again and again.
- Application developers are no longer rewarded for the on-time completion of projects if they do not meet data control and quality standards at the same time.
- Business users are flat out not allowed to produce a report that leaves the enterprise unless it has gone through an approved process for creation and verification.

The term *maturity* is often tossed about in the context of managing information. This book was written with that in mind, but also with another scale—that of learning maturity. My weekend hobby is aviation. I also teach other people how to fly, and I learned a great definition for learning when I became a flight instructor:

Learning occurs when you see a change in behavior as a result of experience.

In other words, just hearing about something is not going to create learning. You need to do it, develop experience, and then look and measure for the change. Frankly, most companies I deal with want a two-week assessment, a four-week road map, and then they somehow think these artifacts and a few hearty commands from management will work miracles. Data governance will require some work and some significant behavior changes. So this book is written with an eye toward changing behavior, and assimilating and managing the work to be done.

The following pages present the steps, artifacts, techniques, and insights developed by my companies over the past 20 years or so. Some of this material can be incredibly dry, so if I sprinkle in a story or amusing metaphor, it is not because I am overly glib. It is because I really want you to pay attention. *This stuff really matters.* Your organization is going to live or die based on how it deals with data. You can do ERP, buy business intelligence tools, or attempt sophisticated analytics. But unless you manage what is going into the infrastructure and control what comes out, you will never be sure you are doing anything correctly.

The following chapters present a comprehensive view of the work and behaviors required to implement data governance. The longer you delay the adoption of some or all of the elements and components, the harder and harder your information management challenges will become. Does your organization want to do advanced predictive analytics? You had better know that the data used by the analytics tools is accurate. Do you want to create single sources of truth for reporting, business intelligence, or just getting your customer list nailed down? Then you need to start data governance *now*. The longer you wait, the harder the decisions will be as the data explosion continues. This is not a trivial request from someone who likes working with data. This is a business imperative.

You will see that data governance can be accomplished by executing a series of steps along with consideration of certain success factors. There are plenty of "nuts-and-bolts" activities to be performed. But there are also cultural, personal, and philosophical changes required to truly treat information as an asset. Data governance is the discipline that encapsulates these changes—but it is also a *long-term commitment to doing business differently.*

Acknowledgments

In the preface, the pronoun "I" is used, but you will notice that in the rest of the book I use "we." This is because I was not the only person doing all of this work over the last 20 years! A lot of battlefield experience is contained in this book—and the people in the trenches with me contributed immensely.

My co-workers and partners in information management and data governance are, or were, Val Torstenson, Ellen Levin, Larry Michael, Richard Lee, John Lee, Donn Vucovich, and Jim Hankemeyer. I must also thank Pam Thomas for educating me as to the finer points of organizational change management as a critical piece of successful information management work. Those behavior changes I referenced in the preface do not happen by themselves. Plus, the topic has become popular on the conference circuit since she and I embedded change management in our classes.

It takes a lot of air cover to do a book while the dragons of commerce are circling. I would like to thank James Kern, Amit Baghat, Michael Demos, and Martin Davies for covering my back on the administrative and client service side of things.

Many thanks to the group who participated in the editing and finishing: Danette McGilvray, Michelle Koch, and Marilyn Thompson for their review and feedback; and Sheila Hultgren and Pam Thomas for their editing. Usually I get to take a span of time to go hide and finish my books. This one required a lot of hotel room and airline time, so I really appreciate the contributions of my reviewers and editors.

I also appreciate and extend thanks to Gwen Thomas for taking the time to write the foreword. Gwen has the rare ability to explain abstract concepts in a clear and relevant fashion and also deliver solutions. Gwen took a sub-discipline of information management and started to give it the attention it required as a stand-alone subject.

I also have to thank my customers who trusted my companies enough to do data governance and information management for them. In particular, the fine people at Erie Insurance, Wal-Mart, and Salt River Project come to mind. Three very different data governance scenarios and very different challenges not only made our work fun, but also really stretched our creativity. In particular, John Collier, Steve Pettinger, Audrey Wiggins, Alan Jamison, Terry Mooney, Greg Whicker, Jim Viveralli, and Felix Orzechowski shared some significant challenges over the past few years.

Many thanks to the various people I get to hang with that share the label of guru or thought leader. They create the forums and intellectual basis for the evolution of data governance as an embedded business function. Tony Shaw has gone above and beyond the call to create conferences and forums that genuinely add value and present great content. Rob Seiner and his newsletter have been the "go to" site for thousands of information management practitioners. Rob and I have also proved that Pittsburgh can turn out very smart and clever people as well as incredible football teams. Dr. Tom Redman is another great guru to work with who is maybe more candid than I am. And thanks goes to Davida Berger for creating the data governance conferences.

Most importantly, if it weren't for Pam Thomas—my business partner, colleague, significant other, and total Sweetie—this would not have happened. Even when I felt the book needed to be delayed or even stopped due to external forces, she would not let me quit. Pam wrote big chunks of Chapters 12 and 13, but declined to be mentioned on the cover. A lot of men would run screaming from the room if they had to work with their wife or partner. I am blessed to live with *and* be able to work with the Love of My Life.

Our opinions do not really blossom into fruition until we have expressed them to someone else.
—**Mark Twain**

INTRODUCTION

While the main purpose of this book is to give the reader a solid head start on the deployment, implementation, or "standing up" of a data (or information) governance program, it is also intended to supplement all other literature written about data governance. If you have a data governance program in place, but it is faltering, there is still plenty of advice in the following pages. In the following chapters, every attempt was made to keep the positions and processes disclosed as neutral as possible. In addition to a large amount of background, definitions, and preferred practices, this book will present a generic version of the steps and activities required to deploy data governance. Some case study examples and a few artifacts will help tie the process together. There are templates included in the appendices as well that serve as starting points for the various deliverables and artifacts that you may need to create, or as supplements for existing programs that may not have addressed all of the necessary factors required for success.

The content in this book represents what we have been doing in our practice over the years. That is why the pronoun "we" is used by the author.[1] A lot of experience and refinement has gone into the material you are about to read. These processes are not the ramblings of one person as to what should be done. This material is battle-tested. Some of the material may vary from other published methods. Where this is the case, we try and point it out.

For example, Gwen Thomas of the Data Governance Institute has a defined data governance life cycle. It is focused on the entire life cycle, from learning about DG to selling the concept to implementing. We focus on implementation.

There are two intended audiences, and for this reason the book is assembled into two layers. The next three chapters (2 through 4) can be considered an executive overview, suitable for CIOs and other organizational leadership. The remainder of the book provides the details to move forward. In this way, a project manager can read the book from start to finish, but a senior leader will also find value by reading Chapters 1–4.

There is a secondary purpose to this book, which is to absolutely convince you, the reader, that data governance (DG or IG) is *not* a new kind of IT or technology project. In addition, DG is not an accumulative program—that is, if done correctly, you do not need to add an eternally funded requirement for manpower and capital. In fact, the perfect deployment of DG will result in nearly or absolutely no visible separate DG area. Therefore, while this book may seem to be a simple "how to," it

---

[1]An early reviewer remarked that we were "channeling Gollum." What a precious comment!

is also unabashedly a treatise to convince organizations to think differently about how to manage their information and data universe. To be clear, real data governance requires that organizations act differently in regard to their use and management of content, meaning data, information, documents, media, et al. You implement data governance by overseeing the management of these instances of content, as well as projects and processes that create, use, and dispose of content.

This book does not distinguish between *data governance* and *information governance*, although some authors do. From a practical viewpoint, there is no real difference. We could conjure up some philosophical argument that there is a difference, but experience has shown these discussions only serve to confuse and reduce the effectiveness of the program.

Data governance is absolutely a mandatory requirement for success if an organization wants to achieve master data management,[2] build business intelligence, improve data quality, or manage documents. However, DG is not an eternally lasting add-on process. This may seem contrary to much of the literature flying about the information industry at the time of this book's writing. There are many articles, for example, on how to design the DG "department," when you are really designing a framework to govern.

At the end of the day, we are modifying people's behaviors and business processes to think more clearly about the care and feeding of data. If we do this correctly, there is no need for large incremental groups of people implementing something brand new. Organizations love to jump on bandwagons and then bang on the "next big thing" until it surrenders. Frankly, this book is determined to prevent that. When it comes to data governance, the devil is in the mindset (as well as in the details).

As stated earlier, the next three chapters form an executive-oriented section. The purpose is to provide background, value proposition, and business relevance.

Chapter 2 will first establish a common vocabulary. The author's practice in this area has determined that the slightest variations in semantics can become huge obstacles. Therefore, we will present a set of terms and definitions as well as context. We will always provide the context of the term as well as refer to the definition. That way, if you read another version of a term like "policy," you at least have a frame of reference.

We will also stick to business terminology. If there is a technical aspect of a topic, it will be presented in business terms. If there is a business metaphor to lock in a point, it will be used in place of a technology metaphor.

Once we establish the terminology, we will cover the basic elements of the DG or IG program. We will present the core managerial and business concepts required for building and operating a DG program. Since DG is a business program, you may feel quite at home reviewing the various pieces and intersections of people, processes, and information technology.

Please thoughtfully read the text that addresses the *scope* of DG. One of the most critical errors that can be made while designing a DG program occurs when an organization has the initial conversation on scope and priorities. This examination also segues into a discussion on the business role of DG. The value proposition of DG needs to be clearly understood by executives if DG is to be successful. Finally, this part of the book is important because if data governance is misunderstood, it leads to a tendency to jam it into another box on the organization chart of the IT department, and this is often a fatal mistake.

The *elements*, *scope*, and *business* role sections are part of an overall segment that provides an overview of the entire DG program. It continues with a detailed examination of who should do the

---

[2]If you are unfamiliar with the terms master data, data quality, and so on, relax—we will define them in the next chapter.

governing, what activities they need to perform, what is actually governed, and how DG looks when it occurs.

The first three chapters present an effective executive-level overview of deploying data governance so a CEO would have enough confidence to hand the book to a subordinate with instructions to develop a plan of attack. In essence, the first section of the book covers the higher levels of business thinking. If we were to view the realm of an enterprise's information architecture as a matrix representing the conceptual view through the physical, we might say the first few chapters address the top two levels of the matrix, or framework.[3] In other words, we cover DG deployment from a conceptual and logical view. Figure 1-1 shows this.

The next few chapters address the middle layers from a level of orientation and understanding. Layer two starts with two chapters suitable for management as well. Chapter 4 talks about the value proposition of DG and Chapter 5 presents an overview of the process to deploy the DG program.

The start of the second layer (Chapter 4) starts with a topic that merits its own chapter, and that is the *business case for DG*. Very often clients will ask for assistance in developing a return on investment (ROI) for a DG program. In most organizations, the largest obstacle to starting DG is the selling—or a business case. This chapter will cover tangible and intangible business drivers for DG. Frankly, developing an ROI for a program like data governance is usually done to accommodate a lack of understanding, political posturing, or plain old resistance to anything perceived as "new." DG is not a "project" that will grant a traditional return. DG does add value, and stating this as part of a business case is about the best way there is to frame its value proposition. We will also leverage the chapter on the business case to learn how to identify the metrics we will use to sustain the DG program.

KEY CONCEPT

As you read, you will occasionally come across a highlighted section (like this). These will be labeled "Key Concept," "Helpful Hint," or "Success Factor." They are there to reinforce the author's point, either through highlighting a point or by presenting an anecdote. For example, the reason that the business case for DG is not traditional lies in its nature. Justifying DG with an ROI-type calculation is like asking your accounting department or even your governing board of directors to justify its existence every year with a stated rate of return tied to a cash flow. You are attempting to justify something in a way that is inconsistent with how it operates. Then again, there is an appeal to the idea of a board of directors justifying itself with an ROI from time to time!

It is important to understand Chapter 5 and the context of the concepts from Chapter 2. If you want to dive into the list of tasks to get you from point A to point B (Chapters 6–13) go right ahead, but you will end up returning to Chapters 2 and 5 to figure out why you are being asked to do certain things at certain times.

Chapters 6–13 review the details of each phase of the process we use to deploy data governance. The activities, tasks, work products, and artifacts are reviewed. To the extent space permits, we present examples and ideas for how to actually execute the activities. Please understand at this point that

---

[3]Figure 1-1 presents a modified view of a common framework us information geeks use to keep track of where it is we are working. It is called the Zachman framework (after the guy who thought it up) and many thanks to John for allowing us to use it. It is an effective presentation to explain how an enterprise needs to link conceptual thinking to physical implementation, which is why we included it.

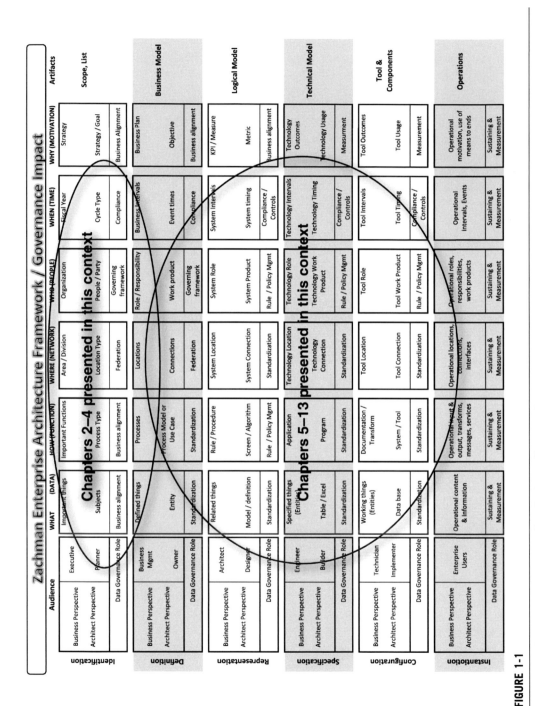

FIGURE 1-1

The scope of this book via the modified Zachman Framework.

a book like this can easily swell to 500 or more pages, so we need to strike a balance between education and writing a cookbook.

Please note that Chapters 12 and 13 focus heavily on managing the behavioral and organization changes required of DG. This is not a culture change management textbook, although reading one of those is advisable. We do delve heavily into those types of activities in the context of DG. Do not take them lightly. If you do not manage the changes associated with DG, you will fail.

Chapter 14 concludes our material with an overview of the technology for data governance, where we will cover what kind of technologies—such as workflow, enterprise architecture, modeling, collaboration, content management, and others—can provide.

We summarize everything in Chapter 15. Under the mantra of "tell them what you are going to tell them, tell them, then tell them what you told them," we will cover a handful of mandatory takeaway concepts. In addition to the usual list of CSF-type bromides, you will find a lot of bullet points you can use for marketing and sustaining your data governance program.

It is our fervent hope you find value on starting and sustaining your data governance effort within these pages. If you already have one, we hope you find some good tidbits in here to give you some ideas and make your success sustainable. If you have any ideas or feedback, please visit the Wiki we have at www.makingeimworkforbusiness.com. Thank you for taking the time and energy to read this book.

Definitions and concepts

Metaphors are hard to implement.
—**John Ladley**

While this chapter is titled *Definitions and concepts*, it is much more than a glossary or repeat of DG bromides. We need to spend some time on the deeper concepts behind the terms that influence the processes to be presented. Also, rather than present a definition and just let it sit there, we will talk about how the term or concept fits into practical data governance practice. In addition, wherever a term or concept is being used in different ways in the real world, we will point out the differences. Either way, we will determine one definition of all the terms you will need to know to get through the remainder of the book. Data governance (DG) is part of a larger discipline that has traditionally been called *enterprise information management* (EIM). In fact, most confusion about the meaning of data governance stems from there being slightly differing views as to how it fits into information management.

Information management is commonly defined and understood as stated in the *Data Management Body of Knowledge*, or DMBOK, for short. The DMBOK labels data management as synonymous with information management. This is fine since we have taken the position that data, information, and content (documents, media, et al.) are all the same fodder for data governance. For the remainder of this book, information management, data management, and content management, as well as data governance, information governance, and content governance, all point to the same concepts and activities.

KEY CONCEPT:

Where possible, we will use the DMBOK definitions unless the definition is not contained in the DMBOK, or industry trends have obviously altered the definition of a term. Even if the author disagrees with DMBOK, we will forge ahead with DMBOK, and work around any heartburn!

CONCEPTS BEHIND DATA GOVERNANCE

Rather than start with the term "data governance," we have to start with what and where is governing happening. Therefore, before we dig into definitions specific to the world of data governance, there are three interrelated and key concepts or terms that need to be understood. They are:

- Data (Information) Management
- Enterprise Information Management
- Data (Information) Architecture

Data Management (DM)

According to the DMBOK, data management is:

1. The business function that develops and executes plans, policies, practices, and projects that acquire, control, protect, deliver, and enhance the value of data and information.
2. A program for implementation and performance of the data management function.
3. The field of disciplines required to perform the data management function.
4. The profession of individuals who perform data management disciplines.
5. In some cases, a synonym for a *data management services* organization that performs data management activities.
6. [i]

Within the context of DG, the reader needs to latch onto these key terms embedded in this definition:

- *Business Function*—Twenty-first–century business and beyond requires organizations to stop looking at data, information, etc., as a convenience. As this book was being written, the author counted four news stories in technology and business publications where mishandling of data had cost business or government organizations enormous sums of money.[ii]
- *Program–Data/Information*—DG is not a project with a discreet start or end point. Once initiated, it needs to operate under a "going concern" concept. Other forms of governance, such as regulatory compliance, are permanent structures. DG is the same.
- *Discipline*—Governance, by its very definition, implies a predetermined rigor. In the early days of computer applications development, new systems analysts often asked, "How do we enforce standards?" The word "enforce" was considered too harsh at the time. Frankly, however, governance is a process that, in part, has an enforcement component—follow the rules, maintain discipline, or expect consequences.

The key concept to take away here is that there is a disciplined, formal process to *manage data*. This is the beginning requirement.

Enterprise Information Management

The DMBOK definition of DM or IM is generic and does require some clarification when talking about an enterprise-level program. This is because, historically, formal data or information management turns out to be a localized function. Any IT group can be more disciplined with information within a specific application or business function. However, in this book the term *enterprise information management* (EIM) is reserved solely for an *enterprise*-level program. Therefore, we need to have a separate definition and concept.

EIM is the program that manages enterprise information assets to support the business and improve value. EIM manages the plans, policies, principles, frameworks, technologies, organizations, people, and processes in an *enterprise* toward the goal of maximizing the investment in data and content.

---

[i]Mosely, Mark, Editor, "The DAMA Dictionary of Data Management," New Jersey, Technics Publications, LLC, 2008.
[ii]Extracts from CNN, *The Wall Street Journal* for August 20–22, 2011. California state medical privacy breach, German Facebook discussion.

FIGURE 2-1

EIM overview.

You cannot deploy EIM by department. EIM represents more of the direction, philosophy, and mindset required to manage data assets. As defined here, information or data management represents the day-to-day "stuff" that actually has to be done to achieve the information asset management. Information management (or data management) is simply the program that manages information as a recognized and formal asset. EIM is the enterprise-level support and mindset (Figure 2-1).

Data Architecture

Another term often heard within a conversation related to IM or DG is *data* or *information architecture*. The DMBOK definition of information architecture, or data architecture, is somewhat convoluted and tilted toward a technical explanation. The entire definition can be read in the DMBOK, but it is summarized next:

1. A master set of *data models* and design approaches identifying the strategic *data requirements* and the components of data management solutions, usually at an enterprise level.

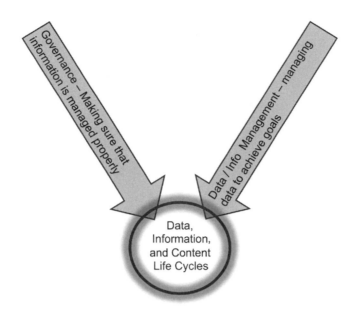

FIGURE 2-2

The Governance V.

2. The "data" column of the Zachman Framework for Enterprise Architecture identifies six different classes of design artifacts, each representing a different level of abstraction. (Note: This is not exactly a business definition like we promised. See Chapter 1 for an explanation of Zachman.)

3. In some common usage, the physical technology infrastructure supporting data management, including database servers, data replication tools, and middleware.

The author would never use the preceding definition when educating management as DG is deployed. Rather, a much simpler version would be used:

• Information architecture is the diagram or picture of the information management environment, its components, and their interactions. This picture, or abstraction, interrelates the framework, people, processes, projects, policies, technologies, and procedures to manage and use valuable enterprise information assets.

  The details of an information architecture would contain elements such as:
  ○ Models, or some other visual abstraction, of how the bits of "stuff" that are used to manage data actually fit together.
  ○ A catalog of standards, which lists the allowable formats, presentation, and uses of data.
  ○ Description of the organization managing data (or information).
  ○ Value statement of the architecture that aligns business priorities and technology.
  ○ Within the context of DG, the information architecture contains an expression of what is actually governed.

DATA GOVERNANCE AND GOVERNANCE

The concept of managing information assets in a formal manner has been established. Now we need a process to ensure that management actually takes place—and is being done correctly. Unplug your technology thinking and turn on your accountant thinking. Accountants manage financial assets. Accountants are governed by a set of principles and policies and are checked by auditors. Auditing ensures the correct management practice of financial assets. This is what data governance (DG) accomplishes for data, information, and content assets.

DG is defined in the DMBOK as, "The exercise of authority, control, and shared decision making (planning, monitoring and enforcement) over the management of data assets." In turn, governance is defined as, "The exercise of authority and control over a process, organization or geopolitical area. The process of setting, controlling, and administering and monitoring conformance with policy."[1] This definition is, of course, roughly synonymous with government.

Slightly different definitions are often stated with an emphasis on the policy and programmatic aspects of DG. The one we use in our consulting work is, "Data governance is the organization and implementation of policies, procedures, structure, roles, and responsibilities which outline and enforce rules of engagement, decision rights, and accountabilities for the effective management of information assets." Regardless of style of definition, the bottom line is that DG is the use of authority combined with policy to ensure the proper management of information assets.

Make sure you do not confuse the *management* of data with *ensuring data is managed*. Let's introduce a concept we will expand throughout this book. We call it the **"Governance V."** (See Figure 2-2).

The left side of the V is governance—providing input to data and content life cycles as to what the rules and policies are, and activity to ensure that data management is happening as it is supposed to. The right side is the actual "hands on"—the managers and executive who are actually doing the information management. The left side is DG, the right side is IM. It is absolutely essential that you keep this next phrase in mind all through your data governance program:

Data governance is NOT a function performed by those who manage information.

This means there must always be a separation of duties between those who manage and those who govern. The V is a visual reminder of this. This is a key concept that business people understand, and IT staff often experience as a problem. For example, in business there are auditors and managers. Managers control, monitor, and ensure work gets done and rules and standards are adhered to. Auditors verify compliance to standards, and define and implement new controls and standards as required. This is exactly the same protocol that is required by data governance. The DG "area" identifies required controls, policies, and processes, and develops rules. Information managers (essentially everyone else) adhere to the rules.

At the confluence of the two lines (the bottom of the V) are the activities that operate the organization through maintaining information life cycles—creation, use, manipulation, and eventual disposal of data, information, and content.

HELPFUL HINT

Keep a version of the Governance V around all the time—you will be amazed at how much it helps.

---

[1]Cite from DMBOK.

An internal definition of DG would take the generic definition of DG, incorporate the Governance V, and tune it to a definition more specific or relevant to an organization. For example:

> *"Data governance represents the program used by ACME to manage the organizational bodies, policies, principles, and quality that will ensure access to accurate and risk-free data and information. Data governance will establish standards, accountabilities, responsibilities, and ensure that data and information usage achieves maximum value to ACME while managing the cost and quality of information handling. Data governance will enforce the consistent, integrated, and disciplined use of information at ACME."*

SOME ADDITIONAL DEFINITION EXAMPLES:

DG is a business process separate from Data (or Information) Management that affects the entire business. *(Data Strategy Journal, October 2007)*

Data Governance is a framework of accountabilities and processes for making decisions and monitoring the execution of data management. *(financial organization)*

…using a horizontal perspective of the organization and focusing on the major "pain points" for our business areas. *(financial services)*

…designating People, Process and Technology. *(Data Strategy Journal)*

…the orchestration of people, process, and technology to enable the leveraging of data as an enterprise asset. It affects all organizational areas by lines of business, functional areas and geographies. *(software company)*

…using rules, monitoring and enforcement with culturally acceptable techniques. *(Data Strategy Journal)*

…a system of decision rights and accountabilities for information-related processes, executed according to agreed-upon models which describe who can take what actions with what information, and when, under what circumstances, using what methods. *(consultant)*

To be clear, it is the exercise of executive authority over business data. *(chemical company)*

At this point, we have explained the concepts of EIM, IM, and DG (see Figure 2-3). It is perfectly understandable that the reader might be thinking, "So what?" However, the time taken to review these concepts is worth it—not for a business person who is reading this book, but for an IT person. Frankly, any businessperson understands these concepts when presented in the context of "hard" assets. Besides the accounting metaphor, we can also use a supply chain metaphor (Figure 2-4).

FIGURE 2-3

EIM Concepts Related.

FIGURE 2-4

Supply Chain Metaphor.

So, for the sake of review:

- EIM is the program similar to supply chain management—an overall philosophy of management toward a goal of efficiency.
- DG is like auditing. Rules, standards, and policies are defined and verified. Data governance is the QA/audit/compliance aspect of EIM. DG designs the rules that information is managed by. IM does the managing.
- IM is like, well, IM. Information management is the same as inventory management—the actual touching, moving, tracking, and managing activities of the assets.

SOLUTIONS

In addition to the aforementioned concepts in this chapter, there are concepts and terms you need to understand that are more related to various business solutions that DG will support. Before we look at the specific types of solutions, however, we need to understand one key theme related to all of these solutions: *regardless of the type of data or content being governed, data governance is essentially done the same way.* That is, from a "how to" data governance perspective, none of the solutions we are defining make a bit of difference in how you deploy data governance.

The three areas that require and usually trigger data governance programs are:

- Master Data Management
- Data Quality
- Business Intelligence

Master Data Management

Master data management (MDM) is actually a revision of another solutions set that started with customer data integration (CDI). The theory was to create a "gold copy" of a crucial data subject (i.e., customer). The gold copy is the single source of truth regarding customer, and all other uses of the concept of customer must be subservient to the central or gold copy. CDI became MDM when the marketing types realized that other subjects, besides customer, required gold copies. Items, products, vendors, etc., are all areas where companies tend to have multiple versions, which are inconsistent or too contextual. In the old days, we called these files master files—hence, master data management.

The DMBOK states that master data is, "…The data that provides the context for *transaction data*. It includes the details (definitions and identifiers) of internal and external objects involved in business transactions. [It] Includes data about customers, products, employees, vendors, and controlled domains (code values)."[iii] Accordingly, master data management (MDM) represents the "Processes that ensure that *reference data* is kept up to date and coordinated across an enterprise. The organization, management, and distribution of corporately adjudicated data with widespread use in the organization."[iv]

Obviously, if MDM represents the process to manage a category of data across an enterprise, then DG needs to come into the picture. Later on, we will talk about DG being mandatory for MDM.

Data governance visibly supports MDM in several ways:

1. Ensures that standards are defined, maintained, and enforced.
2. Ensures that MDM efforts are aligned to business needs and are not technology-only efforts.
3. Ensures that data quality, process change, and other new activity that are rooted in MDM are accepted and adapted by the organization.

Data Quality

Data quality is probably the single most discussed term or concept in the EIM/DG universe. This is easy to comprehend once you understand what it really represents. Data quality is simply the root cause of the majority of data and information problems. Remediating data quality is one of the main drivers of data governance and MDM.

The DMBOK addresses data and information quality separately. As you already know, this book does not separate the two concepts, as governance is governance for both of them. Both are presented here:

- **Data quality** is the degree to which data is accurate, complete, timely, consistent with all requirements and business rules, and relevant for a given use.[v]
- **Information quality** is the degree to which information consistently meets the requirements and expectations of knowledge workers in performing their jobs. In the context of a specific use, the degree to which information is meeting the requirements and expectations for that use.[vi]

Obviously, while the two definitions are different, they are certainly pointing in the same direction. The best way to understand data quality is that the content in question has to be effective or fit for its purpose. This means if your organization feels that customer data is not of "good quality," you need to understand what purpose, action, or context is involved and how the shortfall is measured. Does bad customer data mean a wrong address or excessive duplication? You need to understand that "bad data" does not just appear, and is almost always corrected by a change in processes or habits, or both. That is

---

[iii]Mosely, Mark, Editor, "The DAMA Dictionary of Data Management."
[iv]Ibid.
[v]Ibid.
[vi]Ibid.

why the definition of data quality appears now in this text. It is a key driver of governance, because without governance, data quality efforts become costly one-off exercises.

Data governance supports data quality solutions via:

1. Ensuring that data quality standards and rules are defined and integrated into development and day-to-day operations.
2. Ensuring that on-going evaluation of data quality occurs.
3. Ensuring that organization issues related to changed processes and priorities are addressed.

Business Intelligence

Business intelligence (BI) has grown from a term coined by Gartner Group[vii] in the 1990s. It has since morphed (evolved is too complimentary) into a label that describes a self-perceived cool way of looking at data. Our DMBOK reference states BI is:

1. *Query, analysis* and *reporting* activity by *knowledge workers* to monitor and understand the financial and operational health of the enterprise.
2. Query, analysis and reporting processes and procedures.
3. A synonym for the business intelligence environment.
4. The market segment for *business intelligence software* tools.[viii]

From our DG perspective, we will stick with this definition: *At its roots, BI means one core concept—using information to achieve organization goals.* The rest is techno-speak and not relevant to our discussion on governance. Data governance enhances BI in a number of ways:

1. DG is used to ensure that BI activity is aligned with business activity. Many BI-related efforts never reach potential because they merely regurgitate data back to a requestor versus trying to change the business.
2. DG ensures that data quality is defined and supportive of BI. Data profiling activity is defined in the context of supporting BI data quality, and data quality remediation is occurring.
3. DG is used to ensure consistency in data standards and algorithms. Far too often, multiple business areas define a metric with the same name and different meaning and/or algorithm.
4. Lastly, we promote DG as important to enforcing the defined BI delivery architecture (i.e., make sure that organizations avoid exponential growth of spreadsheets, Acccss databases, and uncontrolled redundancy).

OTHER TERMS

A few other terms we will use frequently are related to actual elements of a DG program. We will review these in detail in upcoming sections. However, it is good to be aware of these before proceeding.

[vii]Power, D. J., "A Brief History of Decision Support Systems." Retrieved November 1, 2010.
[viii]Mosely, Mark, Editor, "The DAMA Dictionary of Data Management."

Principles

At the heart of effective governance are organizational principles. The DMBOK defines them as:

1. A fundamental law, doctrine, premise, or assumption
2. A rule or code of conduct

Principles are statements of philosophy. Think of them as a bill of rights—core beliefs that form the anchor for all policies and behaviors around *information asset management* (IAM). They are beliefs to be applied every day as guidance for procedures and decision-making efforts. Principles are not to be confused with policies (see the following) or rules. Often we see organizations lay out a set of rules—a blend of philosophy, policy, process, and enforcement. This is not an ideal approach; rules do not have the weight of belief, and they are hard to maintain and are inflexible. Data governance is a behavior change, not process revisionism. It may seem heavy handed, but going about it with the structure shown in Figure 2-5 pays off over the long term.

Principles are significant enough that we designed an overarching set of principles that are deliberately modeled on and placed alongside GAAP, or Generally Accepted Accounting Principles. GAAP and the United States Financial Accounting Standards Board set forth the essential and *mandatory* principles and standards for financial accounting. Called GAIP™ (Generally Accepted Information Principles), we urge clients to incorporate these as essential components of their principles. Figure 2-6 presents a summary of GAIP™.

Policies

Policies (or policy) are an area in the field of data governance that can be helpful or destructive for a new data governance function. The definition from DMBOK seems simple:

> *"A statement of a selected course of action and high-level description of desired behavior to achieve a set of goals."*

However, it is too easy for new data governance functions to spew policy without any substance. The real essence of policy is that it is a codification of principles. Policies are enforceable processes. Principles tend to be too lofty to enforce directly. Policies need to be repeatable, and easily trained. Standards, which are important to governance, are a type of policy, or even a characteristic of a particular policy, such as data naming standards or data quality standards.

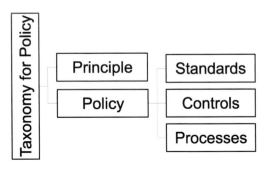

FIGURE 2-5

Structure of Principles and Policies.

| GAIP™ - Generally Accepted Information Principles ||
Principle	Description
Content as Asset	Data and content of all types are assets with all the characteristics of any other asset. Therefore, they should be managed, secured, and accounted for as other material or financial assets.
Real Value	There is value in all data and content, based on their contribution to an organization's business/operational objectives, their intrinsic marketability, and/or their contribution to the organization's Goodwill (balance sheet) valuation.
Going Concern	Data and content are not viewed as temporary means to achieve results (or merely as a business by-product), but are critical to successful, ongoing business operations and management.
Risk	There is risk associated with data and content. This risk must be formally recognized, either as a liability or through incurring costs to manage and reduce the inherent risk.
Due Diligence	If a risk is known, it must be reported. If a risk is possible, it must be confirmed.
Quality	The relevance, meaning, accuracy, and life cycle of data and content can affect the financial status of an organization.
Audit	The accuracy of data and content is subject to periodic audit by an independent body.
Accountability	An organization must identify parties which are ultimately responsible for data and content assets.
Liability	The risks in information means there is a financial liability inherent in all data or content that is based on regulatory and ethical misuse or mismanagement.

FIGURE 2-6

GAIP(tm) - Generally Accepted Information Principles.

SOME FINAL CORE CONCEPTS

Lastly, there are a few more concepts that need to be understood in regard to data governance. These are important to cover now because:

- Data governance programs often do not get started smoothly.
- They are often perceived as expensive.
- They are often scoped incorrectly.
- They contain changes to organizations that are often overlooked until it is too late.

We will go into deeper detail on each one of these but, again, it is good to be aware of them as you proceed.

E for Enterprise

Data governance is an enterprise program. It can be implemented locally, but must never be considered as a localized project. Would you implement financial controls in one department but not in another? We need to view DG the same way.

Business Program

Data governance is for your business or organization. It is *never* an IT program. Later, we will talk about why the CIO should never be in charge of DG. In fact, IT and technology areas are just as likely to be changed or enforced, as is a business area when it comes to managing information. For now, just keep in mind that we are building a business program and that program must add value over time.

Evolution vs. Revolution

Data governance needs to be implemented iteratively, in a carefully designed deployment. You need to learn how to govern. It is not instinctive. It is not a big-bang suitable endeavor. Only the hardiest or most desperate organizations can tolerate a massive shift to governed data from non-governed data. Look at the road to DG logically—if you are reading this book, you are not sure how to do it. You need to evolve through a process to learn how to do data governance. There are four distinct stages to learning, which apply to organizations as well as individuals.

1. Rote–repeat, but not understand—The organization can express definitions of data governance concepts.
2. Understanding—The organization can comprehend the nature and importance of data governance (a lot of DG programs stop here).
3. Application—The organization knows enough to start to apply the concepts of DG, but only as a direct response to a trigger (e.g., data quality is poor, so we start to govern data quality).
4. Correlation—The organization can apply the concepts creatively and to more complex situations (e.g., retrofit some kind of governance to an ERP or MDM program that has gone bad).

Information Management Maturity

A widespread method to view an organization's ability to execute information asset management is through the lens of a maturity scale. There are as many flavors of information management maturity (IMM) scales as there are consultants and vendors providing information solutions. There is a thorough coverage of this in "Making EIM Work for Business"[2] but we have summarized in Table 2-1 the most common expression (a capability-based model) of information maturity. (Figure 5-2 in Chapter 5 shows a comparison of the various expressions of maturity as well.) IMM is a key concept in that it represents a broadly understood means to measure the progress and effectiveness of DG. If IMM improves, DG is working.

Don't confuse maturity with the levels of learning. They are not interchangeable. They support each other. Depending on your organization's culture and environment, you may possibly need to execute all four layers of learning to get through each maturity level.

---

[2]Ladley, John, "Making EIM Work for Business," Morgan Kaufman, 2010.

Table 2-1	Capability-based Information Management Maturity Model.
IMM Stage	**Description**
Initial	The organization is entrepreneurial; individuals have authority over data, so information maturity is chaotic and idiosyncratic. Business rules or criteria for behavior are nonexistent. Data quality is far from integrated, and data handling is costly.
Repeatable	Departmental data becomes the norm. Any sophistication in usage—such as analysis—is departmental, specialized, and costly.
Defined	The organization starts to consider an enterprise view, and looks for some sort of integration across applications and silos. A desire for data accountability evolves. Strategic alignment to the business becomes an activity in IT. Standards are developed, and data quality becomes formal and may centralize. Data usage becomes more common, and efficiency of data management improves.
Managed	Data and content assets are tracked, lineage of all content is understood and documented. Analytical results are used to close process loops. Emails, documents, and web content are also managed, and can be called up alongside "rows and columns." Data quality is built into processes instead of being corrected post facto.
Optimized	There is no need to determine if information assets are managed effectively—they are woven into the fabric of the organization. There are effective measures in place to allow information management to support business innovation. The organization can place a value statement on its content, if not the balance sheet.

Things Will Change

The reason you are reading this book is that something is amiss with your data. By definition, if something is wrong, it needs to be fixed. Fixing anything means making a change to ensure that the fix is never needed again. The bottom line is that data governance is not done with an expectation of "business as usual" across your business and technology functions. There will be changes. Some of them will not be well received. Part of deploying DG means managing changes.

INFORMATION ASSET MANAGEMENT

The last concept has been deliberately positioned at the end of this chapter. So far, we have mentioned that data governance is a key element of managing data assets. We have contrasted DG with information management and reviewed the specific solutions that may trigger IM and DG. Now we need to talk about the asset aspect and frame our concepts within information asset management (IAM). We have found it better to save the whole "information as an asset" discussion until after the relationship of data governance to data management is established.

IAM describes a business-based approach to ensure that data, information, and content are all treated as assets in the *true business and accounting sense*—avoiding increased risk and cost due to data and content misuse, poor handling, or exposure to regulatory scrutiny. Please go back and review that sentence. Applying data governance means treating data as an asset, but not in a metaphorical sense. We truly mean as a real business asset. You may not see your "information value" on a balance sheet, but to be certain, if you view IAM in the true business sense, deploying data governance is a whole lot easier. Metaphors are used to aid in understanding, but metaphors are hard to implement. To be clear, if you are serious about governance or any of the solutions that require its application, you are committing to IAM. Think of another corporate or organization asset that can function without:

• Standards of use
• Accurate financial tracking
• Statement of value to the organization
• Assignment of accountability and responsibility

An asset requires standards, tracking, value, and accountability. EIM, DG, MDM, and all of the other concepts listed earlier, exist to manifest IAM.

SUMMARY

As of the writing of this book, few of the organizations we work with view these concepts and terms as a uniform discipline. Yet they all want "data governance" to be implemented. They want to manage information as an asset. We usually discover they do formal IAM in pockets, but never extract maximum benefit of sustainability. Often the projects related to the various pockets of solutions fail. We can always tie the failure back to not adopting the right mindset. The organizations doing "pocket IAM" go through the motions, hire consultants, and buy the right tools. However, they fall short when it is actually time to *change* the day-to-day treatment of data, information, and content. The solutions do not fully work unless you start to think in terms of IAM. Therefore, IAM is the mindset—the overarching philosophy. The elements of EIM and DG provide the framework (remember the V) that ties the participants together, but clearly delineates a system of checks and balances. What they accomplish together is truly managing data as an asset.

Overview of a data governance program

Laws are sand, customs are rock. Laws can be evaded and punishment escaped but an openly transgressed custom brings sure punishment.
—Mark Twain

DATA GOVERNANCE PROGRAM OVERVIEW

A data governance program really has one clear goal—to disappear. That may seem a bit enigmatic, especially since this book is about making data governance real. Nevertheless, it is true. Remember, you are deploying a new set of principles for treating a valuable asset in a much-improved manner. At the end of the day, the true mark of success is the organization treating its information as it treats its factories, supply chains, vendors, and customers. In the twenty-first century, no manager argues with standards for material handling, depreciation rules, or customer privacy. These are accepted business practices. There is no debate over whether you should have standards or controls. Yet it is easy to spread data all over an organization to the point that (a) it is excessively expensive to manage, and (b) you cannot find it, make sense of it, or agree on its meaning.

Ensuring a good understanding of how a data governance program looks and works is essential to getting participants engaged. Every time we kick off a new governance council or team to design a DG program, we always hear one person say, "I don't get the big picture. What does this look like?" The concept of assimilating data governance into everyday corporate life adds additional challenge, since you are not only defining and implementing a discrete program; you are also attempting to alter behavior to a point that the long-term program is visible only through verification and adjustment.

Regardless if data governance is new, or has become endemic and institutionalized, there is a collection of elements that characterize and describe a data governance program. Understanding how these work together aids in understanding the "big picture." This chapter reviews the scope and content of these elements and their interaction.

THE SCOPE OF DATA GOVERNANCE

We already mentioned that data governance (DG) is an enterprise concept. There needs to be an acknowledgment that the organization will adopt a mindset requiring greater rigor as far as handling its data and information. However, declaring the scope of data governance is a bit more complicated than saying, "We are governing everything!" It means considering some key factors affecting scope, and then making sure you are *very clear* as to the definition of data governance's reach and span in light of these factors. The three factors to consider that affect the scope of DG are:

- *Business model*—The type of organization, its corporate hierarchy, and its operating environment.
- *Content being governed*—The type of content (data, information, documents, etc.), its location, and its business relevance.
- *Degree of federation*—The extent or intensity by which different content is governed.

Business Model

For example, a large multinational company does not have to deploy a global DG program from the initial mention of the word governance. The scope can be a self-contained line of business. Suppose you are a large international chemical company. Your business model may contain pharmaceutical, agricultural, and refining divisions. All of these would operate on a more or less self-contained basis. You may then have three DG "programs" that are each similar in makeup, but separately accountable.

Then again, what if you are a global retailer with a tightly woven international supply chain? The scope of your data governance is most likely global.

In Figure 3-1, Company A is a large multinational organization, but all regions share its data and content. DG would therefore be applied across the entire entity. Remember, applied is not the

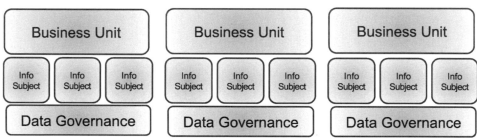

FIGURE 3-1

Data Governance Scope.

same as implemented. We always implement it gradually, but the vision is enterprise-wide. Company B is a large company as well, but has several very distinct business units. They do not share common information, so in this case data governance can be implemented or applied by business unit.

The detailed aspect of the business model is also an area to consider when scoping DG. DG will often require a change in business processes. A typical example is when master data management (MDM) is implemented. It is often the case that the operators entering data into many applications have also maintained the data area in question. Going from many-item master files to one is a typical example of where day-to-day business processes need to change. The scope of DG needs to make clear mention of this possibility.

In addition to the DG scope being dependent on the business model, it can also be dependent on type of content.

Content

Earlier we established that this book does not make a distinction between data governance and information governance. They are philosophical and semantic distinctions that cause considerable confusion, and are not relevant to this discussion. We also do not govern different types of content differently. At the end of the day, the activity to govern business intelligence data, operational data, e-mails, contracts, documents, or even media, is driven by the same reasons and entails the same activities.

While we do not distinguish how differing content is governed, we do need to be clear within a specific organization what types of content are subject to DG. Certainly, master data, BI data, and other forms of structured data are most likely governed. However, a highly regulated company may also need to govern e-mails and contracts.

A company where safety is a major issue may need to place its governance focus on guidelines and procedures. A government body may need to zero in on governing access to public documents while protecting individual privacy.

The types of content subject to DG will heavily impact where the DG program resides, who holds accountability, and how the organization deploys the DG program. It will also influence the types of tools and policies that the DG organization has to define.

Content types are also important because, while DG programs contain the same elements regardless of the content being governed, very often the types of content will influence the detailed governance processes. Differing content types will have unique life cycles. For example, content that is a structured type of data, like a transaction, may come and go within a fiscal year, and governance will tend to focus on the usage of that data within the time period. An unstructured type of data, like contracts and e-mails, may need to be kept for decades and may be subject to legal discovery or strict classifications of privacy or privilege. Obviously, there will need to be consideration of the details of governing these different types.

The development and maintenance of applications and systems should be accounted for in the type of governance as well. Many of our clients have a defined development process, or systems development life cycle (SDLC) for defining and deploying automated systems. Few of them have built any type of consideration for designing around DG policies and standards. Very often, we end up writing enhancements to corporate IT department SDLC methodologies when structured information is being governed. The enhancements take the form of extra artifacts, and branch out to additional tasks, or new approvals and checkpoints. When unstructured information is subject to DG, we often have to modify workflow and document management processes.

HELPFUL HINT

If you want to see a modern example of the need for governance and a precise definition of scope, look no further than your own local SharePoint™ or Notes™ repositories. Frankly, we have never seen a more rapid descent into expensive repositories of data decay and "garbage dump" manifestations. These so-called collaborative tools have become nothing more than document graveyards where old Word documents go to die. Expensive and harmless until a legal case pops up and the company discovers it should really have deleted those a long time ago. The tools themselves are not at fault. It was the total and unequivocal lack of oversight that, in less than a decade, created an enormous corporate data crisis.

Of course, the type of content being governed will require differing types of technology to assist in the management of that content. As of this writing, there are no technologies that can handle structured and unstructured data management under one product.

Federation

One of the most important concepts affecting the nature and scope of data governance is that of "federation." The *Webster Dictionary* definition of *federation* offers some insight:

1. *an encompassing political or societal entity formed by uniting smaller or more localized entities: as a : a federal government, b : a union of organizations*
2. *the act of creating or becoming a federation; especially : the forming of a federal union*

For data governance, this means defining an entity (the DG program) that is a distinct blend of governance functions where the various aspects of DG are touched by the organization. The federation of a data governance program is a definition of where and how standards will be applied across various layers and segments of an organization. This is best understood by looking at another federated organization—the United States government. Politically, the United States is a federation, an organization of states with a federal oversight layer. In the United States, some activities of government are central. There is a central military and reserve banking system. Other functions of government operate at the state or local level, such as medical care and law enforcement. A data governance program will necessitate the same type of definition of the required layers of governance functionality.[1] The definition of federation will influence the scope of your DG organization, its processes, and principles.

---

[1]Federated systems minimize control issues, but do not prevent them. For example, in the United States a few states legalize marijuana to some degree. At the federal level, it is still a federal crime to possess or use marijuana. This leads to some interesting news stories and even more fascinating rhetoric. The resolution mechanism for these issues is the United States Congress and House of Representatives. In your organization, you will require an issue-resolving body as well, but we fervently hope it is more effective.

Federation affects the character and operation of the DG program. Note in Figure 3-2, we show a heat map where similar data assets can be tightly governed (in the center or hot zone), or more loosely governed (on the fringe or the cool zone). The solid areas indicate a governed area called "item," where there is tight control of global items, slightly looser control on regional items, and local items are barely governed. The dotted areas point to another subject, "customer." There is still the tight control for centrally used customer content, but the regional and local are treated the same. So, the federated intensity of DG differs by content type.

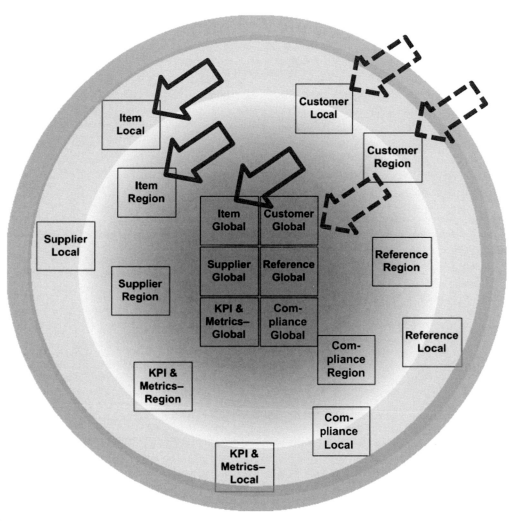

FIGURE 3-2

Federation "Heat Map".

Scope factors that affect the federated layers and activities are:

- *Enterprise size*—Obviously, huge organizations will need to federate their DG programs, and carefully choose the critical areas where DG adds the most value.
- *Brands*—Organizations with strong brands may want to consider this in their DG scoping exercise. One brand may need a more centrally managed data portfolio than another.
- *Divisions*—One division may be more highly regulated, therefore requiring a different intensity of DG.
- *Countries*—Various nations have different regulations and customs, therefore affecting how you can govern certain types of information.
- *IT portfolio condition*—When a DG effort is getting started, it is usually understood at some intuitive level, the nature and condition of the existing information technology portfolio. An organization embarking on a massive overhaul of applications (usually via implementing a large SAP or Oracle enterprise suite) will have definite and specific DG federation requirements.
- *Culture and information maturity*—The ability of an organization to use information and data is referred to as its information management maturity, or IMM. The manner in which an organization gets its work done is usually called culture. In combination, the specific IMM and culture of an organization will affect the scope and design of the DG program. For example, an organization that is rigid in its thinking and has a low level of maturity will require more centralized control in its DG program, as well as more significant change management issues.

MINI CASE STUDY

Don't fall into the scope trap of identifying the scope of DG with size or market dominance. You need to rationally consider influencing factors we have presented, i.e., the business model, the assets to be managed, and what type of federation is required. Let's expand the global retailer example:

Business model—The business model is global, with heavy dependence on economy of scale across the supply chain. So our scope will lean toward the entire organization—we will not be excluding any functions, like merchandising or warehouse.

Content being managed—Obviously there is a lot of content in a large organization, but consider the variety—retail is, at its core, pretty simple. You buy stuff from one place and sell it to someone else. The main content is anything used or descriptive of the "stuff" and getting it sold. Be careful—it isn't just the items—what about the people on the sales floor? What about the trucks and trains to move items about? All are integral to the business. So from a scope standpoint we need to consider almost all of the content within this type of enterprise. The key guidance to apply is—*the scope of data governance is a function of the assets being managed* (i.e., the content and information being governed).

Federation—We have stated the entire enterprise is in scope, and all content relevant to the business model is in scope. We have not narrowed this down much, have we? When we examine the content (remember we are considering all of it), we see that it stratifies into global, regional, and local. This is significant. If a region or locality can buy items to sell, what is the intensity of DG in those supply chains versus the global ones? We have to consider that local data may not be worth close governance and may be okay with a more relaxed level of intensity.

Scope mini case study bottom line: All content is in scope, but due to size, geography, and markets, we need to consciously identify which specific content is managed centrally, regionally, or locally. The organization would state that DG scope is all content relevant to the business model, but the intensity of DG will vary based on a specifically defined set of federated layers.

ELEMENTS OF DATA GOVERNANCE PROGRAMS

In many ways, a data governance program is like any other business program. Many elements of data governance make perfect sense to businesspersons when they first consider DG. For some reason, the people on the technology side of the information management and data governance equation get dazed and confused. Either way, this section will cover these basic program elements in the context of DG. Later on in the book, we will get into the specific design and deployment of each of these elements.

Organization

Like any other activity within a company or government entity, there needs to be a formal statement of roles. The official designation of accountability and responsibility are key factors to the survival of DG. Most important to new DG programs is the concept of accountability for data. This is most likely a very new role. To be clear, it will seem very new and different to hold someone accountable for data quality—especially when accountability means a direct effect on bonuses or promotions. There will also be a perception that the DG program is rather powerful or bold to be making these designations. Assigning responsibility will also be an important activity. In many organizations, the responsible parties have a formal role as designated "stewards" or "custodians." Other implementations of DG may place everyone under a label of a steward, and the responsible parties will be direct supervisors. Either way, you can see that some formal organizational design is in order.

The organization around DG also requires a hierarchy of some sort to enable issue resolution, monitoring, and direction setting. Rarely does this hierarchy of DG become a stand-alone area (i.e., there is rarely a data governance "department"). Most of the time, the DG organization is a virtual organization made up of business and IT personnel.

HELPFUL HINT

Remember that the ultimate goal of DG is to disappear as a stand-alone program. It becomes part of the fabric of business, like financial controls. That is why the DG "department" is really a monitoring structure—much like an audit committee. To be more specific, DG may not really disappear, but it will be very thin. There will always be the need to resolve issues. But like other types of corporate governance, these events become accepted as normal activities, not special programs.

There may be a thin department with participants that roll in and roll out. Some highly regulated organizations may want to have a separate DG department only if it cannot be fit into the compliance areas. This is one of those areas we promised to point out—we differ from many of our peers. Given the long-term nature of DG (i.e., it's not a lot different than financial controls or well-known policies), there is little need for a full time overhead structure. In our opinion, that perpetuates the labeling of information asset management as a program that can be terminated, as opposed to the behavior change it really represents.

A specific time frame for DG to reach the "transparent" stage is hard to define, as it will vary based on scope and organization. The degree of transparency will be tied to your progress up the information management maturity curve, so whatever the timing is of your IMM progress is most likely your timing for DG to fade into the business fabric. If you are using a 5-stage maturity model to measure DG effectiveness, then whenever you hit stage 4 or 5, your DG program should be part of your everyday activity. This may take a very long time. Think about it more as a goal rather than a requirement.

Again, think about financial controls. Few organizations talk about the financial governance program and whether it should be justified to continue or be terminated. That would be unheard of. This perception is what you are striving for with DG.

Regardless of the size of the organization or the complexity of DG, it is key to remember the DG organization is not there to do information management. It is there to guide and monitor. Figure 3-3 takes the V we introduced and shows a typical assignment of roles on the DG side.

The key aspect about understanding the DG organization is that it is a formal definition of roles for assigning responsibility and accountability for managing information assets.

Principles

We touched on principles earlier by way of a definition. In summary, they are general adopted rules that guide conduct and application of data philosophy. Principles are more than just a term to be understood, however. Principles are crucial elements in DG. One client told us they justified the entire program because with principles in place, there were fewer meetings. Principles will succeed where a batch of rules and policies will not. They are foundational. One explanation we use when confronted with resistance to developing principles is to draw an analogy to the "Bill of Rights," the first ten

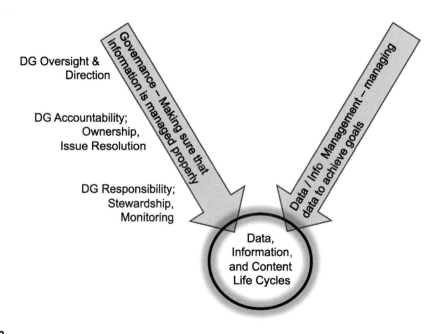

FIGURE 3-3

The "V" with layers of DG.

amendments to the United States Constitution. It's easy to see the historical significance of the application of these principles to United States history. It is the same for data principles (maybe a bit less historical).

As you deploy DG, you will need to revisit and repeat your enterprise-level principles. Not revise, but repeat. Since they are foundational and represent beliefs, repetition will be necessary. Figure 3-4 lists some sample principles we have collected. (Please note that in this book we refer to an organization named "Farfel." This is the name of the fictional company we will occasionally use as a sample case study where we are unable to reveal the real client.)

Policies

Another element we previously defined is policies. Policies are formally defined processes with strength of support—that is, they are a codification of a principle. They give it "teeth." Policies include standards—one area where IT personnel will be very intense as DG becomes real. Most likely, you already have most of your DG policies floating around in the form of a disconnected IT, data, or compliance policy. And, like most places, the policy sits happily in its notebook while life goes on and the policy is disregarded. The marriage of principle and policy prevents this in the DG program.

Functions

We use the term function to describe the "what" has to happen in DG. This is done because early in the DG program these functions will appear to be embedded in the DG "department" but over time they need to evolve into day-to-day activities within all areas. Using the word "process" would immediately

Principle Name	Principle Description
Master principle	Farfel will manage all Enterprise Data and Content as a corporate asset.
Federation	Farfel will specify enterprise standards for all content and data structures.
Information Efficiency	Relevant data, information, and content needs to be available at the right time, at the right place, and in the right format to authorized users/consumers, at an efficient cost.
Business Alignment	Information management applications and technology will be in response to business needs verirfed through a formal annual process.
Information quality	All enterprise data/information will be managed and measured for quality. Quality will be consistently measured to ensure the data can be utilized for its intended purpose.
Risk Management	Appropriate due diligence will be conducted to comply with all relevant statutory and federal laws, policies, and regulations.
Collaborate	Enterprise data will be a shared resource across the enterprise. Data is not a resource which can "owned" by specific business areas.

FIGURE 3-4

Sample Principles.

imply a "where," and that is an operational level of detail that evolves. Some functions will be visible in the DG management framework as stand-alone processes as well as the day-to-day activities that carry out governance. There is no need to design your DG functional model from scratch; we will have a list later in the book. However, recognizing that there will be a formal set of functional requirements (to be manifested as processes) and that they will be executed all the time is a key element to the success of DG. The functions perform two roles. One, they point out what someone has to actually *do*. Second, reviewing the functions required for your organization usually aids in determining which areas or individuals would bear accountability and responsibility.

The DG area will need to consider other business areas where there will be interaction and collaboration, such as:

- Human resources
- Compliance and/or legal
- Risk management
- Large-scale integration projects, such as ERP

The bottom line for this element of DG is that you need to formally consider and build the DG processes and function. They are not instinctive. There is a complete list of sample functions in the appendices.

The process or functional model for DG needs to specify how the V operates. There are processes to develop and deploy DG functionality. In essence, DG has to define the "right things to do."

DG will identify those processes for "doing things right" as well—that is, the hands-on information management activities (the right side of the V).

Metrics

You cannot manage what you do not measure. Over time, your DG program will need to evolve a means to monitor its own effectiveness. Without it, the DG program will certainly fade away. At the outset, the metrics will be hard to collect. After all, you have not been managing data very well, so there is no infrastructure to install a metric. Eventually, the metrics will evolve from simple surveys and counts to true monitoring of activity. Here is a list of common metrics:

- *IMM Index*—Report on information management maturity stated on a scale from 1–5, calculated based on survey and assessment of various elements of the data governance and data management program.
- *DG Stewardship Progress*—Report on counts of individuals trained on DG, counts of specific projects governed, and a count of issues elevated and/or resolved.
- *DG Stewardship Effectiveness*—Alternatively to progress, an effective metric can be based on counts and resolution of issues submitted to data governance bodies.
- *Data Quality*—Data profiling results calculated into a DQ index that represent an average of all of the data-quality profiling measures.
- *Business Value*—We will dive into the business case and business value more in the next chapter, but you can never go wrong with tying the application of DG and data management to business success. Quantifiable and intangible benefits resulting from successful efforts that were governed, or through use of governed and well-managed data should always be reported.

Technology and Tools

The last element that requires high-level consideration is technology. As of the writing of this book, there is not a clear-cut category or market for pure DG technology. Most efforts witnessed have assembled various technologies in support of DG, using SharePoint, Word, and Excel, as well as adapting tools from other disciplines, like data model or data dictionary tools. Specialty tools are evolving and, in general, you will want to consider the following capabilities, but Chapter 14 will cover the application of tools in more detail.

One aspect of tools to understand at this point is you should not feel compelled to buy data governance tools just because you are doing data governance. By definition, a tool exists to improve something you are already doing. If you are not doing formal data governance yet, or if you are doing it poorly, then casting about for a tool to help you deploy DG is a waste of time. This flies in the face of typical IT philosophy, where the tool is usually acquired first. This is a notoriously silly thing to do. However, our work always has us putting the brakes on a tool selection project. It is easy to buy a tool and install it. However, most of the time we witness new tools for data management sitting unused or poorly deployed. This is because no one has mastered the process the tool is supporting.

As you roll out DG and begin to understand the various aspects of your particular program, you will know immediately where you need a tool to "grease the skids." Some features of DG tools that can be considered are:

- Principle and policy administration
- Business rules and standards administration
- Organization management
- Work flow for issues and audits
- Data dictionary
- Enterprise search
- Document management
- Metrics scorecard—data gathering, synthesis, and presentation
- Interfaces to other workflows and methodologies
- Training and collaboration facilities

THE CSFs FOR DATA GOVERNANCE

Normally, *critical success factors* are left for last. Because DG is a business program in some ways, but unique in others, we need to point out the CSFs early on in this book. Frankly, if one or more of the CSFs presented next are totally unrealistic for your organization, you need to reconsider launching a formal DG program as an approach to improving data asset management. Or, at the least, you should call it something else.

1. Data governance is mandatory for the successful implementation of any project or initiative that uses information. Any project requiring reports, business intelligence, cleaning of data, or development of a "single source of truth" requires DG to be sustainable and successful.
2. Data governance has to show value explicitly. This means you cannot do data governance in a vacuum. Something has to be governed, even if it is data quality and you implement data governance as a means to improve data quality. Countless IT shops developed models,

standards, and policies in the 1980s and 1990s, and then went looking for a project to spring them on. You need to show benefit, and that means tying the DG effort to a visible initiative.

3. You must manage organizational culture change. At the risk of being repetitive, you are doing DG because you are NOT doing something correctly. Therefore, something needs to be changed. We have dealt with numerous organizations who wanted all of their data fixed, but did not want to change their views or the behaviors or processes that created the mess. So, you will need to orient, train, educate, communicate, hold hands, encourage, and offer incentives. Then repeat it all again.

4. Data governance must be viewed as an enterprise effort. You can implement it in segments, but it must always have an enterprise perspective. Otherwise, you will end up with conflicting standards and accountabilities.

WHAT ABOUT GLADYS?

We always run into situations where management sets formal organization change management aside. Usually the reasons are [with our response in brackets]:

- We don't have enough time. [It does not take very long…sorry.]
- We cannot afford it. [DG has a net cash cost of zero. Plus, can you can afford to have the project crater?]
- It is squishy. [Anything that, if done improperly, can cost you millions of dollars/euros/pounds, etc., is not squishy; and there is data behind that statement.]

But, in spite of piles of data proving this is not a very bright thing to do, it still happens. If you are experiencing this problem, try telling this story:

Gladys works in procurement in the plant in Iowa. Every day (for the last 20 years), she logs on to four applications to do her job. Once a week, she downloads operational data into a spreadsheet and prints out the weekly inventory updates for her boss. From a data standpoint, she is the sole integration point for three operational systems affecting finance, work orders, and inventory. She is proud of her accumulated knowledge that allows her to accomplish her duties, in spite of the poor data management aspects.

When the company finally fixes the kludge of applications, should the new processes and training be handled via:

a) An e-mail on Friday that comes Monday; she has a new password and the instructions will be on her desk.
b) A change program that has her participate over time to define the new interfaces and processes, including flying her into headquarters to meet others going through the same process.
c) Have the vendor of the new software stop by and do a one-day training class?

Obviously, b) is the kinder method, but b) stems from the change management discipline. Sadly, a) and c) are the more typical approaches because no one ever gets to consider b) since the organizational change effort was squashed.

Hey, Mr. Executive, what if Gladys was your Mom?

SUMMARY

Businesses are accustomed to controls. All organizations have a standard means of ensuring the integrity of financial assets. There is not a single CEO on the planet that would condone multiple sets of accounting standards in their departments. DG is no different. The DG program offers a set of elements that behave like any other business program. It is not easy, but the entire enterprise needs to accept that twenty-first–century organizations' dependence on data assets implies the acceptance and institutionalizing of a data governance program.

The data governance business case

A manager is responsible for the application and performance of knowledge.
—**Peter Drucker**

THE BUSINESS CASE

Data governance is a business program; therefore, it needs to add value to the business. However, since data governance is a program dealing in abstracts (data as an asset), it is similar to other programs where tangible results are hard to see, such as marketing or finance. The CEO will acknowledge the need for marketing and certainly the need for a finance area, but a detailed, hard-dollar justification for these areas (as for DG) is usually not sitting in a folder on a desk somewhere.

Is a business case even required for DG? Suppose the CEO says, "I know we really need this, and it is like marketing—so proceed without a business case." There should be an intrinsic understanding that the treatment of information as an asset leads to a tightly connected business—thus, an information value proposition is not enough. In fact, a business case is required even if it is not requested. There are several reasons for this:

- DG is a holistic effort requiring enterprise attention. But there will be naysayers and you need to be able to handle them. A common form of resistance is for a department head to state there is no time to participate on a new committee or learn new procedures. After all, there is a business to be run. However, it becomes harder to throw resistance up in the face of a business case tied to a goal of making hundreds of millions of dollars for the organization.
- DG will not succeed if it cannot be measured, and the success measures must come from a set of business-oriented metrics.
- There may be a de facto business case for DG tied to a large initiative. There may be overwhelming data-quality issues or strong pressure from regulators. There may be a large implementation of an ERP package planned. DG becomes a necessary part of these projects, therefore it can be launched as part of a larger project. Another common example is in the form of a data-quality effort. All of these scenarios create a risk of developing sets of similar yet non-united DG teams. The bottom line is you do not get a *sustainable* program. DG is "dumbed down" from a business program to a business interest that is then passed to IT where it becomes a project. This progression, of course, directly conflicts with the essential aspect that DG is an enterprise effort.
- Strangely, there is another persistent obstacle facing DG programs. It is the insistence in many organizations on developing a hard-and-fast business case with "real" benefits and strong financial returns that are based on traditional benefits like headcount reduction or reduced business costs. In this event, a business case with tangible returns seems impossible because

managed data and content are "intangible." So, once again, the business case is deemphasized, or we manufacture faux benefits based on technology efficiencies. However, we will soon see that the "hard" benefits *can be* derived.

OBJECTIVES OF THE BUSINESS CASE FOR DG

Obviously, the business case for DG needs to show value. This is accomplished in two ways. First, the value is shown in the form of a tangible direct benefit, where you can tie DG to benefits coming from one of three directions:

- Improvement in efficiency (e.g., integration, faster information delivery)
- Increase in direct business contributors, like revenue, customers, or market share (e.g., post merger economies of scale, efficient supply chains, effective promotions)
- Reduction in risk, either through fewer fines, lower reserves, loss of market share or reduced cost of risk management, such as insurance premiums (e.g., compliance to the Sarbanes–Oxley Act, improved information privacy, improved data quality)

In many organizations, the easiest direct benefit is derived from reduction in risk. Three or four decades' worth of explosive growth of stored data and documents has created enormous amounts of risk. A few examples of this are:

- Privacy violation
- Data security
- Civil liability brought on by poor management of safety or warranty information
- Incorrect decisions brought about by inaccurate or inconsistent data across numerous copies (e.g., establishing reserves too low, or losing track of where you acquire items)
- Regulatory liability by failing to track key documents or respond to a request for documents
- Excessive costs keeping ROT (redundant, obsolete, and trivial) data, including documents, backups, SharePoint, and e-mail

The second form of tangible value is indirect, in much the same way as a marketing program (i.e., the marketing program will support other initiatives that would otherwise fail or falter without the program). In the case of marketing, value is determined by predicting and confirming increased market share or more prospects. Marketing strives to improve visibility of a product that, for example, supports more sales. In a similar manner, the value of information projects stems from where the information is used. Therefore, the DG business case needs to support the activity that ensures good data and information is available to accomplish business goals—without incurring undue risk or cost. You need to look for opportunities where data governance supports business programs that want to increase revenue, lower costs, and reduce risk. Once you have identified opportunities to aid in achieving business targets, then it is time to specifically quantify business benefits and align them, in detail, with the data and content data governance will be overseeing.

Another objective of the DG business case is to build a response to historical shortcomings of IT projects. These are:

- The perception that data and information initiatives always fail
- The perception that spending on "pure" information management projects is wasteful

- Historical criticism of information technology area (IT)
- Ongoing complaints that the IT data is not "correct"—so business areas need to create "correct" data
- A growth of "stealth" or shadow IT in reaction to a poor perception of IT
- Lists of projects that "we will get running with these shortcomings and then fix them later." Of course, *later* never happens.[i]

The business case for DG must address these opinions head-on. To recap, the DG business case needs to accomplish the following:

- Identify where it can support business directly (such as risk avoidance).
- Identify where information is used to move the business forward.
- Associate DG with those IM activities (MDM, BI, etc.).
- Address historical shortcomings of IT projects.

Accomplishing these objectives will provide a multidimensional business case that will make DG a sustainable program.

    If detailed, specific business benefits cannot be quantified easily, you can use industry standards, benchmarks, and papers to provide the metrics for the business case.

CONTENTS OF THE BUSINESS CASE

Several basic components are required to build a business case for data governance. Because DG is a component of EIM, there are similarities in the two business cases. More details on EIM business cases can be found in *Making EIM Work for Business* (John Ladley. Waltham, MA: Morgan Kaufmann, 2010). The basic contents are slightly modified for a specific DG case.

Vision

Vision is perhaps the most abused term in business, but the "big picture" is incredibly important for the acceptance of DG. Remember that you will be telling a large part of the organization to change. Change does not happen among humans without some view of the big picture. In fact, it is rather rude to ask people to change without some sort of explanation.[1] This is your goal for the vision. *What will a day in the life look like when DG is in place? What will you see in the organization? What business goals will be more achievable?*

    One of the big surprises in rolling out DG occurs when the business areas start to comprehend that there will be new accountability for data. Very often an oxymoron will appear. The same business units that insist on their own IT staff and maintain scores of legacy spread sheets and Access databases will also say, "Data accountability is not my issue. Data belongs to IT. Except my data, that is."

---

[i]John Ladley, *Making EIM Work for Business* (Waltham, MA: Morgan Kaufmann, 2010).
[1]While raising children, a parent will take great pains to never say, "Because I said so!" as a justification for asking for a behavior change. In the context of DG, the temptation to say this with difficult cultures or clients will be much stronger.

Never say "better decisions" or "better data quality" as business vision statements. These are not business statements. They have no relevance from a vision standpoint because they are not measureable in terms of business value, and they improperly position expectations. An example of a properly worded business vision for DG might look like this: "ACME Inc. will manage its information assets to increase shareholder value and reduce enterprise risk?"

Program Risks

A business case is also a vehicle to present how a venture will manage risk. While part of the business case for DG will address enterprise risks, you also need to consider risks that the DG program itself may create:

1. *Business Risks*—The DG program fails to do its part to prevent loss of market share and reputation, and fails to hit targets or avoid fraud.
2. *Regulatory Risks*—DG fails to connect with compliance requirements and there are violations of regulations.
3. *Cultural Risks*—The organization fails to engage in the DG process and continues poor data asset management practices that resulted in the need for DG in the first place.

Business Alignment

If the DG program is going to be supporting (directly or indirectly) business initiatives, call out the value points or specific scenarios DG will enable. Your actual business case benefits will come out of these areas, so do not be timid in looking around for opportunity.

Costs of Data Quality

Data quality issues consume an enormous amount of cost and resources. It is the primary manifestation and metric of a functional DG program. Therefore, it is important that your business case mention the current costs and risks associated with data quality.

Costs of Missed Opportunities

There is always the need to highlight what will happen, or continue to happen, without DG. You may cover some of this in the data quality area, but it is good to recap existing issues with data, reporting, poor content management, scary compliance issues, or the high cost of ownership due to extensive redundancy. There may be business actions and scenarios, however, that cannot happen or may be more difficult without DG.

Obstacles, Impacts, and Changes

It is fair to cover possible cultural and other organizational issues. If there is the possibility of technology changes, these can be mentioned (you do not need details, those come later). Any obstacles that are known need to be presented.

Presentation of the Case

The business case for DG is a business document. Even if the CIO is handling this task, you need to avoid three-letter acronyms, techno-babble, and exotic and abstract pictures. You are selling—and any salesperson will tell you that you must be crystal clear and concise.

HELPFUL HINT

Do not depend on a single presentation to sell the DG program. You should be vetting ideas and benefits long before the final PowerPoint blast. Know your audience (i.e., who will be nodding, shaking, or nodding off) before you even schedule the final presentation. The best theme for a final business-case presentation is a 30-minute review with key decision makers and their acknowledgement that everyone is okay to move ahead.

A few themes must dominate the business case:

- DG is a program. (Even if the ultimate goal of DG is to become woven into the enterprise, it is still programmatic in its rollout and lifespan.) You are funding a long-term, permanent change in mindset and behavior but the organization won't embark on this journey without some form of return or perceived benefit.
- DG is supportive of many projects but, most importantly, it is the control and audit function for information asset management.
- Governance and change is mandatory to address the issues that created the need for this meeting. Make sure those issues and history are understood.

At the highest level, a short and concise presentation is required. My guideline for a CEO-level briefing is ten slides or less. If the presentation is done well, the DG team will expect an expression of interest, commitment to proceed, and feedback. The feedback must be an acknowledgment or correction of the business alignment items, and must convey an understanding of the risks and impacts. If this pre-case material is presented to those at lower levels in an organization, then add details around impacts, business benefits, and risks.

THE PROCESS TO BUILD THE CASE

What follows is a brief outline of the process to develop the business case for DG.

Fully Understand Business Direction

Whether you have explicit access to corporate strategy or need to read the annual report, you must form the DG business case in the context of your organization. That means not accepting a boilerplate justification from a conference brochure. Why is DG relevant to your business? If you are forming DG as part of a broader EIM effort via MDM, BI, or both, then confirm that the DG team knows where the business wants to go.

Identify Possible Opportunities

Business strategy begets information opportunities. Again, if an EIM program is being implemented, you may have this information handy. A common direct benefit of governance is in the areas of e-discovery and document management. It is where organizations drastically reduce cost and risk of document handling by simply implementing better governance.

Identify Usage Opportunities

The indirect benefits come from efforts where information is used as a means to deliver a business result, such as a data warehouse. In these cases, DG can help ensure a consistent and relevant result. If there is a large customer MDM effort tied to some sort of customer program, then your DG effort supplies the required governance to the new MDM policies, standards, and processes.

Define Business Benefits and Risks-Management Benefits

Refine the potential benefits in terms of not only a perceived high-level number, but also in terms of cash flow or earnings increase. In addition, describe specific risks. Look for risk across the three risk types—regulatory, civil, and financial.

Confirm

Confirm business benefits you have identified to ensure they are supported by DG. Make sure you do not attempt to support something that is not relevant.

Quantify Costs

Examine current costs of IT as well as other information-related costs. Include all capital costs, depreciation, and overhead. Any analysis of the cost of poor data quality should be factored in here as well. Include costs of departmental end-use databases, spreadsheets, and departmental "mini IT departments." This is a good beginning cost number. It points out how much is being spent now, without governance. The actual cost of governance should be a small fraction of current costs. Ideally, you will use internal resources. Most of the time we initially see a small increase in costs for some consultants or for training, but as DG becomes part of the enterprise, costs will return to prior levels.

Prepare the Business Case Documentation

Apply the various financial benefits and costs to whatever model is used or selected by your organization; then present the results in whatever format is palatable. Make sure you keep it business-like.

Approach Considerations

Many, if not most, companies do a horrible job disseminating their business plans, and that assumes they actually have one. My company(s) has executed dozens of EIM-like engagements over the past 20 years. Few of these companies had a business vision or strategy that was readily available to the very people whose job it was to ensure those plans could be measured. Often the EIM effort would trigger an embarrassing fumbling in a cabinet during an interview and a strategic plan would be produced. Organizations that do publicize their strategies and push this information to all levels tend to have much less challenging information and content needs. This is not a coincidence. If business drivers and goals are endemic, how hard is it really to match up the applications portfolio and business intelligence efforts with the business direction?

HELPFUL HINT

Business Alignment
Any formal business alignment exercise will demonstrate how business and information/content usage is connected. This is what positions the organization for a formal business case. It means taking any business alignment material that you have already prepared and starting to use it.

It is at this point that organizations that have not done business alignment stop, hire a consultant, and then do an alignment exercise. Let us then reinforce the importance of business alignment—it will be done. The issue is to do it early on and in full understanding of the relationship of EIM as a business program within your enterprise.

The typical scenario is that once the business plan has been developed, it is considered "top secret." This is also misdirection from management. Obviously, you can have secret strategies and still give middle and lower management enough to discern business alignment. It is already in their performance objectives, isn't it?

The plain and simple fact is this—if everyone knew where the business was headed, many of the information-management issues we have covered would be minimized or eliminated.

SUMMARY

Even if a business leader clearly trumpets the need for "better data," and is willing to push hard and use political capital to get it, you do not go forth without a business case, otherwise you run the risk of falling into the waste can of failed initiatives. Therefore, there are some business considerations for the business case as well:

1. The business case must feature accountability. If the goals are not met, who is responsible? Historically, it has been very easy to blame IT for a failure to communicate. A clear business case will use business terminology and point out where the business accountability is.
2. Business leaders are poorly incented to do well at information-type projects. The business case for DG must support business accountability and be built into the sponsors' objectives and personal targets.
3. Once IT projects "happen," there is a tendency for interest to wane, and even return to the old alternative. Business areas need to understand that the investment continues beyond deployment, and some effort and willpower are required to sustain the project's goals. The business case must acknowledge the cultural impact and even accommodate the costs and benefits of sustaining the effort while ensuring changes are fully adopted and integrated into the fabric of the culture.

HELPFUL HINT

It is a common statement that a "good business sponsor" is the key to the success of a critical effort. This is only partially true. The business sponsor can be as excited and supportive as imaginable, but if at the end of the year their bonus or compensation is not tied to information management—related goals, forget it. The excitement is political and amorphous. Often, it is merely lip service. It will not hold up to stress or business changes. When you hear that a project has "lost" a sponsor, it is more likely *that it never really had one in the first place*.

The DG team needs to remember that there has to be a sales process of sorts, even if none is requested. One sponsor does not make a successful program. This means examining business opportunities, educating about the ramifications of managing information as an asset, and recognizing that the long-term animosity between IT and business areas must be addressed with a business program. Don't forget there are challengers and naysayers out there. Stating a case with hard dollars will slow down early resistance.

Process overview for deploying data governance

If you don't know where you are going, you'll end up somewhere else.
—Yogi Berra

By "stand up," we mean define, design, deploy, and start to manage the DG program. This does not mean there is no process to get actual approval to proceed with a DG program. Many organizations struggle with the desire to carry out DG, but do not have the commitment from management to do so. However, DG is not a program to do as a stand-alone effort. After all, you need to govern *something*. Our process covers the business case and "selling" DG, but in the context of an organization that acknowledges something needs to be different. We also assume that the process will find a visible benefit to DG. In other words, we are showing the entire process and will not delve into a separate chapter on the debate of selling DG, or if DG has value. If you have read this far, you know that.[1]

This chapter will present an overview of the entire process to "stand up" data governance. The following eight chapters will present each step along with some sample artifacts and relate the steps to our case studies.

If you are considering DG, it means you have acknowledged a problem manifested through lack of governance. Therefore, one path to standing up DG is from the application of a solution to a problem. However, you need to keep the following in mind *all of the time*: DG is a component of an overall enterprise information management (EIM) program. As covered in Chapter 2, DG is applied when various types of EIM solutions are developed, such as business intelligence or master data management (MDM). Even if you are only doing an MDM solution and have no formal EIM program, in effect you are implementing one component of EIM. Since MDM and DG must go hand in hand, your MDM project lays a foundation for expansion of EIM through the DG and MDM efforts.

HELPFUL HINT

We always emphasize that the "E" stands for enterprise when we talk about EIM programs. This is in reaction to the tendency of upper management to say, "First show me it works on a small scale." The same goes for DG. "Govern a little bit" is often heard during the initial days of a DG program. You need to be very careful that the

---

[1]We thought very seriously about inserting a chapter to talk about the justification of DG as a concept. We decided not to. Frankly, if an organization has to debate if DG is "required," or it has to test the legitimacy of the concept, it does not understand what DG is. We have dealt with too many companies where an executive has told the nascent DG team to "do a proof of concept." When we hear that, we embark upon *education*, not selling. "Proving governance" is akin to asking the accounting area to rejustify double-entry bookkeeping. Governance is a required function that most organizations embrace comfortably. Anyone asking for a proof of concept either does not get it or is erecting barriers.

understanding is once the "proof" (i.e., a business case) is shown, there is acceptance that DG is designed and deployed in the context of an enterprise, not a business area.

Whether or not you use the term EIM, DG is crucial for managing information as an asset. The other path to DG is as a component of an EIM effort.

Lastly, DG can stem from concerns originating from a specific set of content. Strangely, while structured or "row-and-column" content is the first target of DG, many companies find themselves building fine DG programs when they clean up and manage documents. Databases and "row-and-column" data sets are governed long after non-structured content, or a regulatory surge makes a company focus on a specific subject area. This happened in 2009–2010 as fallout from the mortgage crisis and recession. Suddenly, DG became "hip."

THE DG "METHODOLOGY"

While we show eight distinct phases, the process for starting and sustaining DG is shown as a cycle because it is usually iterative. Obviously, we need to show what the entire process looks like, but you will execute all or part of this cycle several times. *Additionally, you will not do every step the same way every time.*

Many factors contribute to how the DG programs rolls out:

1. Are you doing DG as part of a single master-data-management effort? If you are doing a typical project to consolidate customer data, you may have to focus your governance on the MDM event. Your organization may not yet have an appetite for enterprise DG. You will execute the entire process, albeit on a more limited scope. This does not mean you treat the DG program as a stand-alone effort. (Remember that you are doing EIM, even if you are not using the name.) Often, there is another MDM project on the heels of the first one (assuming they are successful). Then you will immediately see why DG needs to be treated with an enterprise perspective, regardless of its roots.
2. Do you work in a very large company? If so, our guess is you have simultaneous instances of DG percolating. They may not all be called DG, but they are there. A uniform process allows various efforts to leverage and combine their efforts under a common protocol.
3. Do you have a formal EIM program or IM area? If so, you will execute this approach probably once to stand up the larger DG "area," and then several times as you support various projects requiring DG.

Therefore, the process we are going to review is not a recipe, but rather a methodology that needs to be adapted to your situation.

PROCESS OVERVIEW

There are eight steps or phases to our stand-up process. As we stated earlier, this is a more granular process that focuses on the actual "how-to." This and subsequent chapters will be fairly detailed.[2]

---

[2]We are always asked at conferences or by clients to provide "how-to" advice. Admittedly, it seems many consultants tend to provide "box and arrows" solutions, and seem to be scarce when the hard questions are being asked. To be fair, you cannot understand the detailed steps unless you get a good dose of "box and arrows" learning. So, the earlier chapters were the framing chapters. Now it is time for the details. Remember, you asked for this. You have been warned.

In this chapter, the phases are listed along with key considerations. We provide a list of key activities and an example to provide context. The following chapters delve into the details of the activities and look at specific cases and deliverables.

Each step builds upon the previous one. However, the steps can also be conducted as a "stand-alone" process if the required artifacts or information for that step are available from another EIM-related effort. There is a reference table in the appendices that can be printed or imported into a project plan.

SCOPE AND INITIATION

Anyone who has done any kind of program or project knows you need to start with an understanding of scope. It is no different for deploying DG. After all, there is a great likelihood of affecting several segments of your organization. Figure 5-1 shows how DG can be applied differently based on the type of organization. In addition, there needs to be an understanding of how "deep" the DG program will be going. There are also the traditional activities associated with starting any program or project.

Considerations

For example, right or wrong, most DG programs get started within an information technology (IT) area. If a CIO is gung-ho about cleaning up the treatment of data and making it a powerful asset, she had better verify that the scope of DG includes the creation and enforcement of broad-spectrum policies. If an organization is highly regulated, then the compliance area needs to be brought into the DG effort.

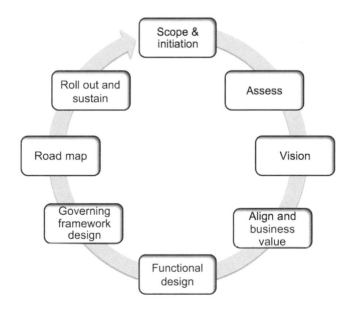

FIGURE 5-1

This figure shows a static view of the stand-up process we will cover.

Defining exactly "what" is governed is also of key importance. For example, are any business areas exempt due to regulatory reasons? Is there a division that, due to its business model, DG would not be helpful? (This happened in our practice. The client had a line of business that dealt entirely in research, so experimental data and research papers were the core information assets. Those folks already took very good care of their data!)

Besides scope restrictions, you may need to consider factors that require a larger scope than initially considered. What about business market factors? A data governance effort attached to a master data project may need to consider a greater scope if a company's market share is suffering and poor-quality data is a contributor. If your company has recently completed or is in the middle of implementing an enterprise-level application project, such as SAP or Oracle ERP, then your data governance effort will need to cozy up to those programs.

The intensity of DG is part of the scope decision. Are the information principles that will arise from the DG effort required to have the weight to cover an entire organization? The same decision goes for policies. Your DG program will create new policies and you need to decide to what levels of the organization you will extend those policies. If appointing individuals with new roles of accountability, or decision rights that are new to your organization will be an issue, then your human resource area needs to be considered as part of the project scope.

It is not a trivial matter that the scope of DG is set by the nature of an organization (i.e., the methods used to set and enforce policy and rules, how decisions are made, and who makes them). If an organization has a culture of accountability, then the scope of DG can be broadly stated. If the organization has operated without blatant accountability for information technology and data assets, then DG scope must be stated very specifically, and mention that accountability will be entering the organization's lexicon.

Lastly, remember the "E" in EIM stands for enterprise. You are defining DG for an enterprise. That means, start with the whole thing, and only reduce scope for specific reasons. There is no such thing as departmental governance. It is a contradiction in terms.[3]

ASSESS

Once scope is understood—and approved—then the DG team can move on to the required assessments. Unlike assessments done for data quality or enterprise architecture, the DG assessments are focused on the ability of the organization to govern and to be governed. We use the alliterative phrase "capacity, culture, collaborate." That is extremely important to determine the current state of the mechanisms and processes an organization will be changing as data governance rolls out.

"Capacity" refers to the capacity to change. Desire to change should never be confused with the capacity to change. For example, the IT organization at a past client of ours knew that data quality was the number one obstacle to developing a customer master data management (CMDM) architecture. Business users across the board openly acknowledged that customer data was, overall, pretty awful. When we came upon the scene, the project was stalled. All of the data problems were known. Many of the processes to correct the problems were designed, but nothing was happening. There were countless

---

[3]Perhaps "departmental governance" will enter the "oxymoron hall of fame" along with military intelligence, jumbo shrimp, and political ethics. Then again, maybe not.

Information Management Maturity Spectrums

Usage basis	Make it happen	Make it happen faster	What happened?	Why did it happen?	What will happen?	Make it happen by itself	What do I want to happen?	How do we make it happen better?	What should we do next?
Content basis	Events	Trans-actions	Reporting	Analyzing	Predictive	Operation-alize	Closed loop	Collabor-ative	Foresight
Capability basis	Initial	Repeatable		Defined	Managed			Optimized	
Organization basis	Operate		Consolidate		Integrate		Optimize		Innovate

FIGURE 5-2

Various Views of Information Management Maturity.

meetings as to how to keep altering scope and the rollout strategy. The root issue was that no business area wanted to be the first one to assume the new discipline required of the CMDM solution. In fact, it did not take long to determine that not a single department was able to embark upon the required changes without major upheaval. The corporate spirit was willing, but the corporate flesh was weak. It took a major effort to prepare the organization for the required changes.

"Culture" is the favorite buzzword, as of this writing, when speaking in the context of the challenges of data governance. However, you cannot say, "Yep, let's manage culture!" and expect to be covered. All organizations have a different way or style of using data and information, even within the same industry. Some may have achieved only mastery of basic reporting. Others may be managing documents and using sophisticated data analysis. That is, they use data and information differently. Since the ultimate goal of a data governance program is better data management resulting in better information, we certainly need to understand where the organization is *now*. Figure 5-2 reproduces an overview of several types of information maturity scales.[4]

It is more important to present some sort of scale than to try to determine which view of maturity is "correct."

"Collaboration" refers to the assessment of an organization to work cross-functionally or to work on a task using teams made up of representatives pulled from various business segments. Granted, this can be considered part of the culture. However, when collaboration enters the DG deployment picture, it is a discipline that requires a thorough understanding of an organization's ability to work collaboratively.

Considerations

Based on the three "Cs" described earlier, the assessment phase for DG deployment entails three types of assessments. Whether you do all of them or only a portion depends heavily on the origins of your DG effort. Figure 5-3 shows what you need to consider along with the three assessment types.

[4]For a detailed discussion on information management maturity, see Chapter 3 of *Making EIM Work for Business*, John Ladley (Waltham, MA: Morgan Kaufman, 2010).

What Types of Assessment Are Needed?

	CULTURE	CAPACITY	COLLABORATE
Assessment types:	Information Maturity	Change Capacity	Collaborative Readiness
Potential targets of DG:			
Support MDM, DW, or other structured information project	Yes - if it has not been done as part of the project		Yes - MDM is, by definition, cross-functional
Support document management, or other unstructured information project	Yes - especially in the context of document management		Yes - document and content management are, by definition, cross-functional
Support data quality	Optional - the data quality effort is usually focused on creating better data so it can be used	Yes - if not already done as part of DQ effort	No - does not apply
Start DG as part of EIM strategy	No - if it has not been done as part of the EIM program your EIM program is not going well		
Start DG as a stand-alone program	Yes - but why? Stand-alone DG is usually really a form of doing a formal EIM program. Better double check what it is you are trying to get accomplished		

FIGURE 5-3

Types of Assessments.

Regardless of what direction, it is perfectly fine to mix and match these assessments. We often combine the "Change Capacity" with the "Information Maturity" survey, usually due to restraints within the population being surveyed or assessed.

The most preferred means of executing these assessments is via an online survey. They work faster, give you a data set that can be analyzed, and can be repurposed. The techniques we least prefer are numerous interviews—mostly because they are too time consuming. Often the assessment will be a blend of online surveys, with interviews of key business leadership.

Activities

1. *Information Maturity Assessment*—This assessment determines the current state of maturity of an organization to utilize data and information in an advanced manner. Understand what the

organization does with the content and information it produces. Focus is on impressions and feelings business personnel have on how well the company uses and manages data to its advantage. Besides identifying a current state, this activity provides a baseline for measuring progress toward future DG effectiveness from an objective, qualitative standpoint.

2. *Change Capacity Assessment*—Understand the organization's ability to adapt to new/changing policies regarding the management of information assets. The focus is on determining how much change the organization can embrace. The assessment will provide an overview of where the DG program will run into resistance and will establish a framework that will influence the design of the sustaining strategy for DG.

3. *Collaborative Readiness Assessment*—This assessment reviews the ability of the organization to operate in a cross-functional manner under a formal program of collaborative processes. The focus is not cultural (i.e., are there barriers to collaborative processes?), but actual ability and understanding of collaborative processes. Most organizations do not grasp the additional abilities and skills required for collaboration. The assessment will develop baseline knowledge of collaborative skills and ability.

HELPFUL HINT

Collaboration is a word that is becoming as cliché as "culture change" due to overuse. Much akin to "governance" and "culture change," it is a term that is easier to understand than to implement. Remember this, the reason you are talking about all three of these terms is that your entire organization is realizing that the way things are being done is *not sustainable.* That means retraining, learning, changing abilities, and adopting new philosophies.

VISION

The "Vision" phase is executed to demonstrate to stakeholders and leadership the definition and meaning of DG to the organization. The goal is to achieve an understanding of what the data governance program might look like and where the critical touch points for DG might appear. Those new to DG but aware of other strategic program processes may initially say this step is superfluous if the organization is totally on board. However, our practice has shown this is a dangerous position to take. It turns out that until you show some sort of "day-in-the-life" presentation, many people do not comprehend what DG means to their position or work environment. In the context of DG, this phase may appear to be more of a conceptual prototype.

Considerations

Since we are creating a very high level, or notional, representation of what DG could look like, you need to translate scope into a definition of DG that is suited to your organization. Then form that definition into a clear simple representation of scope and impact. You may even want to take a run at a notional road map with a comparison of current state to future state. At this stage, you need to do whatever (emphasis on "whatever") it takes to continue to draw more and more stakeholders into accepting the vision. One tactic that has worked with our clients is another more refined version of the governance V, which we present in Chapter 8.

Activities

1. *Define DG for your organization*—Draft a clear, brief definition of DG (see examples in Chapter 2) as well as a brief statement of impact and considerations. Then get them approved.
2. *Define preliminary DG requirements*—The definition and considerations will allow you to organize the first cut at what is going to be governed. Do not start with specific data sources—start with what business goals DG will help achieve. Then move into specific business events, requests, and regulatory areas. If you are deploying DG as part of an MDM or similar program, these elements should already be available. If they are not, then this is the opportunity to orient the MDM effort because if an MDM program is talking only data sources as requirements, it is derailed.
3. *Develop representations of future DG*—Assemble the requirements for DG in terms of where DG will touch business processes. Also, a clear association of DG, business process, and how DG will enable (versus get in the way of) business activity will be invaluable in gaining more understanding of DG. Lastly, a one-page "day-in-the-life" slide is probably the most significant output of this activity. Over the years, this work product has made the difference between proceeding with the program versus bogging it down.

ALIGN AND BUSINESS VALUE

While the vision step helped move more stakeholders toward a greater level of understanding, this phase more specifically develops the financial value statement and baseline for ongoing measurement of the DG deployment. The DG team will examine (in more detail) the business strategy and goals, and develop a link between DG and improving the organization in a financially recognizable way.

Considerations

Two aspects to this phase merit careful consideration. First, you need to consider what else is going on in terms of managing information as an asset. If there is an overall EIM program, or sponsoring efforts like MDM or data quality, then some of the effort described in this phase may have already been done.

You then need to consider that this is a mandatory step in deploying DG. It is good news if some or all of it was performed as part of another effort. Even if there is an associated program (like data quality or MDM), you need to take stock of how DG will support the business, even if it is indirectly through the data quality or MDM efforts. You need to determine what the criteria are for DG success. After all, you cannot manage what you do not measure. To that end, you need to perform this phase to provide the baseline for determining DG performance metrics and measures of sustainability.

Activities

1. *Leverage EIM or DQ business case*—If DG is associated with another effort, most likely there will be some data available to leverage in forming a statement of business alignment. This activity

utilizes that data to tie DG requirements and vision to business needs. Additional details about business goals and objectives are turned into specific value statements where DG enables positive change. For example, the number one area where DG can assist most companies in the BI and reporting areas is to ensure business alignment with BI initiatives and technology. So there needs to be some clear business objectives associated with the BI efforts.

2. *Align business needs to DG*—If there is no other source of an information management business case, then the DG team needs to execute this activity. We have seen this scenario often when the IT department starts an information-centered project. Most notable examples are stand-alone MDM efforts where the CIO tried to integrate core data as a technology effort, or a data warehouse designed as a cure to data quality issues. The DG team needs to fully understand business needs and isolate those actions where correct and well-governed information will help the organization achieve its desired results. This may not be a trivial effort where organizations need to do a lot of things fast with data, or are undergoing multiple large projects. It will mean doing an exercise to map strategies to information projects, an activity that is often met with interrogation as to "why" or outright resistance.

3. *Identify the business value of DG*—This activity is where the DG team identifies specific financial numbers and determines what business metrics will indicate the success of DG. This is also a good place to show the cost of non-governance, or continuing to use information in a poorly managed fashion.

HELPFUL HINT

When you are around the vision or business case activities, you will undoubtedly encounter the first layer of resistance to DG. You will attempt to present to an executive level and three things will happen:

1) A lower level will be told to deal with it. The executives will be too busy.
2) Your sponsors or business representatives will get cold feet when it is time to educate in an upward direction and dilute the message.
3) The executive level will humor you and sit through a presentation, ask some good questions, and then forget you ever met.

Sadly, all three represent a lack of leadership and understanding. Our experience has shown that the highest levels of resistance are usually put forth by the organizations most in need of business alignment! However, repeated education and reinforcement of the message, accompanied by some good metrics will start to open doors. You may have to revisit and repeat vision and business case activities over a period of years as you penetrate more areas of your company.

FUNCTIONAL DESIGN

This phase is where the DG program actually starts to be specified and further details are developed as to how it will actually work. The chief outcomes from this activity are the principles, policies, and process designs. These are the "things" that will occur under the auspices of DG. We use the term "function" with deliberation, as the focus is on the "what" versus the "how." You are now starting to supply details to both sides of the governance V.

Considerations

You are building a program that requires a framework for operation. That means some basic blocking and tackling in terms of Management 101. However, since many DG teams come from technology areas, there is often a major slowdown in the DG effort as people who have never done organization design start to do it. This is *not* an exercise in scraping together a few organization charts.

Another common mistake is to fail to keep the design of information management processes separate from data governance processes. This is usually because the initial staffing of DG is drawn from information areas. Often the initial DG staff are told to "fit it in" to their current roles and responsibilities.[5] It is challenging for these individuals to maintain the separation of duties mandated by the V while creating embedded organizational processes, new roles, and a sustainable program.

Activities

1. *Determine core information principles*—This activity is arguably the most important in the development and deployment of DG. A significant part of Chapter 10 is devoted to these tasks. Simply put, the DG team identifies, documents, and vets the core organization principles that will be adopted to manage information as an asset. Without these, the DG effort is crippled.
2. *Determine baseline DG processes to support business*—All organizations do "stuff." This is where (usually using a list of generic processes) the DG deployment team determines the core list of what DG will be accomplishing. In essence, you add the details to evolve the V—often by developing process models (think flow chart, swim lane presentations, etc.). The team also points out where current business processes are changed. For example, we have often found that a detailed presentation of the DG issue-resolution process is required (i.e., how an issue is identified, recorded, promoted, and resolved—once we even designed a "911" process for emergency attention to data policy transgressions). Lastly, do not fail to consider the IT areas in addition to changes in business-user activity. Processes and methods for developing and managing computer applications will also change.
3. *Identify/refine IM functions and processes*—In a similar fashion, the DG team gathers (or helps in defining) the more IM functions. Remember not to blend the two areas; it will result in confusion and a loss of effectiveness of both areas.
4. *Identify preliminary accountability and ownership model*—The essential lists of DG and IM processes are not at all useful until the DG team identifies who does what, and what the various levels of responsibility are. In this step, the team examines the functions to identify where responsibility and accountability might need to exist to ensure sustainability of DG. This is not the final pass in terms of the new DG "organization"—that happens in the next activity. This is more of a first pass so management can understand the change potential and be able to consider the new DG processes and framework in context and in an intelligent manner.

---

[5]Kudos to those IM staff we have worked with over the years, who, to a person, have all had to do double duty. There are many hard-working people in information management, and we have never seen a management team allow the designated DG deployment team to offload their current duties. Of course, it drags things out, but they hang in there. As for the management who demands the double duty (and does not offer additional incentive) while at the same time saying how important DG is, well, we will refrain from comment.

5. *Present EIM DG functional model to business leadership*—It is very important to educate and present the new responsibilities and accountabilities to management. In most cases, there will be some shift in how management performance is rated. Do not be surprised if there is some back and forth at this point as reality settles in to middle management (i.e., someone is going to be held accountable for data).

GOVERNING FRAMEWORK DESIGN

Once the functions are determined, the next step is to place the functional design for DG into an organization framework. This step is kept separate from the functional design for three reasons:

1. The team stays focused on required processes and workflow without worrying about people and personalities.
2. The actual organization that executes DG will be very different from one organization to another, even within the same industry.
3. In our experience, the organization framework originally proposed rarely resembles the DG organization two years later.

Note also that the term "organization framework" is used instead of "organization chart." We used to call this phase organization design, but that is a misnomer. Given that the goal is to eventually blend in with ordinary day-to-day behavior, you will rarely develop a large separate DG organization. There will always be a small virtual function of DG visible, but only rarely do we see the need for a stand-alone, permanently funded DG "department."

HELPFUL HINT

If you have not done so by this point, drop the idea of a distinct DG now. At the root of successful DG is doing what you are currently doing with information, but *better*. Think about changing other organization behaviors. The audit committee does not take the correct actions to ensure accurate accounting. They make someone else do it. Likewise, you do not want a separate DG organization doing the information asset management tasks.

This phase also entails identifying the stewardship/ownership/custodian population. Please note that our methodology for rolling out DG delays this step until the functional design is completed. Other processes may indicate identifying stewards, etc., earlier. We don't like that because it places people in a position of feeling they need to do something, but that something is usually ill-defined until this point. It also avoids spewing the whole stewardship vocabulary around before you have actually defined what that means for your organization. If you wait until now, you can designate roles and responsibilities and then assign the appropriate label to a specific catalog of DG duties.

Considerations

There are many "standard" data governance organizations available in various articles and books to use as a template. Most of the time a pyramid or other hierarchical presentation represents the DG framework. It is fine to use straw-person frameworks with these, but they should never be proposed without some thought or consideration of the organization's culture and politics.

Also, make sure that the functional model is complete. Reexamine where the list of IM functions and DG functions could intersect. You may discover the need for some coordination that was not obvious earlier.

The most critical concept to consider at this point is the degree of federation. Simply put, some areas or subjects will require more intense governance than others will. We introduced federation in Chapter 3, but to review, the term "federation" is used to describe the level of penetration of DG into various areas within the organization. A typical example for federation of DG appears in the MDM solution area. Assuming that [a?] customer is the subject, we might find in one organization that only a small portion of the content describing a customer needs to be governed. In another organization, you may find that all of the information used around a customer needs to be closely governed. Refer again to Figure 3-2 as a generic example of how we would indicate the type of governance across multiple subjects in a large company. If you do not consider the extent of federation, it will be impossible to design an effective framework. Many organizations strive (naively) for a totally centralized oversight for data (no federation). Others believe they can develop a framework that is totally virtual (totally federated and very hard to sustain). Ideally, there is a middle ground that reflects reality.

Activities

1. *Design DG organization framework*—This series of tasks determines where and what levels will execute, manage, and be accountable for managing information assets. Sometimes forward-looking organizations appoint a DG committee (that eventually supplies stewards and owners) to work with the DG team to design the organization framework. Either way, this activity means an old-fashioned RACI exercise, a definition of the degree of federation, and an identification of the leadership layers for DG. Finally, organization charters will need drafting so that soon-to-be-appointed stewards and owners will have reference material for rolling out DG.
2. *Complete roles and responsibility identification*—Once the RACI is done, the DG team (or committee) will be able to start placing names with roles. Depending on the organization, this may be much harder than just names in boxes on a chart. There are several potential obstacles to the timely completion of this activity:
   * Perceived political threats from some getting "power" over data.
   * Human capital (or HR) concerns on changing job descriptions.
   * Fear that adding additional responsibilities will damage current productivity.

One thing to reinforce at this point is you are not creating a new job description or position. Our good friend and practitioner, David Plotkin, put it this way: "Data stewardship is not a job. It is the formalization of data responsibilities that are likely in place in an informal way."[i] The DG team should coordinate with HR to identify potential revisions in performance goals for the new roles. Finally, the DG team will suggest the makeup of the DG oversight bodies or committees. These oversight bodies take on different names. Figure 5-4 shows an example of the various names and layers. Note the example uses the V structure, not a pyramid. This representation clearly shows not only layers, but also where communication needs to occur.

---

[i]David Plotkin, extract from "Presentation to Enterprise Data World, 2010."

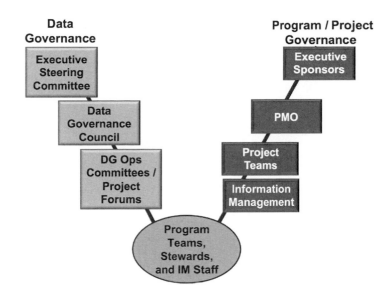

FIGURE 5-4

Example of an Evolved "V".

Over the years, we have used the following names based on position and role in the DG framework:

- Council—The DG council usually is the primary monitoring and issue resolution body. In larger organizations, there can be an executive council as well as an operational council.
- Committee—When the executive level council is advisory, we call it a committee.
- Forums—In large companies, there are multiple varieties of governance. Very often, we need to set up sub-units that focus on one topic. We call these forums.

Regardless of the eventual structure, each major level of DG needs to have a charter developed. A sample outline is provided in Appendix iii, but it will contain the mission, vision, and major activities for the respective DG layers.

3. *Review and obtain approval of DG framework design*—Once the RACI exercise, roles, and names are identified, the obvious step is to present the list of proposed layers and functionality. Typically, there will be some back and forth regarding the roles and availability of higher-level resources. The DG team needs to be aware that this step may take a while, as the approval of such structures usually occurs among personnel who only get together once a month, at best. Once the various layers and functionality of DG are approved, the actual appointment of accountable parties must occur. This is not an exercise to be taken lightly. Many DG efforts come to a total halt here. Once business leadership sees that someone in their area (or even themselves) will be exposed to additional accountability, the hands go up and the hollering starts. This is why the change capacity assessment is so important. Hopefully, a savvy DG team has identified the individuals who will balk, and worked behind the scenes to address any issues. We had one client who took six months to go through this one activity. They were able to move on and begin to rollout DG, but their story is more rule than exception.

4. *Initiate DG socialization*—Approval of structure and personnel is only the beginning. Now the new stewards and their stakeholders must be oriented and be prepared for the new approach to managing data assets. The leadership of DG, including executive and steering councils, needs to be communicated with as to the nearness and details of the upcoming G activities. You may need to—in fact, you should—plan on one-on-one conversations with the members of your executive teams. This task can be considered the beginning of the wholesale rollout of DG. One way to view this activity is the initial pass of orientation and education.

ROAD MAP

This phase is the step where DG plans the details around the "go live" events of DG. The team will define the events that take the organization from a non-governed to a governed state for its data assets. In addition, the requirements and groundwork are laid to sustain the DG program (i.e., detailed preparations to address the changes required by the DG program).

Considerations

Understand that the team may be creating a tactical plan that will take several years. This is not a light-duty activity. Often the "road map" that is produced from this step integrates DG activity with other projects and initiatives. In fact, most of the time you will need to "piggy back" DG on other efforts (unless you are doing DG because of another effort).

Regardless of how the rollout phase is developed, make sure there are frequent checkpoints and opportunity for feedback. Again, you will be changing behavior. Don't let circumstances and lack of attention create a situation where the organization can make an excuse to "defer" DG.

Perhaps the most important consideration of this activity is to make sure that output (communications and training plans as well as a road map) are all tuned to the organization's culture. Too often we see generic results from this step (i.e., a few newsletters, a mass "training class," and a one-page Gantt chart. Frankly, most of these will be overlooked. The DG team will receive a full-on response of "been there, done that." These tasks require some creativity.

Activities

1. *Integrate DG with other efforts*—DG needs to be woven into the fabric of everyday business. This is where the DG team jumps on board with other efforts. Sometimes the DG committees, forums, etc., need a little refinement or additional orientation, so don't hesitate to go back and reorient. The DG road map or detailed schedule is produced. Remember, if there is a program "sponsoring" DG, like MDM, you need to integrate with that program's plans.
2. *Design DG metrics and reporting requirements*—It is often said that you need to measure what you manage. DG requires some sort of metric-based feedback to ensure its continuity. If you cannot show demonstrable effect, it's too easy for naysayers to slap the program down when the changes start to take effect. Therefore, the DG team needs to define some solid progress metrics and reports.

The audience, collection, and delivery mechanisms for progress reports are determined in this step. It will be important to vet the data being reported with leadership as well, in case there are business-driven reasons to adjust the measurement and feedback mechanisms.

3. *Define the sustaining requirements*—The first step of managing the changes that will occur is to plan those changes. There will be many cultural elements that need to be addressed if there is to be a successful DG rollout. This activity determines these elements and how they are coordinated. The team reviews the change capacity assessment, stakeholder analysis, and any other findings gathered during the previous activity with the intent of developing the requirements for ensuring the DG program is sustainable. The number one pet peeve in our practice is the deployment of, well, almost anything, without considering what will need to happen one or two years down the road. In addition to training and communications activity, which are obvious, there will need to be an ongoing measurement of the rate and amount of change, as well as the attitude and morale of the DG team and stakeholders. Change efforts require long-term sponsorship, so the DG team will be looking for an individual to act as a change sponsor.

A key segment of any effort requiring changes in process, policy, or behavior is consistent, clear, and unambiguous communication. The plan for communicating is developed at this point. Two other adjectives that help here are *simple* and *straightforward.* The DG team will invest time creating the message and brand for the oncoming changes. The timing, type, and intensity of the communications are all specified. Lastly, the communications plan is reviewed and approved by DG leadership.

Similar to the communications plan, a training plan is developed to reflect the required audiences and delivery vehicles suitable for the organization's culture, along with the review and approval of the training approach. The key here is to avoid "one-size-fits-all" orientation slide decks—also known in our practice as "Death by PowerPoint." There are three distinct levels of training:

   a) *Orientation*—Setting the stage and high-level view of DG
   b) *Education*—Awareness and ability to use policies and procedures
   c) *Training*—Actual hands-on development for use of new tools and procedures

4. *Design change management plan*—The requirements for change lead into the development of a formal change management plan. This will entail metrics to measure change (not to be confused with the metrics for DG effectiveness) and the development of reward structures and compliance activity for stakeholders who are moving into a world of well-managed data assets. The change management plan is fairly detailed and should encompass a period of one to three years.

5. *Define DG operational roll out*—Once the requirements for change are understood, the details of the rollout of DG are put together. The actual steps to start DG, including details for the stewards and custodians, are presented.

HELPFUL HINT

The successful deployment of DG will be viewed as yesterday's news unless it is kept visible (and someone important gets credit for its success), and that is the purpose of the sustaining phase. We approach the planning and rollout of DG with the viewpoint that modern organizations, especially modern corporations, have the attention span of a two-year-old. This may or may not be true, but it helps with the planning.

ROLLOUT AND SUSTAIN

Earlier, we mentioned the need to ensure that DG was sustainable. This phase represents execution of the activities related to sustainability. This phase is not really a phase with a distinct start and stop date. In essence, once you have started to sustain DG, it never stops. Until DG is totally internalized, which may take years, there will be the need to manage the transformation from non-governed data assets to governed data assets.

Any material on sustainability provided in this book is really material based solely on the business discipline of culture change management. In our practice, we have evolved to using the term "sustain" simply because it's more understandable and accepted than "culture change."

During this phase, the DG team (actually the entire DG framework) works to ensure the DG program remains effective and meets or exceeds expectations. At times, there will be reactive responses to open resistance. There will be proactive tactics to head off resistance. The main emphasis will be to ensure that there is on-going visible support for DG.

Considerations

DG is not self-sustaining. First and foremost, this must be accepted. While we stand by the statement that the net cost of DG, over time, is zero, there must be the understanding that formal activity is required to ensure you reach the zero-sum state. Remember that the eventual goal is to make DG institutionalized and not a separate concept. This phase should also reflect periodic replanning, as personnel and business needs will change. The DG program needs to adapt without losing focus.

The activities in this phase are not linear. Most of them will occur in parallel, or even intertwine. They are presented next by topic to aid in understanding.

Activities

1. *DG operating rollout*—At last. The DG team, along with whatever the appropriate project teams and DG forums are, actually start to "do governance." Whatever initial groups have been designated (via the road map) are indoctrinated into new processes. This means, of course, training and communications. It also means publishing many of the artifacts that have been developed (e.g., guidelines, principles, policies, etc.). The DG stewards and owners who are responsible for reviews and audits start these activities as well.
2. *Execute the DG change plan*—All of the activity defined to address sustaining DG occurs here. Communications, training, check points, data collection, etc. Any specific tasks to deal with resistance can be placed here. Over time, training and educational material will require updating. Additional staff will require orientation. Management will need to hear about the bright spots and not-so-bright spots. All of these elements of the culture change can be listed in this activity. Initially, the most effective tasks to be defined are the ones where resources need to be involved in communicating, training, or addressing resistance.
3. *Confirm operation and effectiveness of DG operations*—The DG framework needs to be scrutinized for effectiveness. A separate forum or a central DG group will carry this out if one exists. Principles, policies, and incentives need to be reviewed for effectiveness. There is a need to separate effectiveness of the framework (the federation of responsibilities and

accountabilities) from the general effectiveness of DG. This entails data collection and the generation of metrics that report on effectiveness of policies and standards, as well as the activity of designated stewards and owners. Focus groups, interviews, and surveys are common techniques used to assess how the rest of the organization views DG. If changes are required in DG policies, then this activity triggers the necessary adjustments.

DG OVERVIEW SUMMARY

This chapter provided an overview of a methodology for "standing up" DG, with an overview, considerations, and activities for each step. The following chapters will provide specifics on the tasks and work products necessary to deploy DG. The main concept to take away from this chapter is that DG deployment, while being programmatic in nature, still requires a process and rigorous management.

CORE SUCCESS FACTORS

There are three core success factors we want to make sure are identified at this point:

1. DG requires culture change management. By definition, you are moving from an undesirable state to a desired state. That means changes are in order.
2. DG "organization" is not a stand-alone, brand-new department. Ideally, in most organizations DG will end up being a virtual activity.
3. DG, even if started as a stand-alone concept, needs to be tied to an initiative.

Much of what has been presented is not rocket science. However the basic "blocking and tackling" activities are often overlooked by personnel who are new to standing up an organization.

Scope and initiation

In preparing for battle, I have always found that plans are useless, but planning is indispensable.
—Dwight D. Eisenhower

As we said earlier, starting the deployment of your DG program entails standard program startup activities. Therefore, we must ensure that scope and span are adequately understood, and then produce a plan that will sufficiently guide the team through DG deployment.

As with any other effort related to EIM, our practice has observed that, simply stated, it is difficult to get started. This is usually due to the need for some specialized activities. Most companies have experience with projects but bog down in starting the new activity. Like any other EIM-type effort, there will be the need to execute new activities that are unique to data governance. This chapter will cover those in detail.

OVERVIEW

Remember that traditional activities such as timelines, participants, project administration, and communications need to be established. Additionally, if you are working under an MDM or similar effort, there will or should be documents that need to be reviewed. Gather them up or find out where they are, and get permission to access them, if permission is required. Like any other strategic effort, knowing what you have and what you need to dig up makes a large difference in estimates. Lastly, remember that this phase will confirm a common understanding of the DG program's success measures. Figure 6-1 and Figure 6-2 show the details and flows of the DG "Scope and Initiation" phase.

Please do not assume this is a casual exercise. In our practice, the typical program/project plan deliverable from this phase averages 400 tasks. We have produced DG deployment plans that span three years and contain nearly 1000 discrete tasks. You may not follow each and every task, but you need to comprehend the amount of activity that can possibly take place, and how the workload will be addressed. Hence, the quote at the beginning of the chapter—the planning activity sets the tone and the team. Perhaps the most well-planned activity in history was the Operation Overlord invasion of Europe (sometimes referred to as D-Day). That event took two years to plan. The invasion was successful, but the plan was quite fluid once the event started.[1] Therefore, the plan itself will change over time, but the focus and artifacts will help sustain the DG effort.

---

[1] Near as we can tell, the planning and execution of the Normandy invasion gave rise to the quote, "The reason you have a plan is so some SOB can change it." We never have been able to track this one down, but it certainly captures the essence of DG planning.

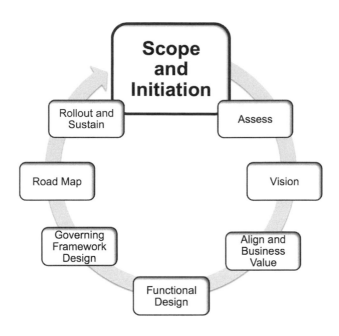

FIGURE 6-1

Process Overview.

FIGURE 6-2

Activity Overview.

This chapter and the seven that follow will be presented in the same format. The activities for each phase will be described along with a breakdown of tasks, work products, and benefits. Where appropriate we also present a sample work product.

Activity: Identify Business Unit(s) and/or Organizations Subject to DG

The scope of data governance is actually a function of span and the anticipated degree of penetration. For example, a large financial services organization may require a wide span of DG given the nature of its products and regulatory environment. The same organization may require a very deep level of penetration where DG policies will manifest themselves in all aspects of the business. List those segments of the business that will most likely come under the influence of the DG program.

Activity Summary Table

Objective	Determine candidate business units and/or organizations that can come under the oversight of the DG program.
Purpose	Begin to understand the possible span and depth of the DG program.
Inputs	Business model, organization charts
Tasks	1. List business units/divisions that may be subject to DG. 2. Identify key divisions in business units. 3. Understand significant strategies and initiatives. 4. Determine if divisional differences merit different DG. 5. Develop list of organizational units in scope of DG.
Techniques	None
Tools	Word, PowerPoint, or similar
Outputs	1. Business-area candidates for DG 2. Divisional candidates for DG 3. High-level business strategies driving DG 4. Scope drivers of DG 5. DG program scope
Outcome	A declaration of scope for the DG program

FIGURE 6-3

Activity Summary Table.

Business Benefits and Ramifications

DG is a business program. The business will benefit from this activity by getting a sense of how large (or small) the DG program will be. On one hand, a realistic image of the extent of the effort becomes evident. On the other hand, this realistic image may create some positive debate on where DG can work.

Approach Considerations

Obviously, some explanation of DG is in order before this happens. Even though this book is focused on deployment, it probably will be valuable to the nascent DG group to verify that there is adequate understanding of DG to develop a realistic scope statement. They need to verify:

- Is there a working definition or perception of what DG actually is?
- Is DG truly sold? Is more selling needed?
- Is there at least a notional understanding of the long-term success factors and impact of DG?

If the answer to any of those questions is "No," then the subsequent activities need to add effort to reinforce DG concepts.

Sample Output

Figure 6-4 shows sample scope. Since there is one business model (in this case, retail), the scope is functional in nature. Figure 6-5 shows the scope for an organization with multiple business models, so scope is along the lines of brands, or units.

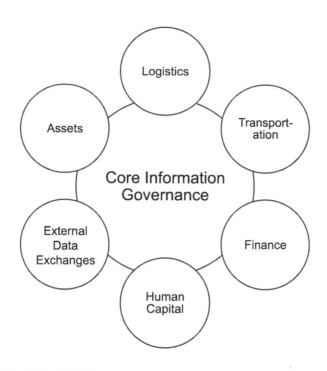

FIGURE 6-4

Initial Scope Data Governance—Retail.

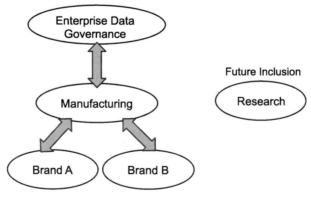

FIGURE 6-5

Initial Scope Data Governance - Manufacturing.

Tips for Success

The data governance "team" is usually a few folks who are told to lay out DG for an MDM project or similar effort—or they are enhancing ongoing information management efforts as part of an overall EIM strategy. Therefore, they will seem to be revisiting old concepts. It is very important to make sure the nascent team gets sufficient "air coverage" (i.e., be introduced or initially sponsored by a respected executive). If an MDM project is initiating DG, then the project sponsor needs to kick this off.

Activity: Propose Scope and Initial Approach to Define and Deploy DG

This set of tasks develops the plan for the definition and rollout of the DG program. Any required constraints are applied and any required assessments are determined.

Activity Summary Table

Objective	Define the final areas subject to DG. Based on a standard definition of DG, adjust the scope based on any constraints such as timing, market conditions, or regulations, then define the DG rollout plan.
Purpose	Refine the proposed scope based on realities of timing and develop a detailed approach to deploying the DG program.
Inputs	1. Initial scope 2. Basic DG deployment template (see appendices)
Tasks	1. Define DG specific tasks. 2. Define known constraints within proposed scope. 3. Define required assessments. 4. Define standard startup tasks.
Techniques	None
Tools	Word, PowerPoint, or similar
Outputs	1. DG tasks 2. Known constraints (e.g., market, time, regulations) 3. Required assessment tasks 4. Standard enterprise program startup tasks (if any)
Outcome	DG project plan

FIGURE 6-6

Activity Summary Table.

Business Benefits and Ramifications

When the team starts the detailed planning, the full extent of required activity will become apparent. Scope can be adjusted here. This prevents the DG effort from possibly going after too much at one time. For a program-driven DG effort, such as one under an MDM umbrella, the benefit comes from beginning to grasp the impact and interactions with the sponsoring effort.

Approach Considerations

Obviously, the final scope determination will be dependent on whether the DG program is based on a program like MDM or is part of a larger EIM program.

Sample Output

There is a sample DG project plan in Appendix 1.

Tips for Success

Remember that you can be developing a rather large plan. Even if you are constrained to managing DG only for a specific MDM effort, there are a lot of moving parts to coordinate. If time is of the essence, develop detailed plans for the next few months and then add details as necessary, as long as you keep a good three-month detailed tactical plan at the ready.

Activity: Develop DG Rollout Team Structure

Once you understand the approach, establishing the ongoing DG team is necessary. This includes all levels (i.e., hands-on individuals who can write policy and design functional models, as well as decision-making steering bodies).

This is not to be confused with defining the ongoing organization to operate DG. At this point, you are collecting some smart folks together to define the program. Make very sure the organization does not insert the team deploying DG with the ongoing practitioners. The steering body or sponsors at this point may also be focused only on the program rollout. There may be carryover of individual persons, but there is no overlap in mission or method.

Activity Summary Table

Objective	Identify the on-the-ground team members, the steering committee, and other key stakeholders.
Purpose	Determine who will be available to assist in deploying DG, including leaders and "hands-on" individuals.
Inputs	1. Initial scope and plan 2. Organization chart
Tasks	1. Identify DG team and key stakeholders. 2. Identify DG steering body. 3. Perform SWOT analysis on participants.
Techniques	1. Facilitation 2. SWOT analysis (strength, weakness, opportunity, threat) 3. Team building
Tools	Word, PowerPoint, and similar
Outputs	1. DG team and stakeholder list 2. DG steering body names 3. DG participant SWOT analysis
Outcome	A proposed DG team that will be able to stand up the DG program

FIGURE 6-7

Activity Summary Table.

Business Benefits and Ramifications

Note that there is a SWOT (strength, weakness, opportunity, threat) analysis in this activity. A SWOT analysis is a well-known technique to assess a team's potential. Every individual is assessed by what strengths they bring, weaknesses they may have, and what opportunities or threats participants may

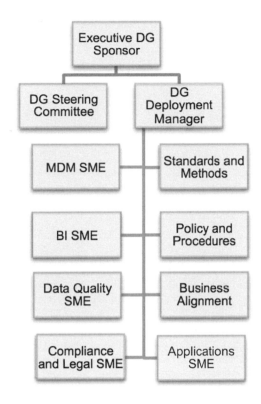

FIGURE 6-8

Typical Roles on the DG Team.

pose. You will start to run into politics, ignorance, and even resistance at this point. Here are some symptoms that the team is not taken seriously:

- Viewing the DG team as the programmer "graveyard"—usually IT staff are the first members of the DG team. Often, individuals will be submitted for membership because they do not fit anywhere else. This means someone is not taking DG seriously. The DG deployment team needs to be experienced in internal politics, know the players, and be able to think outside traditional information-management functionality. Typical roles are shown in Figure 6-8.
- Getting a steering committee that immediately delegates attendance to non-decision makers. Again, DG is not being taken seriously. More education is required, so add it to the plan.

Approach Considerations

There are two alternatives when the rollout team runs into obstacles. Note we said *when*, not *if*.

1. As part of an MDM or similar effort, the project sponsor discovers a brand-new issue that is related to the DG program. (Normally, it is something along the lines of "No, you cannot use that resource anymore.") The DG team needs to submit an issue to the PMO or similar body over the MDM project. This is one of those weird transitional things that happen, but it will certainly occur.

2. If the DG team is part of an EIM effort, then they should proceed with whatever staff they are offered, and then build in additional time for training and team building. They either will get the extra time or will have a solid case for getting other people assigned.

Remember that this rollout team is not permanent. They will be able to go back to their prior duties.

Sample Output

The sample DG deplyent plan in Appendix 1 is representative of this activity.

Tips for Success

If the team is not getting any additional resources, then the DG effort is poorly formed. We worked with a client who assigned one person to stand up DG in an organization with over 500,000 employees on three continents. The DG organization was designed and laid out in a vacuum, so when it was eventually presented for implementation, not much happened.

The deployment team should include some experience in data management and data quality. They will have the skills to recognize data issues. Business subject matter experts (SMEs) and someone with a good knowledge of the applications portfolio are also valuable.

You do not need hordes of people to stand up DG. Even the large company mentioned earlier only needed four to six FTEs to get it right eventually. The key is having a powerful steering body or sponsor.

Activity: Approve Scope and Constraints

This set of tasks will present the desired team to leadership and get the support to move forward. The steering body has to acknowledge the team's commitment to their day-to-day work areas. They then need to publicly voice support so there are no resources pulled back.

Activity Summary Table

Objective	Obtain approval of the DG team and deployment scope, approach, and schedule.
Purpose	Establish that DG has true, realistic support to move forward.
Inputs	DG plan, team structure, scope
Tasks	1. Review scope with proposed steering body. 2. Adjust based on feedback. 3. Develop final statement of DG scope.
Techniques	1. Presentation 2. Selling 3. Facilitation
Tools	Word, PowerPoint, and similar
Outputs	1. Proposed DG scope 2. Feedback adjustments 3. Final DG scope statement
Outcome	Approval to proceed within a well-defined scope

FIGURE 6-9

Activity Summary Table.

Business Benefits and Ramifications

Obviously, approval to proceed with management consensus is a good thing. Additionally, the DG team now has, albeit modestly, the ability to say they are real and have some authority.

Approach Considerations

Make sure you are getting true approval based on the scope and approach. Too often we see a "rubber stamp" and then shock and surprise when the leadership teams starts to see resistance. The approval process should contain a good walkthrough of the process.

Sample Output

Again, there is a sample deployment plan in the appendices.

Tips for Success

The concept of "authority" is critical here. As long as the DG team has some perceived authority, it can proceed. If you have been staffed with marginal personnel, you can train them.[2] Then, plan more training. If your steering body is weak, then develop tactics to be noticed (in a diplomatic way).

SUMMARY

Remember our earlier mention that most DG programs get started within an information technology (IT) area. While not ideal, this is okay. Just remember to build in the effort to engage the correct personnel in the future.

The main emphasis of this phase is to get started. Scope may wobble a bit; the project plan will definitely change; staff will come and go. However, just getting started is decidedly the hardest aspect of any type of effort in the EIM universe. It is important to remember that the main driver of the scope and plan will be where the initiative of DG is coming from. MDM, whether brand new or repairing an SAP implementation gone ugly, will provide a focused scope. General DG as part of enterprise EIM or data quality will require some thinking as to the nature of DG, or the areas that will be first exposed to DG.

---

[2]We have never really run into anyone who was totally incapable of adding some value to the DG team. After all, you are doing someone (who probably is a source of resistance) a favor by taking a resource off his or her hands. But, in a more idealistic light, we are often surprised that individuals we are assigned who have been perceived as marginal performers actually just need a breath of fresh air, and we always find something we can leverage in them. This drives the author's staff nuts, by the way. We never throw anything back.

Assess

Seeing, contrary to popular wisdom, isn't believing. It's where belief stops, because it isn't
needed any more.

—**Terry Pratchett**

The "Assess" step gathers data about the organization's ability to do governance, and to be governed. These assessments can overlap greatly with other assessments done in conjunction with data quality, MDM, BI, or other EIM solutions. They can also be derived as subsets of overall EIM assessments. They identify the "perceptions and means an organization deploys to use data, and how the organization is positioned to carry out its day-to-day work while adopting the philosophy of IAM. The current state of an organization's information abilities, maturity, and content effectiveness are examined."[1]

While we can get what we need from other assessments that are often happening around DG, this chapter focuses on them solely from a DG perspective. However, since there is overlap, a great deal of this chapter is similar in tone and content to Chapter 19 of *Making EIM Work for Business* (Morgan Kaufman, 2010). To see more assessment examples, as well as these assessments in a larger context, please refer to that work.

In the context of the DG assessments, the bottom line is that you need to understand if the organization can truly manage information as an asset. *Information asset management* (IAM) creates the philosophical basis for data governance. Therefore, the philosophy must be accepted currently or you need to start identifying the gaps that are preventing IAM from being adapted.

Assessments are more than just lists of questions that are asked in a stream of interviews.[2] They need to present an accurate, verifiable account of the current state—and they need to do it in a timely fashion. Interviews can certainly accomplish this but are rarely timely. Therefore, the assessment for DG tends to be better accomplished via survey or other data-gathering techniques.

---

[1]John Ladley, *Making EIM work for Business* (Waltham, MA: Morgan Kaufman, 2010).
[2]The author developed a mild and short-lived reputation as a radical from a presentation entitled "Interviews Are Dumb." It got people's attention. Consultants got panicky since the default starting position for anything seemingly MUST be an interview (it is not). Business personnel in the audience went "PHEW…thanks!"

All assessments in the realm of EIM (including data governance) need to cover the following dimensions:

1. *Organization*—There are many aspects of the organization itself that will affect DG and, in turn, be affected by DG. This covers organization charts, distribution of staff, the maturity of personnel related to information usage, and the level of understanding of their data assets. It also covers the need for the basic skills required to exist in a governed information world.
2. *Alignment*—This dimension addresses, foremost, the business alignment to the actual current state of IT and information use. Are IT projects done within a managed portfolio, and is information a key consideration? A very significant reason that DG efforts go awry is a lack of business alignment to information. Without alignment, there is no business visibility of what is essentially a business program. It gets lost in the noise and dies.
3. *Operations*—This dimension looks at the facilities that create and contain content. Whereas technology looks at the wire and pliers, operations looks at the usage of technology. Does the organization have operational processes and facilities in place to handle content efficiently? Are applications and systems process-heavy or data-oriented?
4. *Technology*—Does current technology adequately support information use and creation?
5. *Information*—What is managed in terms of information? Are privacy and security a concern? Are there rules and models?[3]

FIGURE 7-1

Process Overview.

[3]Ibid.

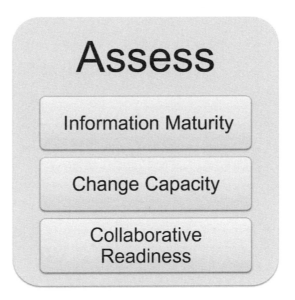

FIGURE 7-2

Activity Overview.

OVERVIEW

Activity: Information Maturity

The *information management maturity* (IMM) of an organization may seem like a driver for data governance versus a characteristic of DG. After all, if we were "mature" we would not need DG. It is a bit more involved than that. Anecdotal and hard evidence leads to the conclusion that organizations with a more proactive approach to information achieve better results. The key aspect of any discussion around maturity is that IT organizations, at a grass roots level, are beginning to see that there is a predictable maturity curve to climb around information production and usage. This, in turn, influences the definition of what the intended level of information maturity needs to be. There are definite stages of IMM along the way that can be described and measured.

While we review *how* the organization produces information and content, the main objective of this activity is to understand *what* the organization does with the content and information it produces. Usually, this assessment is performed online over the company intranet. Questions focus on the relative impression management has regarding how well the company uses and manages data to its advantage. This includes use for decisions, communication, and analysis, as well as critical functions such as R&D or compliance when required by the business. Figure 7-4 is a brief sample of some of the survey questions.

Activity Summary Table

Objective	Understand what the organization does with the content and information it produces. The focus is on the impressions and feelings business personnel have as to how well the company uses and manages data to its advantage.
Purpose	Improving the leverage and quality of data and content is a core driver for data governance. This activity provides the baseline for measuring progress toward future DG effectiveness from an objective, qualitative standpoint.
Inputs	This activity requires the development of survey-style questions. Input would be a template from this book or a similar process. Respondents must also be assured, and have controls in place, to maintain anonymity.
Tasks	1. Determine scope of the survey instrument. 2. Select or develop a maturity scale. 3. Identify all participants by name and group. 4. Orient respondents on importance and anonymity. 5. Agree on survey delivery (online, written, group focus). 6. Review and modify maturity template. 7. Produce final form for delivery. 8. Deploy survey instrument. 9. Monitor online survey OR 10. Distribute and monitor written version OR 11. Prepare and deliver focus session(s). 12. Collect and evaluate data. 13. Derive maturity score based on selected scale. 14. Collect existing standards, procedures, and policies for information management, info, resource utilization, prioritization, and controls—and map to IMM scale. 15. Prepare findings for presentation.
Techniques	*Survey respondents must be assured their answers are anonymous.* There are three techniques, listed in order of preference: 1. Online survey using intranet tool—most efficient means with highest response rates 2. Focus groups, with groups segmented by management level—do *not* mix upper and lower management groups 3. Written survey to be "check boxed"—this takes forever and response rates are low Develop the IMM score with the team, and have the sponsor review and concur.
Tools	Online survey tools—most large companies have one licensed, or find one on the web (e.g., Survey Monkey™). Use Excel to modify/develop the survey template.
Outputs	1. Survey results are evaluated and are usually produced in the form of charts or graphs. 2. A statement on the existence or lack of data governance can be made. 3. Specific outliers or extreme results must be evaluated and addressed.
Outcome	1. IMM score and presentation delivered. 2. Results may include recommendations for next steps. 3. Sponsor concurs with findings, even if they are controversial.

FIGURE 7-3

Activity Summary Table.

Business Benefits and Ramifications

This activity provides an objective view of the level of sophistication in regard to information use. Often the survey will stand on its own to make a framing statement for the need for DG.

Approach Considerations

Most likely, the length of the survey will be of concern to your sponsor or initial DG leadership team. A sponsoring CIO will be concerned with alienating stakeholders or ruffling feathers. Determining the scope of the instrument will be a function of determining what data you must collect for IMM, and whether or not you are combining this survey with another. The survey should take no more than 15 minutes in its online form or response rates will be too low to use.

The actual questions need to be very unambiguous. A significant portion of respondents will try to second-guess the survey. When we blend surveys, we always throw in a few questions that have obvious answers to indicate possible attempts to influence the results.

Of course, you want as many responses as possible. Respondents should represent, at minimum, middle and upper layers of management. We prefer to segregate the responses of various groups, as their answers are almost always very different. In addition, there must be a mechanism to provide an incentive to take the survey, as well as monitoring and follow-up processes to deal with laggards.

If the assessment is being done via facilitation or interviews, attempt to make the meetings as structured as possible. A group session should fill out the survey via a form, then tally and review the results. Interviews should cover a core set of questions in a survey format. The interview should also be used to collect personal impressions from interviewees. The population for interviews will be much smaller, so make sure the sponsor understands the IMM survey will be more anecdotal than statistical.

This activity is not considered optional, although it can be merged in with a change readiness assessment.

Sample Output

Figure 7-4 shows a sample of some of the types of questions asked. All the surveys we use take this form of answer scale (called a "Likert scale"). We feel it provides a decent distribution regarding the answers and gets us closer to seeing how the organization really feels about how data and content are used.

Figure 7-5 shows two panels from the IMM results from the case study in *Making EIM Work for Business.* (UIC is the fictional company.) The maturity scale ended up as a 1.8 (subjective based on concurrence with the sponsor and executives).

Tips for Success

Surveys have become a very popular means within organizations to measure just about everything. As a result, any attempt to survey may be met with suspicion or people may feel that they are not worth the investment in time. Depending on how survey results have been used in the past, you may be surprised at how far you need to go to convince personnel they will remain anonymous. If the survey history in your organization makes it a poor choice for you, consider facilitated focus groups conducted by individuals outside the DG organization. It will take longer but may lead to better results.

	Strongly Disagree	Disagree	Neutral	Agree	Strongly Agree
	1	2	3	4	5
The enterprise has published principles on how we will view and handle data and information.					
There are standards for how data is presented to all users, and standards within IT for describing data.					
There are policies for managing data that are published.					
The data policies are understood and adhered to consistently.					
There are rules for sharing and moving data in and out of the organization.					
There is a widespread understanding of the importance of data quality.					

FIGURE 7-4

Sample IMM Survey.

Timeframes for this activity should average two to four weeks with the attention of a full-time resource from the DG team and assistance from an internal survey group. A short timeframe is a success factor here. If there is a need to do focus groups, then assign two resources and get the groups processed within a month. Avoid the perception of "analysis paralysis." Remember there are people out there who will be looking for symptoms of the "same old IM project."

HELPFUL HINT

Try your marketing or HR organizations for help. They usually do all kinds of surveys and are adept with them, and they can help you with focus groups, if you go that route.

Activity: Change Capacity

All organizations are unique in how they carry out their mission and activities, even within the same business arena or market. This set of behavior patterns or style of an organization represents its culture. Part of any culture is its capacity for change. Obviously, organizations vary as to how easily or rapidly they

Question #	Percent Positive	Survey Question
26	49%	I understand the key indicators that measure my organization's performance.
5	72%	There are rules for sharing and moving data in and out of the company.
29	79%	I use data analysis to make changes in my work processes to improve results.
21	85%	My department has several databases, spreadsheets, or other data stores that we build and use to do reports.
28	94%	I collect and analyze information related to my work.

- There is general belief that management understands the measures of organizational performance.

- Given the insurance regulatory environment, the strong positive response to question 5 is not surprising; however, it conflicts with general perceptions regarding data quality and controls.

- UIC management generally believes that it uses analysis to analyze and improve work processes.

- The high percent positive score for questions 21, 29, and 28 that pervasive "shadow IT" may be exposing UIC to risks or higher costs

- Question 28 indicates that most of middle management could be spending more time collecting and analyzing data than managing, and requires further review.

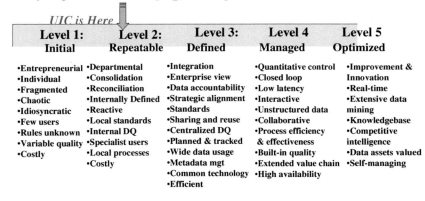

FIGURE 7-5

Sample Change Capacity Survey.

can accommodate changes. Therefore, the objective of this activity is to measure this capacity for change and locate potential resistance points. If you do not do this, you risk missing vital information that will allow the EIM team to accommodate and leverage your culture rather than fight it. In addition, the earlier the cultural issues are identified, the sooner any large obstacles will be recognized and addressed.

Activity Summary Table

Objective	Measure the capacity for the organization to change behaviors required for adapting IAM. Secondarily, identify potential resistance points.
Purpose	It is vital to assess the risk to DG that will originate from culture change issues. The DG program must be sustainable, and it cannot be made so without vital information that will allow the DG team to accommodate and leverage the organization's culture. The results are used to adjust the "Sustaining" phase, and will even influence the rollout of information projects and policies.
Inputs	None, unless your organization has a standard change-management process, which always includes an "Assessment" step. The "Sustaining" phase may ask for this assessment to be revisited to measure how the organization is adapting to required changes.

Tasks[3]	1. Determine the formality of the assessment. That is, an informal structured meeting format or a formal survey instrument.
	 2. Determine the target audience.
	 3. Define the survey population or interviewees.
	 4. Define the approach—structured meeting, written, or online.
	 5. Administer the survey OR conduct meetings.
	 6. Analyze and summarize findings.
	 7. Determine if additional investigation is required.
	    a. Leadership alignment
	    b. Leadership commitment
	 8. Determine what will be reported now versus sent to the EIM team to use during subsequent phases.

Techniques	If the human resources (HR) department has a change management team or organization development practitioners with change management expertise, utilize their skills. If time is short, an informal, anecdotal exercise will be sufficient until the "Sustaining" phase. Another informal technique is to maintain the structured meeting questions as a checklist, and review those with various groups as different personnel move in and out of the EIM effort.
Tools	Online survey tools—most large companies have one licensed, or find one on the web (e.g., Survey Monkey). Use Excel or Word to modify/develop the survey and questionnaire forms.
Outputs	The results may take the form of a report or presentation. Individual responses need to be held confidential within the EIM program, while aggregated results need to be widely communicated.
Outcome	The culture capacity assessment is complete when results are acknowledged and accepted by the executive team or sponsor.

FIGURE 7-6

Activity Summary Table.

Business Benefits and Ramifications

The data collected from this step will be used throughout the program design and for a long time after the rollout. It provides an excellent baseline to measure EIM adoption as well.

Approach Considerations

This is a strongly recommended effort. There really is no optional path—it has to be done. It can be done in two passes: a brief informal iteration now and then a detailed formal pass during the Road Map or Sustaining phases. The most common approach is to do a survey that is geared to reveal any glaring issues now, afterward revisiting the change capacity assessment during the Road Map and Sustaining phases.

Some organizations will resist any assessment of culture from any sort of "technical" team. If the DG team cannot overcome this obstacle, bury the most telling aspects of the change-capacity instrument in the IMM survey.

The target audience is all management, as well as knowledge workers or departmental analysts. The population to be surveyed needs to be segregated, with results kept by whatever segments you choose. At a minimum, segregate upper management, middle management, and all others.

This assessment is in the form of a survey and is best done online. If an online survey option is not available, switch to focus groups. Given historically low response rates, the last resort is a form to be filled out. If the focus group or paper form options are used, allow several weeks to get focus groups scheduled. Then, allow two weeks for forms to come back, but expect three weeks during which they actually keep showing up.

If there is a hint of sweeping changes, or known resistance areas are already identified (i.e., a prior attempt at information management failed in some way due to resistance), then a formal instrument is strongly recommended.

Sample Output

A simple visual is the best means to present results. Figure 7-7 shows a strong, but not insurmountable, resistance to change.

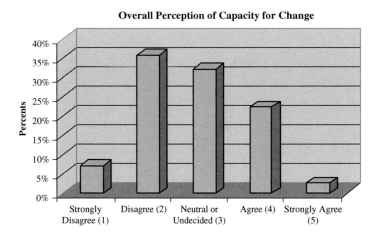

Overall Perception of Capacity for Change

FIGURE 7-7

Change Capacity Sample Output.

Tips for Success

Often, business or technology executives that have not engaged in formal business change programs will resist performing this step. In fact, a lot of the Road Map and Sustaining phases are spent dealing with resistance. It will seem "squishy." However, any root-cause analysis of the failures of large technology efforts over the decades shows the reoccurrence of a number of significant factors—poor communication, no alignment with the business on what is to be delivered, ineffective training, and lack of business sponsorship, to name a few. These change-management issues have cost organizations millions of dollars in failed programs. If you want to do better with your DG program, you *must* formally manage the changes required.

The standard change management tasks used to support implementation of DG can be taken from any number of prominent organizational development industry sources or authors, including Prosci; Change Guides, LLC; John Kotter; William Bridges; or Daryl Connor. Please see the footnotes and bibliography for these sources. There is an *enormous* amount of material available for very little (if any) cost, and it is easily adapted to DG.

Activity: Collaborative Readiness

A specific area of cultural readiness is the ability to collaborate. This activity measures the amount of collaboration or other cooperative behaviors in existence and, in some organizations, may include Facebook-type constructs or even Twitter. This assessment is important when content management, document management, and workflow are within the realm of the DG team. Additionally, the assessment is handy if the business has picked up on social networking as a possible enabler of business goals. This assessment is usually done via examination of the technology available, its extent of deployment, and its usage. Additionally, a brief survey, similar to the "Change Capacity," can be used to see if the organization even wants to collaborate.

This is not a trivial subject. As organizations become more sophisticated in their ability to reach across organizational boundaries, the need to leverage and manage the collaboration increases. There is also an opportunity to improve how an enterprise makes decisions by instituting and managing collaborative and social technologies. If anything like this is on the enterprise radar, then this assessment should be considered. Lastly, often companies have a situation where SharePoint or Lotus files are out of control. This assessment offers a chance to zero in on this issue.

Activity Summary Table

Objective	Determine the capability and/or the need for an organization to institute collaborative elements into the use of data and content.
Purpose	If there are elements such as workflow, document sharing (e.g., Notes, SharePoint), document management, and social networking-type facilities, then there are significant resources being used. These can present as much "information asset management" opportunity as any database.
Inputs	Most of the time, the IMM or "Change Capacity" surveys will trigger the need for this. When planning the entire

FIGURE 7-8

Activity Summary Table.

	assessment phase, however, consider this activity beforehand. This will help with shaping the "Readiness" approach. Typical inputs are the questions related to cooperation, from the IMM or change capacity assessments, or determinations that the business needs to consider workflow from the readiness assessment.
Tasks	1. Determine the assessment's scope. Does it include: a. Websites and content b. Documents and sharing c. Seeking and identifying existing communities of practice or interest d. Workflow e. Collaborative products f. Contemporary facilities like instant messaging, texting, Twitter, or Facebook 2. Determine assessment approach—interviews, document reviews, surveys, or a combination. 3. Collect existing standards, procedures, and policies for document sharing, workflow, internal wikis, blogs, etc., for review. 4. Collect inventory of SharePoint, Notes, or other work-share facilities. 5. Determine scope of survey instrument. 6. Select or develop a survey scale. 7. Identify all participants by name and group, if necessary. 8. Orient respondents on importance and anonymity. 9. Identify interviews of focus group participants, if necessary. 10. Agree on survey delivery (online, written, focus group). 11. Produce final form for delivery. 12. Deploy survey instrument. 13. Monitor online survey OR 14. Distribute and monitor written version OR 15. Prepare and deliver focus session(s). 16. Collect and evaluate data from surveys, documents, and meetings. 17. Develop collaborative readiness statement based on predetermined scale. 18. Prepare findings for presentation.
Techniques	Interviews, surveys (online preferred), and facilitated sessions are techniques of choice.
Tools	On rare occasions, large organizations may actually track work and content use through their intranet, and this data may be available. Otherwise, Excel and Word are the tools in use here.
Outputs	The readiness information from this assessment is used to shape the DG vision, in that collaboration may be a new topic for many organizations. DG can be an impetus to cross functional accomplishments.
Outcome	This step is done when the assessment is reviewed and accepted by the DG leadership.

FIGURE 7-8

(Continued)

Business Benefits and Ramifications

Collaborative business intelligence communities often establish more efficient relationships that drive new business actions as information and knowledge residing throughout the organization are optimized. The benefit of managing collaboration is that business areas, once fully engaged through these collaborative communities or mechanisms, can be measured and given feedback that they can use to improve not only the business, but also their own work processes.

Approach Considerations

The existence of large amounts of Lotus Notes or SharePoint data may require a spin-off assessment, as many organizations wake up one day to find out they cannot control or afford any more Notes and SharePoint sites. They tend to multiply like rodents. Otherwise, this is a fairly straightforward assessment.

Sample Output

Figure 7-9 shows some interview and survey results from another case study: Farfel Emporiums. Farfel has one collaborative mechanism, FarfelNet, which was developed to support the merchandising area. It is a website that allows access to merchandiser notes, proposals, supplier catalogs, and purchase orders for merchandise.

Collaborative Assessment Results Summary
1. FarfelNet keeps the merchandiser in front of the desktop waiting for information, rather than in front of the supplier making the deal.
2. The catalog information is always one quarter old. During the holidays, it is useless.
3. All merchandisers have their own "system" for managing suppliers, looking for trends, and maintaining catalog entries.
4. Representative FarfelNet survey responses:
a. The overall organization of FarfelNet needs to be simplified. I find it very difficult to find presentations, brochures, etc. Navigating through the Menu ultimately results in a search, and the search box most often results in no documents found.
b. Very often, I'm not able to find what I'm looking for or the relevant documents are not so immediately in evidence.
c. Why do we use SharePoint? All we do is spread out old messes into new messes. We are wasting the potential for sharing.
d. Also, I find it hard to have to look at multiple websites for competitors.
e. FarfelNet does not provide the productive work environment the Farfel merchandisers require to meet corporate objectives.

FIGURE 7-9

Farfel Collaborative Readiness Assessment.

Tips for Success

Understanding just what is being assessed can sometimes be a challenge. Large organizations, such as big companies or government agencies, have enormous amounts of content and many islands of local "knowledge stores." Blend this with the examination of current state, as well as there being a huge pressure to use more and more collaborative technologies, and scope becomes a problem. If there is a large amount of content in question, then make sure there is adequate time to conduct an effective collaboration assessment, or spin off a project to add to the DG rollout Road Map.

SUMMARY

The assessment phase for DG provides understanding and starts to seed the core data required to form the business-aligned architecture. The DG team—and, more importantly, the business sponsors—will start to see the importance of building blocks, like an aligned business model, data governance, and the role of culture.

The assessments need to be tailored to your situation, but some version of the key assessments of IMM and change capacity *must* be done. It is fine to take a lighter approach due to time or other constraints, as long as the remainder of the DG program development and sustaining activities incorporate the details. At some point, you will address the details for the required assessments if you intend to treat data as an asset. Tailoring them means choosing *when* to assess, not *if*.

Vision

Few things are harder to put up with than the annoyance of a good example.
—**Mark Twain**

The "Vision" phase shows stakeholders and leadership what DG will look like. This means a bit more than a one-page picture, although that is important, too. This phase also includes work on the mission statement, and both vision and mission are defined in detail in the coming sections. A vision establishes a picture of where an organization would like to be at a certain point in time in the future. The mission talks about how to get there. The goal is to convey understanding and comprehension of what DG means and what the organization wants to do to get there. This vision reinforces the fact that the business of enterprise information asset management *is* the business.

This phase can actually result in a stalled effort if ignored or done poorly.

"Vision" can be an abused term. It implies fluff and waste to many disillusioned executives. With DG, however, there is a profound need to convey the "big picture." Earlier in the book we mentioned the need for organizational change management. A key aspect of a change program is maintaining a future vision in front of those undergoing the changes. Change does not happen among humans without some view of the big picture. This is your goal for the vision phase. What will a "day in the life" look like when DG is activated? What will be visible? What business goals will be more achievable?

These activities are simple and should not take long, but we caution you to avoid defining a stated period for *fulfilling* the vision. Although nice, it is unrealistic at this juncture and, frankly, could alienate middle management who might perceive such statements as arbitrary.

OVERVIEW

Activity: Define DG for Your Organization

During this activity, the team will work with necessary stakeholders to draft a clear, brief definition of DG. They also need to develop the mission and vision statements as well as a brief statement of impact and considerations. In addition, we have found it advantageous to begin to define some of the success metrics for DG. There is a natural connection between the impact of DG and how it is measured. The metrics often help clarify the meaning of DG for business people. An "elevator speech" is likely to be the most visible result from this step. Experience has proven that an elegant elevator speech adds tremendously to long-term comprehension. (Yes, there is some marketing going on here.)

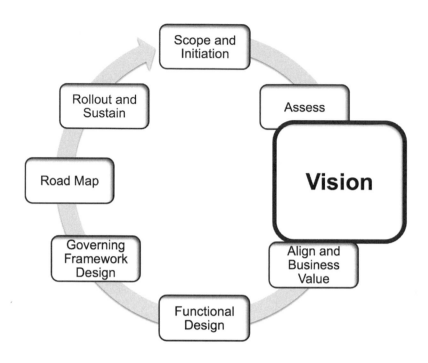

FIGURE 8-1

Process Overview.

FIGURE 8-2

Activity Overview.

Activity Summary Table

Objective	Draft a clear vision and definition that are relevant to the organization.
Purpose	Ensure that the enterprise (or program) has a clear definition of data governance.
Inputs	Assessment results, sample definitions of DG
Tasks	1. Define IAM for enterprise (if not defined elsewhere). 2. List possible DG measures. 3. Develop DG mission and value statements. 4. Develop straw-person DG definition. 5. Build DG elevator speech.
Techniques	Mission and vision statements facilitation
Tools	Word, PowerPoint, or similar
Outputs	1. Definition of DG/IAM philosophy. Draft brief impact and considerations document. 2. Initial list of DG metrics 3. DG mission and value 4. Notional definition of DG 5. DG elevator speech

FIGURE 8-3

Activity Summary Table.

Business Benefits and Ramifications

Starting the vision with a clear first cut at the definition of DG will result in a smoother process to define a vision. The resulting elevator speech is something that the entire team and, eventually, the DG managing framework should memorize.

The business will begin to recognize that data governance is *part* of the program to manage enterprise data and information—*not the end*. It is the *means* to achieve the end. Hopefully, this was stated in your vision that ties DG to ensuring a faster, more effective, and efficient organization that is positioned to achieve competitive advantage in a dynamic environment.

Approach Considerations

Keep in mind that you are looking for comprehension. It is not going to come easily. (We learned this the hard way.) Regardless of how wonderful you believe DG is in concept, remember that nearly everyone you are dealing with thinks:

- It is already being done (they will be surprised).
- DG does not merit the same status as financial controls or compliance because it is just data.

Be simple and elegant in your definition. The proof of elegance will come from how concise the elevator speech is.

Sample Output

The following is a batch of sample definitions, all of which are the real deal and are in use:

— Data governance is a business process separate from data (or information) management that affects the entire business by designating people, process, and technology using rules, monitoring, and enforcement with culturally acceptable enforcement.
— Data governance is a framework of accountabilities and processes for making decisions and monitoring the execution of data management. *(financial organization)*

— Data governance uses the horizontal perspective of the organization and focuses on the major "pain points" for our business areas. *(financial services)*

— Data governance is the orchestration of people, process, and technology to enable the leveraging of data as an enterprise asset. It affects all organizational areas by lines of business, functional areas, and geographies. *(software company)*

— Data governance is a system of decision rights and accountabilities for information-related processes, executed according to agreed-upon models which describe who can take what actions with what information, when, under what circumstances, and using what methods. *(consultant)*

— To be clear, data governance is the exercise of executive authority over business data. *(chemical company)*[1]

— Data governance represents the program used by ACME to manage the organizational bodies, policies, principles, and quality that will ensure access to accurate and risk-free data and information. Data governance will establish standards, accountabilities, and responsibilities, and ensure that data and information usage achieves maximum value to ACME while managing the cost and quality of information handling. Data governance will enforce the consistent, integrated, and disciplined use of information at ACME. *(energy company)*

— Data governance is the organization and implementation of policies, procedures, structure, roles, and responsibilities that outline and enforce rules of engagement, decision rights, and accountabilities for the effective management of information. *(generic definition used by author)*

Examples of an elevator speech are just as varied:

— Data governance will support our information asset management, ensuring we maintain our market share and achieve cost targets.

— We are going to support cost management and market growth, in part due to the more disciplined management of information assets.

Lastly, examples of mission and vision statements are also varied. A few are listed here:

Mission Statement—Retailer

To implement a shared, integrated enterprise data environment that always reflects current and future business requirements, and to promote its exploitation as a valuable resource.

Vision Statement—Retailer

An organization positioned to act faster, more effectively and efficiently in a dynamic business environment due to a cost-effective data resource managed as an enterprise asset.

Mission Statement—Energy Company

Ensure that information management provides the resources, processes, and enabling technologies necessary to manage information as an asset throughout its life cycle.

Vision Statement—Energy Company

*… will manage its information in a **disciplined** and **coordinated** manner to optimize the value of our investment in information assets, support effective and efficient operations, mitigate legal and regulatory risk, and improve the delivery of services to our customers and stakeholders.*

Vision Statement—Insurance

… will use information management and governance to enable employees, customers, and business partners to have easy access to the information they need any time, any place, and in any format, to

---

[1]*Data Strategy Journal*, October 2007.

reduce the cost, or improve the value of investments in information architecture, and ensure data accuracy, quality, and consistency.

(We did not recommend the insurance example, as it was in existence when we got there. It is a little too focused on information technology, but it set a baseline for measuring and achieving the mission, so it sufficed.)

Tips for Success

This activity is, fortunately, one where it is effective to gather many examples from elsewhere. Be certain that the definition contains elements that are meaningful to your organization. If discipline will be a challenge, mention it. If authority is important to success, mention it.

Ideally, your MDM project or EIM area will have mission and vision statements that can be leveraged. If not, you will need to assist in these efforts by creating them. Remember the fundamentals of *mission* and *vision* statements.

- A *vision* statement should provide a picture of where an organization would like to be at a certain point in time in the future. As such, it must clearly state what is to be accomplished, therefore supplying a foundation for measurement by framing the goals and objectives. For example, a vision of "we are going to be the best" is not very clear.
- A *mission* statement is a carefully worded statement of what an organization does in support of its vision, goals, and objectives. Each word of the mission statement is chosen for a specific reason.

The elevator speech needs to be positioned similarly. You also should fold in what DG will do for the company, using terms such as "ensure value, increase revenue," etc.

Whatever you do, *never* use words such as "better data," "improved decisions," or similar terms. They are vague and irrelevant to most executives.

Activity: Draft Preliminary DG Requirements

This activity goes hand in hand with definition, metrics, and elevator speech. The definition and considerations will allow you to organize a first cut at what is going to be governed. This activity starts with business needs. In addition, known issues, requests, and works in process are factored in to create a view of what is going to be governed. The team will need to consider specific business events, application maintenance requests, and regulatory or compliance obligations.

If MDM, BI, or data quality efforts are driving the rollout of DG, it is likely that much of this information will be available. Remember, DG is a program to ensure that BI, MDM, DQ, etc., all "stick." The drivers for these are also drivers for DG. Interestingly, it is not until we assist clients in getting the DG effort going alongside the other efforts (MDM, DQ, etc.) that they actually catalog and examine the business drivers of MDM. They are aware of the drivers in an anecdotal sense, but they do not sit and catalog and consider them. You might be able to sneak MDM in without a lot of consideration of business drivers (as long as you have a good sponsor and are solving a business problem). However, DG requires consideration of the business drivers and documentation of the following:

- How lack of DG-induced discipline could affect project sustainability.
- How lack of DG-induced discipline could increase risk by affecting the ability to comply with regulation, loss of market share, or potential lawsuits.

- Where DG processes, IM processes, and project-related processes intersect.
- The effects and details of long-standing requests to "fix" data in major applications.[1]

If you are standing up DG as part of MDM or something similar and cannot find any business drivers, you will need to execute a business-alignment exercise. The MDM team is in a lot of trouble but does not realize it.

Activity Summary Table

Objective	Develop an initial view of DG requirements that shows how DG will support business needs.
Purpose	This activity will provide focus for the DG team, help identify stakeholders and stewards, and provide more insight into metrics and additional tasks to help sustain DG.
Inputs	1. Business drivers, goals, and objectives 2. Data artifacts affected by DG 3. Outstanding application issues 4. Knowledge of organization risks
Tasks	1. Gather levers or stated goals and strategies and examine required content to enable them. 2. Gather existing artifacts such as data or process models or DQ surveys. 3. Examine backlogs of report requests, website updates, and requisitions for external data, data issues, and anecdotal requests for DG. 4. Identify obvious targets for improved quality or those that would benefit from external scrutiny. 5. Examine significant business events and activities for content affecting risk such as safety, regulated products, rate filings, etc.
Techniques	
Tools	Word, PowerPoint, and similar; requires management tools, and strategic planning or enterprise architecture tools
Outputs	1. Business goals affected by DG 2. Data artifacts affecting DG 3. Direct and indirect requests for DG 4. Data quality opportunities for DG 5. Risk areas benefitting from DG

FIGURE 8-4

Activity Summary Table.

---

[1]After several decades of doing this type of work, we are always amazed that among all of the needs and issues we document, all organizations can be counted on to have at least one of the following two DG drivers. First is the eternally lasting request to fix an old operational applications database. This application is the one that is so old no one can actually risk touching the code—so they try to fix the data, but the request has always fallen off the priority list. Second is that every organization has its legacy "data dumpster"—the ancient database that the data warehouse (and the second-generation data warehouse) was supposed to replace. There is one individual who has mythical powers and is able to navigate and support this database. Managers lay awake at night when they realize she will retire someday. Our theory is that all of the people supporting the legacy data are related, and originated from an ancient medieval guild.

Business Benefits and Ramifications

We stated earlier that some resistance to DG is inevitable. This step consolidates the reasons you need to do DG. In conjunction with the elevator speech, you are beginning to develop the compelling message that will be required for successful organizational change.

Approach Considerations

Take the time to consider business needs, as well as the other information mentioned earlier, in a formal manner. Do not throw it all in a document and say, "there it is." Remember, DG is all about making sure that information asset management is being done, so you need to examine all of the points where information management affects what the business wants to accomplish. At a minimum, you should break major business needs into subject areas or content used and identify what types of policies and standards may be required.

Sample Output

Representation of Initial Data Governance Requirements

Business Strategy	Driver / Lever /Objective	Information Assets	IM Artifact Governed	DG Touchpoint
Increase Value	Increase customer store visits by 2 per year	Customer, Customer analysis, Store activity, Store analysis	Customer data model	Customer MDM project
			Workflows and standards for consistency	Data migration and data quality remediation
		Business results from Store activity - Business Intelligence, reporting, analytics	Strategy Map of information levers and business benefits	Ensure aligned business vision of reporting, BI, and analytics
				Aligned BI architecture blending significant business information requirements into a uniform presentation
			Dictionary of core metrics and KPIs	BI and reporting requirements and development
			Defined framework to deliver information	BI users

FIGURE 8-5

Sample Initial Data Governance Requirements.

Tips for Success

Sadly, we often run into a lack of transparency when trying to align business needs with information management pursuits, including data governance. If your organization is the sort where IT is told to "do what you are told," and information has evolved into the inevitable rat's nest of applications and shadow IT, look to external sources. Most industries have trade journals. Many companies must publicly disclose intentions. Use this type of data to interpolate a business plan.

Activity: Develop Future Representation of DG

The DG requirements will enable the team to get an idea of where and how DG will enable business activity. This activity is where the team designs a clear representation of what that "day-in-the-life" will look like. The emphasis is again on simple and straightforward.

Activity Summary Table

Objective	Produce a visual represen tation of the DG vision.
Purpose	Develop the deliverable that will serve to convey the value and purpose of the DG program.
Inputs	DG requirements, mission and vision statements, and elevator speech
Tasks	1. Identify single-page abstract of DG vision. 2. Identify notional DG touchpoints. 3. Develop "day-in-the-life" picture.
Techniques	
Tools	Word, PowerPoint, and similar programs
Outputs	1. Visual DG vision 2. Refined DG business value proposition 3. "Day-in-the-life" slide

FIGURE 8-6

Activity Summary Table.

Business Benefits and Ramifications

Besides the obvious advantage of the organization being able to comprehend what DG means, there is also the beginning of seeing the specific areas where DG can clearly add value.

Approach Considerations

If you are doing DG for a very visible effort or for a large organization with a wide scope, then consider some professional help with regard to messaging, the picture, or even animated media.

Sample Output

Figure 8-7 is an example from a client (modified for privacy) to show where DG fits. A large company was doing a global DG effort and the big picture was very important. It had to say that:

1. There was executive-level direction to use data to be a game changer.
2. Data governance was going to be applied to all layers of their strategies.

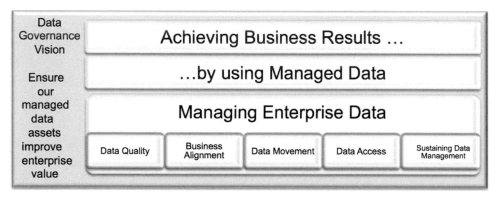

FIGURE 8-7

Sample Data Governance Vision.

Figure 8-8 demonstrates a much different example. A smaller financial services organization, well known for excellent service and execution, really needed to understand what happened day to day. Many graphical examples were produced and none clicked. Again, simplicity won the day—a simple pro forma agenda for possible future meetings showed what a "day-in-the-life" would look like. (Note that they referred to DG as IG [information governance].)

Tips for Success

Frequent vetting and consultation of the results and vision presentation will help achieve buy-in and avoid surprises. You really want to strive for a review meeting where everyone nods and says, "Yep, that's what we talked about."

Striving for an elegant message is also important because you will be repeating that message many, many times. This should not be a point of frustration. As long as you are being asked to repeat the message and demonstrate the vision because people want to understand the value, you have a sustainable effort. If the repetition is requested because no one "gets it," you need to repeat this activity!

UBETCHA Financial Services Enterprise Information Governance		Thursday, November 21, 2010 2:30 – 4:00 Main Conference Room	
Meeting Topic:	Quarterly Information Governance Council Meeting	*Type of meeting:*	Update, Issue resolution
Invitees:	Executive Data Strategy Council, Info. Governance Council		
AGENDA			

- Information Governance Value Update
  - IG and IM Scorecard Review
    - Data Quality Metrics
    - Business results from information projects
- Issue resolution
  - External business intelligence "cloud" package acquisition by Marketing
  - SAP Project - Location and Supplier Coding conflicts with current Ledger package
  - Marketing area absent from stewardship training
- IG Compliance items
  - Review IG Steward training progress (see issues)
  - Review status of BI and reporting governance
- Cross functional Collaboration
  - Report on recommended enterprise data controls
  - Report on policy revisions for information accuracy
  - Report from Compliance on revised Privacy and Security policies

FIGURE 8-8

UBETCHA Financial Services.

SUMMARY

Framing the data governance program in a comprehensible manner is a key step. Experience has shown that not everyone "gets it." If you combine the newness of formal information asset management with some of the "dubiousness" of business executives (who choose ignorance or are soured on information projects), then you can see that this phase, while short, is very important.

Align and business value

Efficiency is doing things right; effectiveness is doing the right things.
—**Peter Drucker**

You cannot manage what you do not measure, and this phase gives you the ability to measure the success of managing data governance. One thing to be clear on as you read this section:

- If you have a business case that is aligned with business needs, then this will be a very short phase. If there are no business value statements, ROI, a business case, or anything else resembling the business case for managing information as an asset, then it will be a bit longer in duration, and you *must do this phase.*

The steps to be taken are almost identical to the steps taken to generate a business case for all other types of enterprise information-management efforts. This is covered in detail in *Making EIM Work for Business.*[i]

This chapter, therefore, will focus on the particulars regarding data governance. For example, an exercise to do the business alignment for a refit of a data warehouse would (or *should)* focus on the business benefits that will be derived from using more accessible data or having powerful analytics. In the context of data governance, we want to make sure that the business benefits are actually achieved (i.e., the right things are done to ensure successful use of the new data warehouse). This may seem like a faint distinction, but it is very important when your DG program is asked to justify its existence. Your business value for DG is stated through the same lens as the value of a Six Sigma program or a compliance program. DG is a necessary underpinning.

People being people, however, will rapidly declare any program an inconvenience unless you hold up a paper that says, "If you do not do this, it will cost you $$$$$$."

Alignment refers to the direct linkage of the efforts to manage information assets to business strategies and measuring these information and knowledge projects against the anticipated benefits.

Therefore, the DG rollout team needs to make sure that the link between IAM, business strategy, and DG are apparent. This provides the baseline for sustaining the DG effort.

OVERVIEW

Activity: Leverage Existing EIM (or Other) Business Case

You should have business needs and a business case identified as a result of DG supporting another effort if you are going to do this activity. All you will need to do is tie DG activities to the business

---

[i]John Ladley, *Making EIM Work for Business* (Waltham, MA: Morgan Kaufmann, 2010).

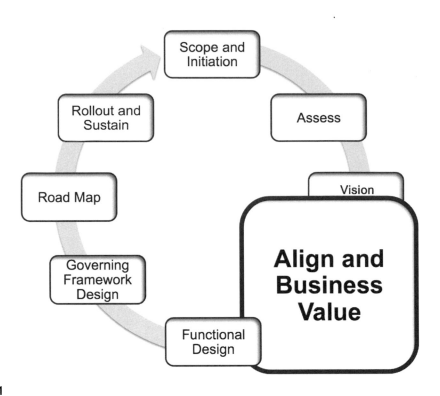

FIGURE 9-1

Process Overview.

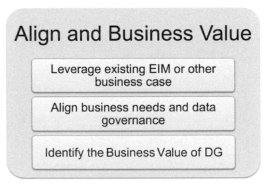

FIGURE 9-2

Activity Overview.

objectives. If you do not have any business case or your organization is averse to developing one, go to the next activity and forget this one.

The DG team needs to sit down and review any prior efforts at business alignment or building a business case. A thorough understanding of what the business defines as success is key.

The team can then determine where the benefits are that have been identified and start to discover points where DG can affect or ensure usefulness of data and content. After a thorough understanding of the business needs, metrics, and organization goals, they can go to the last activity in this phase and place a value on the organization's DG program.

Activity Summary Table

Objective	Start to tie DG into meeting business needs.
Purpose	Familiarize the DG team with business needs and deepen the position of DG as a business program.
Inputs	Organization goals and objectives, business cases, and ROI documents
Tasks	1. Review business documents, earlier findings. 2. Confirm future relevance of goals and objectives to DG. 3. Confirm measures of goals and objectives. 4. Clarify possible DG role in achieving business goals. 5. Ensure each goal or objective is measurable.
Techniques	Interpreting business goals and objectives into metrics
Tools	Excel, Word
Outputs	1. Business goals and objectives, findings from earlier activity 2. Confirmed business goals relevant to DG 3. Metrics for confirming business goals 4. DG roles in achieving business goals 5. Confirmed metrics

FIGURE 9-3

Activity Summary Table.

Business Benefits and Ramifications

There are benefits to examining benefits. If the DG team is not tuned into business needs, it will start to see where they can clearly speak to the value of DG. We are astonished in our DG practice as to how many employees in all varieties of large and/or well-known companies have no idea where the company is supposed to be headed.[1]

Besides the ultimate assignment of some financial value to DG, the business gets the material to think of DG as a business program versus an annoying IT effort.

Approach Considerations

This is not a "read-it on-the-train" activity. It is a "team-around-the-table" activity. There should be a summarization and presentation of the business programs that may require the application of DG to their information underpinnings.

---

[1]While it is poor form to do so, we often want to take executives aside and educate them that the idea of informing employees of business goals is a good thing. They have a "need-to-know" or "elitist" mentality that assumes the person in the mailroom is incapable of understanding the goals of the company. While we certainly understand the need to keep *strategy* close to the vest, sharing the bigger picture with employees is an incredible contributor to an effective culture. (Everyone else will read about the strategy on the Internet anyway.)

FARFEL EMPORIUMS SUMMARIZED GOALS			
Driver	**Goal**	**Documented Objectives**	**Measurable Attributes**
Improve Market Share	Recover lead market share in category	Regain market share of 25%	Market Share
	Increase top line sales across all categories and stores	Increase same store sales 15% over three years	Same store sales, Forecasted versus actual
Increase Customer Interactions	Improve Customer experience	Increase visits per store from 3 - 4 per year	Store visits, Market basket return
		Improve service environment, highlight differences	Surveyed opinions
	Improve effectiveness of web site	Improve web sites sales 15% without cannibalizing store sales	Percent sales from website
		Integrate store and web site offerings	Frequency of assortment refresh New products per season
	Increase repeat visits with more household awareness	Capture customer feedback, integrate findings into marketing	Store traffic
Product Innovation	Offer an improved selection of products and services by channel	Beat competitors to market on new products	Time to market averages for specified product
		Implement the most appropriate and profitable product mix, with brand consistency and neighborhood variation.	Same stores sales, Category product turns
	Maintain accurate merchandising processes	Improve procurement and store communications	Elimination of missed products or out of stocks
	Improve R&D to improve recognition of new opportunities	Gain insight into Generation x, y buying patterns	Demographic, psychographic trends
Improve Operational Efficiency	Improve management of merchandise inventory assets.	Reduce weeks of supply across appropriate product classes	Weeks of Supply
		Improve cash flow and asset management to improve current ratios	Current ratio, Inventory turns and Weeks of supply
	Identify business processes that can be improved to increase profits.	Improve processes through more efficient collaboration	SG&A expenses, Cycle times, Division results
	Optimize store performance	Monitor and assist stores with declining performance of more than 3% gross sales decline	Same store sales, Geographic and demographic sales potential
		Eliminate / relocate bottom 5% of stores	Same store sales, Geographic and demographic sales potential
	Reduce SG&A	Reduce "shadow IT" to competitive or industry standard levels	Total cost of ownership for data usage, IT and business areas

FIGURE 9-4

Sample List Information Management Needs.

Sample Output

Figure 9-4 shows an initial list and assignment of information management and, therefore, DG needs. The Farfel case is being used as an example, and we will tie samples to that case study from here forward. The columns represent the hierarchy of business alignment we use:

- *Drivers* are industry- or market-inspired trends, usually stated in terms of a direction. These tend to be categories of business goals.
- *Goals* are refinements of drivers, expressing the general trend in terms that indicate desired accomplishments within a timeframe.
- *Documented objectives* are the specified measurable criteria for achieving the goals and drivers.
- *Measurable Attributes* are aspects of the business to be measured. These become metrics or a category of metrics.

Tips for Success

There are occasions when DG is initiated as part of a project with very good business justification and alignment, but the team is not privy to that information (see the footnote diatribe above again).

This is not a showstopper. It means you need to add another businessperson to the team—one who can speak to business needs. In addition, do not hesitate to have the DG team sign an internal confidentiality agreement if the business goals are such a super-secret deal. If there is a total roadblock, then look to the next activity to gather business needs.

Activity: Align Business Needs and Data Governance

This activity should be done only if there are no other forms of business alignment. So don't confuse yourself—you do this activity OR the prior one. It depends on your situation. If there are no obvious business cases tied to any information management-type solutions, then you need to do this. The most typical scenarios we see are:

- A CIO starts an MDM project strictly as a technology effort.
- An ERP software package is used to integrate data with no business drivers.

Remember, DG needs to support the business. It is a business program. If you cannot state its outcomes in business terms, then the simple, ugly fact is you may not succeed.

This activity is presented here because all too often the CIO is told, or tells some subordinates, to "Get some data governance running." When the typical scenarios presented earlier happen, the projects tend to leave a smoking crater. Then the realization sets in that data governance should have been deployed as part of the MDM or ERP project. In these settings, there has been little business input, so the outcomes of DG cannot be defined even if the DG team manages to get them up and running.

This activity serves to collect and analyze business objectives, goals, and drivers and, in effect, replace the missing business case(s) that should be there. They, in turn, state how an organization is trying to improve itself and are presented in terms relevant to the business area being described. Most methodologies and analysis systems have a hierarchy of goals, objectives, etc. For this text, the hierarchy is as follows:

- *Drivers* are industry- or market-inspired trends, usually stated in terms of a direction. These tend to be categories of business goals.
- *Goals* are refinements of drivers, expressing the general trend in terms that indicate desired accomplishments within a timeframe.
- *Documented objectives* are the specified measurable criteria for achieving the goals and drivers.
- *Measureable Attributes* are aspects of the business to be measured. These become metrics or a category of metrics.

An example of a driver is *customer intimacy*. A goal would be *improve customer retention*, and the objective would be *increase customer retention to 97 percent this year.*[ii]

This activity is not as detailed as it could be if the team was doing a full-on enterprise information strategy. There is just enough analysis to show how DG can hold up its end in the business environment.

Since this section is essentially an abridged version of the full process for EIM business alignment, we once again reduced some text from the book *Making EIM Work for Business*. For consistency, we will follow the Farfel case shown in Figure 9-4.

Lastly, the acronym BIR is going to appear. BIR stands for *business information requirement*, which is the label given to any data, information, or content required by an enterprise to get its work done. Most of the time, BIRs are manifested in the form of metrics or business events; however, they can also be documents, regulatory mandates, or industry-standardized reference data. Remember this, because we use it a lot.

[ii]Ibid.

Activity Summary Table

Objective	Derive the organization's goals and objectives and look for DG opportunities to support business objectives.
Purpose	Develop sufficient business information to provide input for the DG team to determine some financial impacts of DG.
Inputs	Business plans, external research, internal project ROI, budget, and management by objective (MBO) type documents

Tasks	1. Gather/verify collective business goals and objectives.
	2. Develop a list of known business challenges, problems, and potential opportunities.
	3. Turn challenges and opportunities into business directions.
	4. Ensure each goal or objective is measureable.
	5. Convert goals and strategies into data requirements.
	   a. Gather metrics and indicators from other BIRs.
	   b. Identify standard industry metrics (if not done yet).
	   c. Map DG opportunities to BIRs and metrics to verify model relevance.
	   d. Optional: Map measures to source systems where data quality may be a concern.
	6. Connect BIRs to data issues.
	7. Build data usage/value worksheets, if required (these show specific business activities that will use information to accomplish business goals, so it is a collection of use cases).
	8. Determine the business context to present benefits of DG.
	9. Schedule facilitated sessions with business leaders or subject matter experts.
	10. Capture business benefit results in the session, or refine results after presenting them.
	11. Confirm the future relevance of goals and objectives to DG.
	12. Confirm measures of goals and objectives.
	13. Clarify possible DG role in achieving business goals.

Techniques	Business alignment, strategy mapping, use cases
Tools	Enterprise architecture tools, Excel, planning tools
Outputs	1. Organization goals and objectives 2. Categorized business goals, etc., into opportunities, challenges, problems 3. Business opportunities 4. Confirmed objectives and business metrics 5. Enterprise data requirements 6. Consolidated metrics and BIR list 7. Standard or industry metrics 8. BIR/metrics to data model cross reference 9. Metrics/BIRs to data quality issues cross reference 10. Enterprise DG touchpoints 11. Usage value/info lever worksheets or information usage cases 12. Enterprise value context 13. Business discovery session schedule 14. Discovery session results 15. Confirmed business goals relevant to DG 16. Metrics for confirming business goals 17. DG roles in achieving business goals

FIGURE 9-5

Activity Summary Table.

Business Benefits and Ramifications

This step captures, in business terms, how the enterprise needs information and content to achieve its objectives. The DG (and all of enterprise EIM) can be tied back to this list, ensuring that information assets are used and managed to meet business needs.

Approach Considerations

This activity should take only a day or so if the business plans are readily available. Otherwise, it may take between one and two weeks, depending on the span of DG in the organization. The most time-consuming efforts in this activity will be document research and review. Additionally, if interviews or reviews of findings are necessary, additional time will be required for scheduling sessions with management.

When you do not have access to business plans, you need to take the "guerilla approach" to business directions. The DG team should look outside your company at the business environment. Mass media, trade publications, and regulatory filings are excellent sources of business-direction tidbits that can be used to support information asset management and DG.

"Business drivers" can also be a vague term. Most organizations have goals and objectives or strategies. There are many layers to corporate and organizational strategies. Most list drivers as some sort of influencing factor. Therefore, be cautious of semantics. A great deal of the time, goals, objectives, and/or drivers can be discerned from corporate documents. The key is to look for material that lists or implies *measurable* goals and objectives. There are several fundamental reasons to take this perspective:

- The ability to share data is not of prime interest to a CEO. What is important is lower costs and more revenue. Period. If sharing data leads to those, fine; if not, don't bother them.
- Most executives have been interviewed into a stupor. However, few DG or EIM teams know enough about the business to replace executive insight—so other techniques are called for.

Business measures (and BIRs in general) are objective, and we always end up with the same level of information from exhaustive interviews. Your collection of objectives and goals will be decomposed into their component parts. It is the nature of these component parts that indicate where DG will be needed. If you are in guerilla mode, it will become evident very soon that you are collecting real business drivers versus ones that cannot be decomposed. For example, if you start to nose around and are compiling drivers like the following, then you are barking up the wrong tree:

- Inability to share information across the organization
- Multiple inconsistent sources of data
- Lack of ability to generate reconcilable financial reports

What you are really getting are requirements of some EIM-type project, and this is not suitable material for business alignment. What component parts of "better access to data" can be governed?

This activity also requires the team to examine where the business objectives, BIRs, and business activity intersect.

Once the goals and objectives are discerned, then it is very important to consider what the enterprise is like with IAM. Where does IAM fit into the current business? This means we need to start to recognize specific actions that the business will take. This also means creating a list of specific activities where the business will use information to accomplish goals. Feel free to use business use

Usage Value Category	Data, Information and, Content used to improve or achieve goals through:
Processes	Improve cycle time, lower cost, improve quality
Competitive Position	Capture competitive intelligence and differentiate yourself
Product	Create package and market unique, higher margin products
Asset/Intellectual Capital	Prolong leadership, embed knowledge into products and services
Enabler	Foster employee growth and empowerment
Risk	Manage risk, of various types, that threaten value by increasing liability

FIGURE 9-6

Usage Categories for Data, Information and Content.

cases as a technique here as well. We use a cheat sheet for this by listing the basic generic activities that take place around data and content (see Figure 9-6).

It is a simple matter to take an objective and "bump it" against this list. Your goal is to see which of these basic uses of data can be applied to help achieve the business goal you have identified.

Sample Output

See Figure 9-4. It represents the summarized output from this activity, and you should derive the same type of work product. Figure 9-7 is another example in the form of a strategy map, which is now a more common presentation that is based on the approach by Nolan.[iii] (It is the same type of document as Figure 9-4, only flopped on its side; it is an example from an insurance company case study.) Figure 9-8 shows an example from the Farfel case of how the generic uses of data (Figure 9-6) were applied.

Tips for Success

If you have scarce or low-level sponsorship, you may be questioned as to how you reached certain conclusions in terms of business needs and direction. Maintain all of your research so you have an audit trail. It does help when presenting your business findings, and hopefully management will take note. The DG team is likely to get the attention of management since there will be the appearance of some serious strategy work going on—without management's involvement. Of course, the best critical success factor (CSF) is to have executive sponsorship and presence as soon as possible.

[iii]Nolan, *Strategy Maps*.

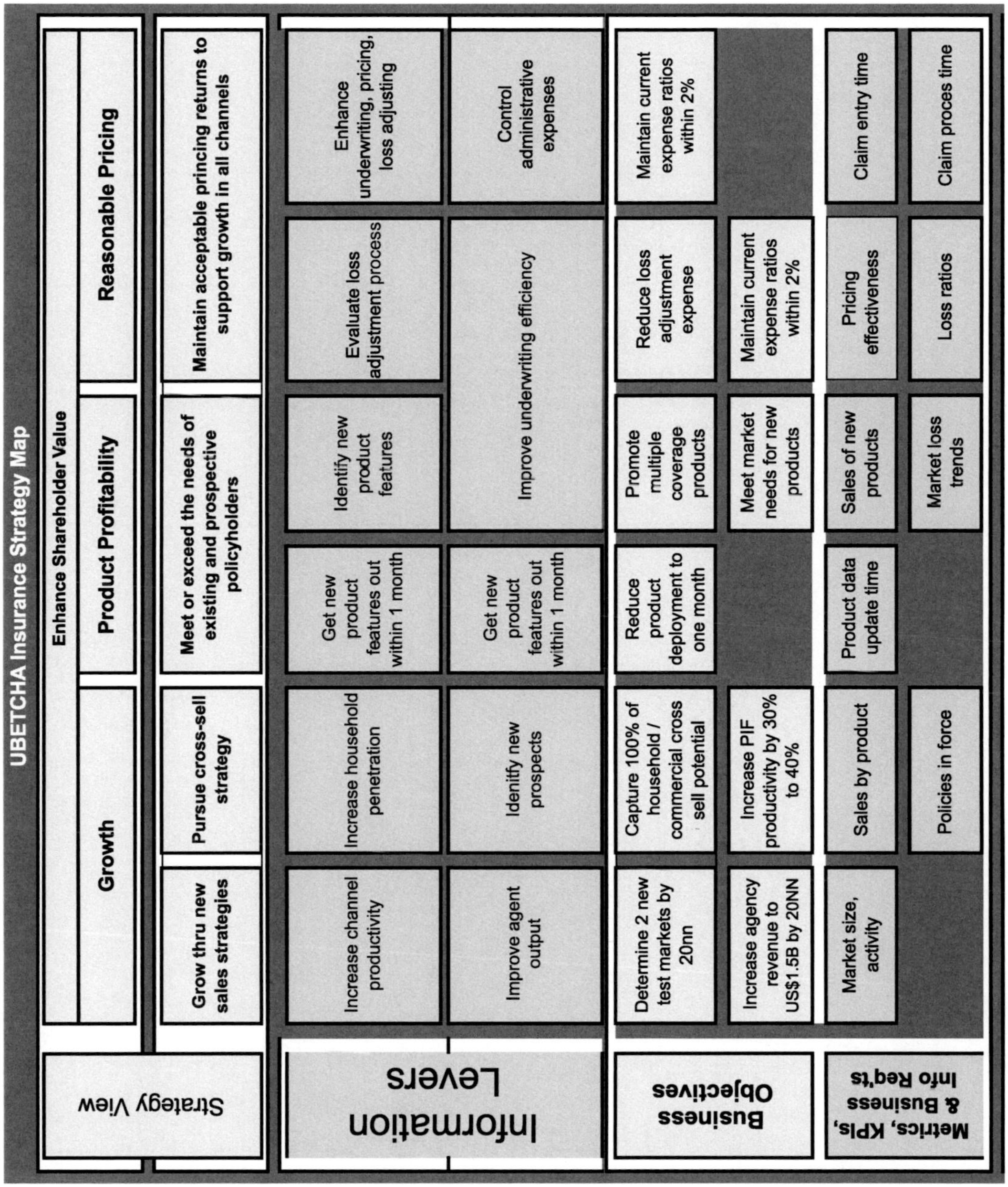

UBETCHA Insurance Strategy Map

Enhance Shareholder Value

	Growth	Product Profitability	Reasonable Pricing
Strategy View			
Information Levers	Grow thru new sales strategies; Pursue cross-sell strategy	Meet or exceed the needs of existing and prospective policyholders	Maintain acceptable pricing returns to support growth in all channels
	Increase channel productivity; Improve agent output; Increase household penetration; Identify new prospects	Get new product features out within 1 month; Get new product features out within 1 month; Identify new product features; Improve underwriting efficiency	Enhance underwriting, pricing, loss adjusting; Evaluate loss adjustment process; Control administrative expenses
Business Objectives	Determine 2 new test markets by 20nn; Increase agency revenue to US$1.5B by 20NN; Capture 100% of household / commercial cross sell potential; Increase PIF productivity by 30% to 40%	Reduce product deployment to one month; Promote multiple coverage products; Meet market needs for new products	Reduce loss adjustment expense; Maintain current expense ratios within 2%; Maintain current expense ratios within 2%
Metrics, KPIs, & Business Info Req'ts	Market size, activity; Policies in force; Sales by product	Product data update time; Sales of new products; Market loss trends	Pricing effectiveness; Loss ratios; Claim entry time; Claim proces time

FIGURE 9-7

Sample Strategy Map.

BUSINESS GOALS → INFORMATION USES FROM USAGE CATEGORY ↓	PROCESS		PRODUCT		ENABLER		ASSET		WEAPON
	1. Touchpoint information allowing Farfel to improve customer relevancy	2. Decrease customer cycle times by providing products in a timely manner	3. Leverage brand image and affiliated product/services to create additional opportunities	4. Offer additional products and services based on affinity to core offerings	5. Empower employees with customer and market model information	6. Use knowledge of customer to increase customer retention and loyalty	7. Leverage product information collected at the touchpoints to develop a service relationship	8. Holistic view of customer purchasing behavior to enable analysis of customer value	9. Increase high value market share
Improve consumer experience by 10% per year	X	X	X	X					
Develop programs for customer data capture through research and customer touch points. Provide a means of accessing the data at all necessary locations	X						X	X	
Ensure that assortment and refresh plans reflect the needs of selected customer segments		X	X	X	X	X			X
Increase trial and repeat purchase, household penetration	X			X		X			X
Offer an improved selection of products and services by channel			X	X					
Improve Supply Chain Management processes		X	X						
Design and deliver tools to facilitate access to operational data					X	X			
Streamline end-to-end data access, integration, and delivery processes. Use web platforms to simplify access to info		X	X	X					
Identify business process that facilitate the storage and maintenance of business critical data in non-corporate structures (i.e. Access databases)		X			X				

FIGURE 9-8

Sample Application of Value Usage.

HELPFUL HINT

We did such an exercise for a large company where the business goals were "not for our eyes." Our team did the research and data gathering required to find business needs that matched up to IAM and DG. We then developed a strategy map and presented it to the DG steering committee. The uproar was astonishing, and we were interrogated immediately as to where we had found this information and who was responsible for "leaking" it. The lesson learned was to vet the findings within the team and executive sponsorship first, and then drive to the final deliverable of this phase, which is an idea of the financial impact of DG. You may never get to show your wonderful work to anyone.

As an aside, when confronted by management the author revealed that the "top secret" sources were *The Wall Street Journal* and the CEO's letter in the company's own annual report.

This activity may take a few lunchtime sessions with peers, but a mildly facilitated discussion will enable a small group to derive a list of 10 to 15 items. You will have collected sufficient business data if you have items that, if addressed, would reduce risk or drive good numbers to financial statements. There should also be items that reflect product or service changes, efficiency changes, or customer-relationship improvement.

When deriving the levers and examining how data will get the business where it needs to be, we facilitate a meeting where selected business personnel view each goal or objective and look at each of the six usage categories. Often, we have them complete a phrase: "ACME Company will use data/content to _____ as a means to achieve (insert the goal here)." The answer to the phrase is a specific opportunity for DG to support business value. For example, a completed version of the phrase might be: "ACME Company will use data/content to target healthy lifestyle messages to members as a means to achieve higher member retention and lower health care costs."

Again, you are doing this for the purpose of stating the value of DG, so while the ideal scenario is a room full of inspired and authoritative business leaders, this may be a team exercise done solely for making sure DG can measure itself and be sustainable.

Activity: Identify the Business Value of Data Governance

This activity is where the DG team identifies specific financial numbers and determines what business metrics will indicate the success of DG. This is also a good place to show the cost of non-governance, or in continuing to use information in a poorly managed fashion. Regardless of whether the team arrived at a business/data governance intersection from the first or second activity mentioned earlier, this activity is required to put some numbers together.

For example, if we take an example from Ubetcha Insurance—the goal of improving our agents—we can ask, "If this happens, what is the anticipated impact on financial statements?" Since we have an idea of what application of data might do here, we can either claim the whole amount for IAM (and DG) *or* take partial credit based on how much of the resulting business action may or may not be directly enabled by good data. If agency growth contributed $10 million in new premiums, and we discerned from our levers that good data and content would enable or help improve half of the business actions taken to grow the agent force, then we can, pro forma, write down $5 million. The Farfel example states that it can improve equity through customer loyalty and product innovation. What does a financial analyst say in terms of stock price or retained earnings? Granted, this is early, but the goal here is *not* to develop an accurate forecast of business benefits; the goal is to show that without DG the likelihood of these benefits is reduced.

Activity Summary Table

Objective	Assign financial value to DG program.
Purpose	Create baseline for determining DG success and set goals for DG to achieve.
Input	Business goals, objectives, levers, initial BIRs

Tasks	1. Connect data issues with business needs.
	 2. Identify potential cash flow from business goals.
	 3. Extract levers and other opportunities for using content and data.
	    1. Identify touchpoints where new managed content or data will touch or be leveraged by levers or other processes.
	    2. Isolate the processes that create value or achieve the goal related to the originating action.
	 4. Apply the various financial benefits and the costs to whatever benefit model is in use.
	 5. Create value statements of the interaction of data and business goals.
	 6. Publish results to the DG team and/or steering committee.
	 7. Align business data needs with DG benefits (show connection between business goal, required information, and data governance activity).

Techniques	Strategy mapping, business case development
Tool	Excel, strategic planning tools
Outputs	• List of known data issues cross-referenced with related business needs • Business cash flow from affected business issues • Possible value points for new processes • Detailed actions in business processes achieving results through managed information • Financial benefit model for DG • DG value statement • DG value presentation • DG business value

FIGURE 9-9

Activity Summary Table.

Business Benefits and Ramifications

At this point, the DG sponsors and management will begin to see DG as a business program. At any rate, the foundation for the ongoing reporting of DG value is in place.

Approach Considerations

If your EIM program is of a formal nature, or you have a large, well-sponsored MDM effort underway, this exercise is a matter of reloading numbers and assumptions. If not, this and the second activity in this phase may take several weeks.

Related Goal	Information Usage as a Product—Build into offerings		Information Usage as a Process—Improve cycle times, lower costs		Data Governance Touchpoint	Benefit Potential
	Business Actions	Objectives/Results	Business Actions	Objectives/Results		(000's)
Improve Customer experience	Determine level of attention (or avoid harassing) in-store shoppers Determine easier product location layout	Increase customer shopping satisfaction Increase re-visits Improved Customer Satisfaction Increased sales	Explore use of self-checkout Develop on-line order, in-store pickup capability	Increase customer shopping satisfaction Increase re-visits Improved Customer Satisfaction Increased sales Increased store/web traffic from targeted customer segments	Definition of Customer Order data quality Consistent metrics BI and analytics governance	$6,306
			Develop customer profile / score at POS touch points to offer promotions, affinity cards Store on line information securely to avoid re-entry	Increased promotional sales More effective sales into more profitable segments	Definition of Customer In store information security Customer privacy	
Offer a selection of products and services most profitable for target segments	Analyze internet activity to adjust in-store inventory and products	Beat competitors to market on new products Decreased carrying costs Increased customer satisfaction Increased sales in targeted areas	n/a	n/a	Definition of Product Web site information security	$2,523
	Target specific demographics based on product type / customer propensity	Implement the most appropriate and profitable product mix, allowing for regional and local variations	Offer products based on profiles and propensity ahead of time via e-mail notifications	Increased customer satisfaction	Definition of Customer In store information security Customer privacy BI and analytics governance	
Improve R&D to improve virgule recognize new opportunities	Fine tune product offerings in store and web site sections	Gain insight into Generation x, y buying patterns	Order big demand items to grab market share before competitors	Increased sales in targeted segments	Business alignment to web site BI and analytics governance	$1,261
Increase repeat visits with more household awareness	Capture customer feedback, integrate findings into marketing	Decreased mailing costs via target e-mails, or household mailings	Offer up-sell promotions at POS or web site to targeted households	Increased repeat customer purchases Increased product awareness Increased repeat visits	Definition of Customer In store information security Customer privacy BI and analytics governance	$6,306
Improve management of merchandise inventory assets	Provide better demand data to suppliers to reduce in-store stock levels	Decreased support and system costs Increased employee satisfaction (no longer have to go in circles to get the product info they need - regardless of department) Wider product selection, increased store traffic and selling opportunities	Reduce weeks of supply across appropriate product classes through "just-in-time" restocking	Shorten cycle times to restock Improved cash flow, balance sheet	Definition of data controls BI and analytics governance Supplier data quaity	$1,081
	Improve cash flow and asset management to improve current ratios	Improved Current ratio, Inventory turns and Weeks of supply	n/a	n/a		

FIGURE 9-10

Sample Business Case.

Sample Output

Figure 9-10 shows the Farfel example with prorated benefits applied to business actions. For the real client, we took a conservative 5% of benefits from improved cash flow. These were stated in the client's pro-forma projected balance sheets.

Tips for Success

One other subtle event that can be leveraged is that now the naysayers will take their chance to shoot holes in the program. Make sure there is the audit trail that was mentioned earlier. Between that and backing from a good sponsor, you may be able to elevate DG a bit higher.

SUMMARY

Do not despair if you feel this set of activities will result in a pro forma or artificial number. After all, business benefits tend to sail right past any sort of information project and land at the feet of the business area. Even if your team used a guerilla approach, you still have a quantitative means to monitor DG. The main benefit here is formal consideration of how DG will contribute to the business; not to data quality or other efforts, but to the business.

Functional design

Our principles are the springs of our actions. Our actions, the springs of our happiness or misery.
Too much care, therefore, cannot be taken in forming our principles.
—**Red Skelton**

This chapter covers the process of designing the DG program from the standpoint of "the what" and some of "the how." The next phase addresses "who." Some very significant program artifacts are developed that will remain with, and be used by, the DG program for as long as it is in operation. The DG deployment team will provide the list of processes that will occur on both sides of the "V."

The focus on the V is important. Your team will be defining (or refining) information management functions, *in addition* to the DG functions. As stated earlier, most organizations do some kind of information management as well as governance—however, they are less disciplined than is desirable. Therefore, what is really happening in this phase is the *formalization of a functional model for DG and IM*.

An obvious question might be, "Why should we build the DG program by identifying information management activity?" The answer was stated in Chapter 2—you have to govern something and information management is the main subject. You need to specify what is governed. You also need to be very clear about what the DG program has to do and who is accountable. Likewise, the same needs to be done for IM (i.e., what functions are undertaken to do the hands-on management of information assets). The eventual makeup of the DG operating framework depends on a clear result from these activities.

If DG is to be a "net zero" or minimal increase in cost, where does the oversight come from? If the V is focused on separation of duties, don't we need more people to handle oversight while others are working on information projects? In reality, very few organizations can afford to add a 100-percent-dedicated DG staff. (Those that can are unwilling.)

The answer is found in how you assign the various duties. For example, if a business leader is sponsoring an MDM project, then obviously that person cannot be responsible for the data governance of that project. Therefore, another business leader is given the duty to provide oversight. If there is a governance council, then the members of the council participating in the project are recused. If the business leader of another project requires DG, then perhaps the first business leader does the DG activity. In other words, they take turns.

OVERVIEW

Activity: Determine Core Information Principles

This activity sets the tone and foundation for the entire DG program. Principles are statements of values and philosophical beliefs that the organization wants to adopt. There are a few ways to look at the benefits to be derived from development of the enterprise information principles.

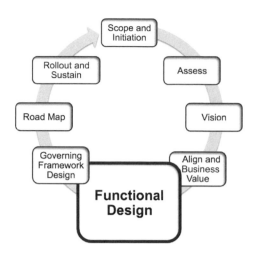

FIGURE 10-1

Process Overview.

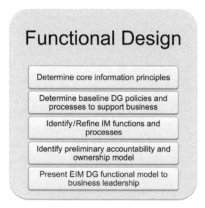

FIGURE 10-2

Activity Overview.

1. The principles anchor the formation of policies. The core information principles expressed in this step will be used to frame the procedures required to enact DG. It is not hard to see that there are some ramifications requiring policy and process if we examine the most common principle—that is, "we will treat information as an asset."
2. The defining and vetting of the new principles create a deeper layer of understanding of DG's meaning to the organization. DG concepts and impacts come into sharper focus if leadership is still uncertain as to their meaning.
3. The review, refinement, and publication of the principles establish the relevance of the DG team.

This is not a task to take lightly. We often see a list of principles lifted from a published source, plopped into a document, and then mailed out with a decree that these are the principles. These rarely succeed. Without review, participation, and buy-in, it is impossible to extract relevant, realistic processes and policies. If the DG team and the constituents of the DG program are not immersed in the principles, then there is no intellectual connection between policy and philosophy. The principles need to be derived and refined formally, not casually.

While it is good to start with a "seed" list of principles, which usually comes from external examples and existing internal belief statements, we also apply an internally developed technique to act as a framework to ensure your information principles provide adequate coverage. Called the GAIP™ technique, it is based on a set of core principles that apply to data and information at a pure business level. Refer back to Chapter 2 for more background on GAIP. Once the seed list has been identified, we walk through each one of these core principles to ensure coverage.

GAIP™ - Generally Accepted Information Principles	
Principle	**Description**
Content as Asset	Data and content of all types are assets with all the characteristics of any other asset. Therefore, they should be managed, secured, and accounted for as other material or financial assets.
Real Value	There is value in all data and content, based on its contribution to an organization's business/operational objectives, its intrinsic marketability, and/or its contribution to the organization's Goodwill (balance sheet) valuation.
Going Concern	Data and content are not viewed as temporary means to achieve results (or merely as a business by-product), but are critical to successful, ongoing business operations and management.
Risk	There is risk associated with data and content. This risk must be formally recognized, either as a liability or through incurring costs to manage and reduce the inherent risk.
Due Diligence	If a risk is known, it must be reported. If a risk is possible, it must be confirmed.
Quality	The relevance, meaning, accuracy, and life cycle of data and content can affect the financial status of an organization.
Audit	The accuracy of data and content is subject to periodic audit by an independent body.
Accountability	An organization must identify parties which are ultimately responsible for data and content assets.
Liability	The risks in information mean there is a financial liability inherent in all data or content that is based on regulatory and ethical misuse or mismanagement.

FIGURE 10-3

GAIP(tm) List.

Activity Summary Table

Objective	Determine core information principles.
Purpose	Establish statements of enterprise-level beliefs regarding data governance.
Inputs	GAIP external examples, current organization belief statements
Tasks	1. Use seed principle. 2. Apply GAIP. 3. Align with existing enterprise principles and policies. 4. Add rationale and implications for each principle. 5. Submit and approve principles to DG steering body.
Techniques	GAIP application
Tools	Microsoft Word
Outputs	1. Initial list of information principles 2. Verification of principles to GAIP 3. Adjusted and rationalized principles to reflect other principles or policies 4. Draft enterprise information principles 5. Approved information principles

FIGURE 10-4

Activity Summary Table.

Business Benefits and Ramifications

Let's reinforce the importance of the review and refinement of principles. This is best illustrated by examining the results from two very different organizations (seen in Figures 10-5 and 10-6). Our consulting practice has assisted many companies in the rollout of a DG program, but these two stand out due to the marked differences.

As we worked with these companies to develop principles, we started at the same point. We used a "seed list" (as described earlier) and the GAIP technique. We also made sure that the principles clearly demonstrated alignment with business direction and philosophy. However, we came out with two very different sets of principles. Both companies are in the same industry, but the names have been altered due to nondisclosure requirements. Figure 10-6 is a large company. Figure 10-7 is a mid-sized company. Note the difference in tone and granularity. Both sets of principles are effective. Both sets had different ramifications for their respective organizations.

Approach Considerations

The duration of this phase depends entirely on the ability of the DG team to tune the principles to their organization and get sincere and effective review from leadership. These activities can be a great opportunity to build consensus and increase the internalization of DG, or they can drag out and dissolve into a seemingly typical exercise of irrelevant meetings. If your organization starts to spend more time on "wordsmithing" principles so as not to offend anyone, you have encountered one of two cultural issues.

1) The principles represent changes that are perceived as an admission that the organization is deficient, or "bad," which the sponsor needs to assuage.

2) The participants in the process fear being pointed at as instigators of bad things. The sponsor needs to make sure the team knows it is covered and someone has their back.

Guiding Business Strategy/Philosophy	Information Principle Name	Description
Increase Shareholder Value	Data and Content as an Asset	All BigCo Enterprise Data and Content will be managed as a corporate asset, using formal Principles to guide quality, compliance, value, and use of information
Improve Efficiency	Right Person, Right Time, Right Place, Right Cost	Business stakeholders will get information and content delivered at the right time, location, and amount as efficiently as possible
	Relevance	BigCo will designate federated enterprise standards and guidelines for all metrics, data structures, documents, and content
Business Alignment and Proper Federation	Business Alignment	Information management applications, technologies, and implementations will be aligned with business needs, and not driven by technology
	Share and Collaborate	BigCo data will collaboratively apply analytics and other uses of information to address business opportunities and challenges
Accountability	Accountability	There will be accountability for overall integrity of enterprise data and content
	Governance	Data that is designated as "governed" will be under the oversight of existing business areas that have appropriate authority and accountability to define and establish how information, data, and content is managed, controlled, and disseminated
Risk Management	Risk Management	Management of enterprise information will reflect compliance with statutory and federal laws, policies, and regulations; such as but not limited to security, privacy, confidentiality, and data reporting

FIGURE 10-5

Sample Data Governance Principles.

Do not forget to spend time with the implications and ramifications of the principles. It is only fair to be able to explain why a principle has come about (the rationale). The implications are very important, not only from a perspective of understanding, but also because implications almost always provide requirements for policies.

There can be a lot of wordsmithing associated with the development of your principles. You may find yourself in a frustrating loop of tweaking the words. If this happens, the leader of the DG deployment will need to declare the principles are good enough. They will evolve slightly anyway, so there is not much risk in starting to publicize them and begin policy development.

The general outline for a principle should contain the following elements:

1. A short description of the principle
2. A long description and full definition of the principle
3. A rationale, or statement, as to why the principle is necessary
4. Implications, or statements, of potential and known impacts that the principle will have

The most common mistake with principle development is to create policies and call them principles. If your principles are showing any of the following warning signs, you have entered the next activity:

- There are more than ten principles. While not unheard of, when you have more than ten principles you are starting to get very specific about what they mean.
- Using the description to declare how the principle will be enforced.
- Mentioning specific business areas or functions within the principle.

In general, you will start with 12 to 14 principles and then whittle them down to 7 to 9. They will usually lend themselves to some sort of consolidation.

Sample Output

The sample below is the textual version of an entire principle.

Information Should Be Authoritative

Short Description

There should exist a single authoritative source that may be interrogated to determine any fact about any subject or object of interest.

Long Description

There should exist a single authoritative source that may be interrogated to determine any fact about any subject or object of interest. This does not preclude creating certified copies of data and information (this is understood as "managed" redundancy).

Rationale

- A verified, accurate source for enterprise subject area data is critical to achieving comprehensive data integrity and reduces confusion, complexity, and cost.
- Data is collected from a variety of internal and external sources, resulting in inconsistencies that must be resolved to provide a single, accurate view.
- The shift in focus from a product-centric to a customer-centric organization requires easy access to accurate and consistent data that spans functional business units.
- Common and consistent data is required to present customers with a single view.
- Costs associated with unnecessary movement and maintenance of redundant data must be eliminated and access latency must be reduced.

Benefits

- Reduced risk from disconnected applications projects
- Improved business alignment due to structural need to collaborate
- Reduced costs associated with data and information movement
- Reduced costs associated with the proliferation of departmental databases
- Increased accuracy in business measures based on consistent data elements

Implications

- There will be a single, clearly identified, authoritative source for each managed enterprise subject area data element.
- The authoritative source and definitions will need to be easy to find and determine.
- Multiple data stores may exist within a managed environment, but one is designated as authoritative.
- Data location will be transparent to strategic business units (SBUs).
- Procedural discipline (governance) is required to consistently establish this practice.
- There will be a single source of authoritative data regarding customer satisfaction and loyalty for enterprise users, dealers, vendors, field personnel, and others.

- Data stewardship for enterprise subject area data will be established.
- IT and business data stewards will need to show unified support for this principle.
- Enterprise data management policies must be defined, communicated, and followed.
- The enterprise information resource must be managed with an approach that requires a centralized data management function (central authority). This function must be clearly responsible for ensuring a single, authoritative source exists for enterprise information.
- Replication and extraction must only be used as required for optimizing performance or for supporting controlled, local data updates. A governance process for replication and extraction will be required.

The following are the two aforementioned example list of principles from two organization in the same industry. Figure 10-6 may have one or two extra principles, but this organization felt that policies would not hold up unless made a part of principles.

Tips for Success

Some of the discussions around principles can become dry. Even the most enthusiastic data architect or business member of the team can start to nod off. Keep review sessions short. Also, divide the work.

Information Principle Name	Description
Information is an asset	Information is an asset that will be leveraged across MidCo to improve operational efficiency, enhance competitive advantage, and accelerate decision making.
Information should be representative	Information will represent the authentic and faithful model of MidCo's real world and its objects.
Information should be authoritative	There should exist a single, authoritative source that may be interrogated to determine any fact about an object of interest.
Information should be accurate	All available facilities, such as controls, standards, and governance, will be employed to maintain the accuracy of MidCo's information.
Information should be timely	The value of information decreases rapidly in proportion to any decrease in its timeliness and should only be retained for the duration of its useful business life.
Information should be shared	The value of information to MidCo increases in proportion to its appropriate use.
Information should be secure	Like any asset of MidCo, information should be protected from intentional or accidental corruption or destruction.
Information should be intelligible	Information at MidCo will be managed to remove risks from misinterpretation and misuse.
Information and content should be catalogued	The degree to which information is applied consistently depends on its ability to be found and shared.

FIGURE 10-6

Sample Principles.

Principle Name	Principle Description
Accountability	Enterprise data will be governed by a formal organization, with appropriate authority and accountability to define and establish how information, data, and content is managed.
Standardization	Have enterprise standards and guidelines for all metrics, content, data structures, codes, values, and data naming.
Authoritative	There should exist a single, authoritative source that may be interrogated to determine any fact about any subject or object of interest.
Right time, place, cost	Data, information, and content needs to be available at the right time, at the right place, and in the right format to authorized users/consumers at an efficient cost.
Business alignment	Information management solutions will maintain business alignment, and will only be in response to business needs vs. business area requests.
Information asset quality	There will be parties that are accountable for overall integrity and quality of enterprise data and content.
Risk management	Enterprise information management processes will manage risk and must comply with all relevant statutory and federal laws, policies, and regulations.
Collaboration	Data is a collaborative asset, to be sha ed and made available when it meets business needs.

FIGURE 10-7

Sample Principles.

Have a few people write some of the principles while another group writes the others. Then have them exchange and critique.

The first pass will result in many principles that should be policy. It is not uncommon to feel you need 20 principles, but this is akin to saying there are 20 commandments or 200 rights in the Bill of Rights—you dilute the power of the philosophy and belief. Figure 10-7 represents final list. The original worksheet of principles was actually too large to include in the book!

Occasionally approval of principles becomes an issue—executives feel that there are too many principles and policies. Even if it takes a while to get the principles approved, do not stop. You can continue working on other activities in this phase. The principles affect ideas, beliefs, and behavior. You can continue to work on the "nuts and bolts."

Activity: Determine Baseline DG Processes to Support Business

Every process has a step where the ideas, concepts, and philosophy must become real and tangible. This activity is that step for data governance. The mission and vision of DG, along with the principles and business drivers, converge to identify the policies that codify data governance as well as the actual processes that will be required for a functional DG program.

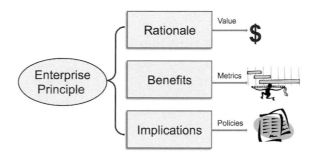

FIGURE 10-8

Principles Support Other Aspects of DG.

Some of the processes for DG will have the weight of carrying out policy, so be aware that policy and process are not mutually exclusive. Other processes will make sure the activities of DG are carried out. For example, there will be functions to determine or revise data policies and there will be functions to audit and verify compliance with data policies.

The actual activity occurs along parallel efforts. Figure 10-8 shows how the principle provides input and inspiration for other components of DG. First, the information principles need to be evaluated for implied policies. Review the "Authoritative" principle we reproduced earlier. Each implication points to a potential policy—that is, how to make sure you have dealt with each implication.

While that is going on, another part of the team can start with a generic list of processes (a sample of which is in this book's appendices) to begin to develop the process list. Another consideration during this activity is the development of the processes (and process flows) for managing the artifacts and outputs of the DG processes. These essential processes, such as issue resolution, need to be detailed. Policy maintenance can be overwhelming in a large organization, so that should be addressed as well.

Activity Summary Table

Objective	Define the required processes for information management and data governance.
Purpose	Develop the details to make the data governance program operational.
Inputs	Information principles, DG mission and vision, DG requirements

Tasks	1. Draft initial policies from principles rationale.
	2. Identify DG processes.
	   a. Gather any existing information and governance policies.
	   b. Identify processes to sustain key business measures or metrics models.

FIGURE 10-9

Activity Summary Table.

	c. Identify processes to support standards, controls, and policy.
	   d. Identify processes to support master data and ERP projects.
	   e. Define/support regulatory drivers.
	   f. Identify requirements and processes for enterprise data model standards and procedures.
	   g. Identify requirements and processes for reference and code policies/procedures.
	   h. Identify any planning or management functions.
	   i. Identify processes to administer policies and standards.
	3. Ensure processes and policies are not in conflict.
	4. Optional: Work with finance and compliance to perform a pro forma "Information Risk Forecast."
	5. Identify gaps in the current state of data management.
	6. Specify adequate controls.
	7. Specify privacy and security concerns.
	8. Specify compliance and regulatory concerns.
	9. Specify key DG process flows.
	   a. Define issue resolution process.
	   b. Define process for DG policy and standards changes.
	   c. Define DG and project interaction.
	   d. Develop new organization performance objectives.
	10. Identify other DG detail processes.
	   a. Identify changes to SDLC processes.
	   b. Design DG process details, deliverables, and documentation for SDLC integration touchpoints.
	   c. Develop revised process/policy alignment plan (Review/update existing policies and processes related to data governance and EIM).

Techniques	Process modeling, process design
Tools	Process modeling tools

Outputs	1. Draft DG policies
	2. Metrics and business information requirements and management processes
	3. Standards and controls management processes
	4. MDM and ERP DG processes
	5. Regulatory DG processes
	6. Data standards DG processes
	   a. DG planning and management processes
	   b. DG administration processes
	   c. Policy/process cross reference
	   d. Reference and code DG processes
	7. Information risk forecast
	8. Processes to close current DG deficiencies
	9. Data controls
	10. Privacy/security controls
	11. Compliance and regulatory DG processes
	12. DG issue resolution flow
	13. Policy and standards maintenance flow
	14. Project DG flow
	15. DG performance objectives for business areas
	16. SDLC change requirements
	17. SDLC changes
	18. Revised policies affected by governance

FIGURE 10-9

(Continued)

Business Benefits and Ramifications

The primary benefit is the ability to see the activity that is required to operate the DG program. Of course, the downside could also be that the business gets to see what is required to operate the DG program! The bottom line is that you have moved from abstraction to reality.

Approach Considerations

The information principles (and specifically the implications) are used as a basis for initial identification of policies. The team will merge these with a generic set of processes typical to a DG program. The essential DG processes need to address a basic functional cycle of *plan*, *design*, *manage*, and *operate*, while also covering processes to:

- Sustain key business measures or metrics models
- Support standards, controls, and policies
- Support master data and ERP projects
- Support regulatory drivers
- Manage enterprise data model standards and procedures
- Manage processes for reference and code data
- Plan and manage the DG program itself, including processes to administer policies and standards

Once the DG team has assembled a list of DG processes, they can work through a rationalization process and make sure there are no policies in place that could conflict with the new DG processes.

Separately, the team can address regulatory items, such as security, privacy, and compliance.

Data controls are also important, especially in a financial services environment. Many of our clients base their data governance on COBIT, a standard framework for data control and financial governance.

Don't forget processes to support compliance, regulatory, security, and privacy areas. These will be very visible DG functions. Most organizations have security and privacy areas in place, so coordination and leverage with existing policies in this area are important. If the policies already exist, make sure they are adopted into DG.

Lastly, the team needs to strongly consider some process design, especially for key functions such as issue resolution or maintaining and implementing new policies. Walking through these will give a great indication of the amount of change the organization will undergo. This includes changes to the development methods used by IT to implement systems. These are referred to as the *system development life cycle* (SDLC) *methods* and can take a variety of forms (Agile, waterfall, iterative, etc.). Regardless of form, the DG program will require changes to internal SDLCs.

Sample Output

Figure 10-10 shows an example of the standard list of DG functions we use. The entire list is in the appendices, including the basic IM functions. Sorry to force you to the back of the book, but space is limited for these larger lists.

Tips for Success

If you receive feedback upon review of your functional design that it is "too much," remind the critics that business functional areas have similar sets of activity.

A common mistake is to fail to keep the design of information management processes separate from data governance processes. The next activity gets specific about information management processes. The lack of separation is usually because the initial staffing of DG is drawn from

Mgmt Phase	Basic Enterprise Information Governance Functions	Function Area		
		IM	DG	Change Mgmt
Plan	Identify essential information principles	x	x	
	Recommend new IG processes		x	
	Refine current governance practices		x	
Define	Define data meaning & business rules		x	
	Develop application code management requirements for reusability and consistency	x	x	
	Design privacy and security standards		x	
	Establish standards for rules, models		x	
	Define EIM policy guidelines		x	
	Define data linkage policy		x	
	Define info lifecycle mgmt policies		x	
	Define enterprise master data management standards		x	
	Determine IG technology requirements		x	
	Define naming standards and policies		x	
Manage	Refine data governance roll out strategy and metrics		x	
	Recommend new IG Processes		x	
	Assess current governance practices		x	
	Audit applications and other projects for EIM compliance		x	
	Elevate IG issues to appropriate body			
	Measure and report progress of IG		x	
	Assess effectiveness of IG		x	
Operate	Implement business processes & systems for data privacy	x	x	
	Review processes to support data controls		x	
	Operate IG steering bodies - meetings, agendas, issue resolution		x	
	Implement regular metrics and measurement of IG implementation		x	
	Enforce use of integrated and managed data		x	
	Mediate and resolve conflicts pertaining to data		x	
	Enforce enterprise MDM (policies, design, processes)		x	
	Enforce data principles, policies, & standards		x	

FIGURE 10-10

Sample List of DG Functions.

information areas. Often, the initial DG staff are told to "fit it in" to their current roles and responsibilities.[1] It is challenging to these individuals to maintain the separation of duties mandated by the V, while also creating embedded organizational processes, new roles, and a sustainable program. Remember, you must identify the IM functions as well as the DG functions.

Activity: Identify/Refine IM Functions and Processes

This is a short activity to identify the IM functions. During this activity, the team collects and identifies processes that are for the information-management area. This is done to make a clear distinction between the governed and the governors. Business areas do not have a difficult time understanding they are subject to oversight. Business leaders often interact with all kinds of compliance requirements. But Information technology (IT) staff, as well as information managers of an organization, occasionally have difficulty seeing the distinction. The prior activity added details to the left part of the V. This activity adds details to the right side.

---

[1]Kudos to those IM staff we have worked with over the years that, to a person, have all had to do double duty. There are many hardworking people in information management, and we have never seen a management team allow the designated DG deployment team to offload their current duties. Of course, it drags things out, but they hang in there. As for the management who demands the double duty (and does not offer additional incentive) while at the same time saying how important DG is, well, we will refrain from comment here.

Activity Summary Table

Objective	Define the functionality that the information management area will need to perform.
Purpose	Provide visibility to the difference between IM and DG processes.
Inputs	DG functions
Tasks	1. Identify IM processes. 2. Separate IM functionality from DG.
Techniques	Process modeling, process design
Tools	Process modeling tools
Outputs	1. Revised IM processes (not DG) 2. Separate lists of IM and DG functionality

FIGURE 10-11

Activity Summary Table.

Business Benefits and Ramifications

Separation of duties is an important concept. If the same people who are handling DG activity must also maintain databases and manage data models, then you do not have proper oversight. There will be an inevitable conflict between the projects they are assigned to and the governance of those very projects. The same goes for the business sponsors and stakeholders of projects. They cannot be expected to be motivated by project deadlines and then stop and audit compliance to governance policy. Inevitably, the governance falls by the wayside.

Approach Considerations

Make sure you provide examples that show how DG and IM functions operate independently and together. About this time, some confusion may be setting in with the project teams as to who does what. The complete list of IM and DG functions should be presented together. See Figure 10-15 below.

Sample Output

Figure 10-12 lists a sample set of IM functions.

Tips for Success

Please use the templates we provide. They have evolved over many years of IM and DG work. We also refresh them periodically. There is a website address (www.makingeimworkforbusiness.com) with the templates if you want to download the latest versions.

Activity: Identify Preliminary Accountability and Ownership Model

This activity adds the details to the DG processes (i.e., the specifics of "who does what"). The V evolves more with specifics of who is required to manage the various DG processes. While we are not declaring the entire design of the operational framework and organizational aspect of DG, we are taking a shot at what the various levels of DG might look like. We evolve our V model by identifying possible names of the various levels and some lines of communication. These will be verified and approved later in the process but are addressed now since it is inevitable that the Plan, Design, Manage, Operate model will translate to organization levels.

Mgmt Phase	Basic Enterprise Information Management Functions	Function Area		
		IM	DG	Change Mgmt
Plan	Align information architecture with enterprise business strategy	x		
	Establish priorities for information projects	x		
	Assess information maturity	x		
	Establish data technology infrastructure	x		
Define	Confirm enterprise architecture principles with Information principles	x	x	
	Develop processes for enterprise information content and delivery (data models)	x		
	Develop & establish enterprise metadata management environment	x		
	Define IM usage metrics to determine effectiveness of IM	x		
	Define reference data	x		
	Develop application code management requirements for reusability and consistency	x	x	
	Define enterprise master data management (policies, design, processes)	x		
	Design metadata layer	x		
	Define business requirements for information systems	x		
Manage	Manage data architecture, models, & definitions	x		
	Track and leverage industry trends in EIM	x		
	Manage EIM BI projects	x		
	Manage EIM MDM projects	x		
	Develop processes for information management	x		
	Ensure data quality & integration (by subject)	x		
Operate	Secure data	x		
	Implement business processes & systems for data privacy	x	x	
	Execute processes to support data access	x		
	Execute processes to support data controls	x		
	Support the new IM and DG vision, not contradict it	x	x	
	Develop customer/vendor/other subject area hierarchies	x		
	Assess data quality throughout all systems life cycles	x		
	Monitor and tune IM technology	x		
	Oversee data integration & transformation	x		
	Design & maintain metadata layer	x		
	Enable appropriate access to data	x		

FIGURE 10-12

Sample List of IM Functions.

Activity Summary Table

Objective	Develop the initial view of who will perform the various roles in the organization after DG is deployed.
Purpose	Provide leadership with a preliminary view of new roles and accountabilities.
Inputs	The IM and IG functions and processes
Tasks	1. Examine processes requiring DG accountability. 2. Identify business area touchpoints with DG functions. 3. Define preliminary operating DG layers.
Techniques	Facilitation, organization design
Tools	Excel, Word, or similar
Outputs	1. Processes with accountability list 2. Touchpoints between DG and rest of the organization 3. Preliminary view of DG operating layers

FIGURE 10-13

Activity Summary Table.

Business Benefits and Ramifications

There will be the perception of more ramifications than benefits during this activity. Anytime new responsibility or accountability enters the picture, organizations react. The reactions can range from a few raised eyebrows to a request for a full-blown human resources engagement.

The benefit of this activity is the raising of organizational flags at a relatively early stage. Once leadership starts to digest the accountability and responsibility inherent in DG, then you will know where they really stand and where your support is located.

Approach Considerations

Focus on processes where DG will touch the business in the form of individuals being accountable for DG success (e.g., the oversight of stewards).

Sample Output

See Figure 10-15 for the results of both this activity and the next.

Tips for Success

Have the DG team address this work product before any discussions or reviews are held with other stakeholders. This will help the team tighten any loose ends and prepare explanations of the meanings of certain processes.

There will be many perspectives on how the layers may shake out, and there will be disagreements. If necessary, use smaller sessions (in terms of attendees) to gather as many perspectives as possible.

Activity: Present EIM DG Functional Model to Business Leadership

You are now at a critical step in the process to activate DG. At a minimum, you need to review a summarized version of your functional lists. The DG functions are new activities that will seem disruptive to many stakeholders (even though they are not).

The realization of new accountabilities will often stall DG efforts at this point, even if the full "green light" was given. Therefore, this is not a casual presentation. While you are looking for acceptance in principle and understanding of the details, you are not looking for a detailed review of all processes. The DG team needs to be aware that this step may take time, as the approval of such structures usually occurs among personnel who only get together once per month, at best.

Activity Summary Table

Objective	Gain approval of the functional approach to data governance.
Purpose	Ensure that there is support and understanding of the DG program before assignments are made.
Inputs	The functional models for IM and DG
Tasks	1. Prepare a DG functional presentation. 2. Gain acceptance of data governance processes in principle.
Techniques	Facilitation
Tools	PowerPoint or similar
Outputs	1. DG functional presentation 2. Approved function list

FIGURE 10-14

Activity Summary Table.

Business Benefits and Ramifications

The obvious benefit in this activity is either increased buy-in or the reinforcement of existing buy-in. You will also be able to see the reaction of management to the functional model for DG. There are a few benefits of demonstrating to management a visible picture of what needs to happen to rein in data.

- Many of the functions you are defining already happen in multiple places and are redundant or create conflicts.
- The functions that are not occurring open the organization to risk.
- The functions that are occurring currently should also be made as efficient as possible.

Most of the time, the responses range from "this is a lot" to "is this what we are supposed to do?" You will need to be very clear with leadership that these activities are, more or less, *already* done.

Approach Considerations

Use the V or a similar format. The key interest here will be the accountabilities. While the next phase will accomplish the definition of organization, it cannot be helped but to consider the various assignments of who goes where. Keep the reviewers focused on the accountabilities and responsibilities. Are they appropriate? Are there cultural or policy-level barriers to the potential management layers?

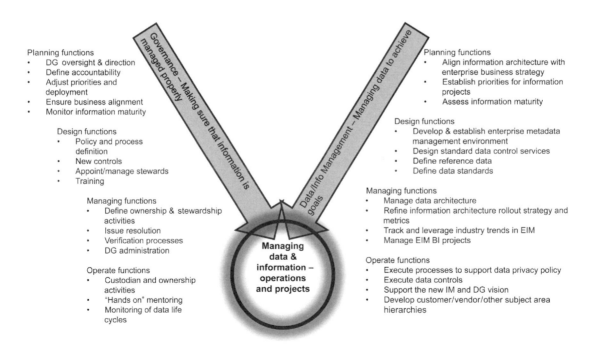

FIGURE 10-15

Functional View of the "V".

Sample Output

Tips for Success

Try to brainstorm the various types of questions that may be presented to the DG team. Remember, most reviewers will go immediately into forming mental organization charts. It is very easy to pick the model apart if that is allowed to happen.

Be careful when presenting the results of this activity to leadership. Very often too much detail is presented. You may want to focus on a version of the V along with a list of functions by DG and IM. Hopefully, the details will be left to the DG team.

SUMMARY

At some point, data governance needs to make the transition from a cool concept to an operational model. This phase conducts the first half of that transition. It is the step where the realities of data governance start to run into the realities of organizations realizing the need to approach information differently.

As a result, some engineering is required. Relevant principles of information management are defined. The principles form a foundation for belief that is critical. They also provide implications and rationale, which then frames policy development. Then the required functions for plan, design, manage, and operate DG can be defined. We are not done yet, though. We still need to identify "who" and determine "where" the data governance happens. However, we do have a firm grasp of the "what." From the principles to the detailed processes, you need to complete this activity with a good understanding of an operational model and a clear presentation of data governance for your enterprise.

Governing framework design

The ability to convert ideas to things is the secret to outward success.
—Henry Ward Beecher

During the past few decades, as we started to make data governance an integral part of information projects, we did not pay much attention to how the organization would operate after all the new data, tools, and neat things were turned on. After all, how hard could it be? Appoint a few stewards, give them power to enforce standards, and away we go. Reality soon hit us right between the eyes and we realized there had to be additional formal treatment of how organizations implement DG.[1] There had to be some engineering to show people what it was they needed to do, and then they had to be appointed to do it. This had to be done in a form that allowed us to monitor it all. In other words, we had to design and staff an organization framework of sorts to actually carry out DG.

Also, note that the term "organization framework" is used instead of "organization chart." Because the goal is to eventually blend in with ordinary day-to-day behavior, you will rarely develop a large separate DG organization. As our experience in developing DG "organizations" matured, we stopped using the term.

This phase entails identifying the stewardship/ownership/custodian population. We nail down what will be done where and who will do it. The assumption is that there is a functional design of DG for your organization, not just a list of "things" to do, but a true design. Other defined processes for DG indicate identifying stewards much sooner. As stated earlier, we do not consider this a good practice. Up to this point, any members of the DG team are part of the process to get started. They may or may not be formal stewards over the long term. Think about it, if you have defined stewards before you have a functional organization, you have given responsibility without:

- "Air cover" of a defined process
- Formal means to monitor activity
- Training
- Organizational acceptance of one definition of "steward"

---

[1]Strange as it may seem, most human beings are not genetically disposed to be data stewards. There is no "data instinct" from birth. Therefore, taking an approach of defining a few standards and a mandate to "go forth and govern" usually ends in a bad way.

KEY CONCEPT

A moment for stewardship

We are not talking about a portion of a Protestant church service—we are talking about the definition of stewardship in the context of data governance. The term "stewardship" has been overused, and we look at it as more of a function than an individual role. The entire DG framework is essentially the vessel for data stewardship. Rather than focusing on assigning a body to a title, focus on defining accountability and responsibility.

This activity takes the functional framework and refines the various layers required to do governance. Then the responsibility and accountability can be identified. The federation (if required) of DG is also determined and specified. After that, the process of approval and socialization of the new framework for governance can start.

At the core of this activity is the final arrangement and definition of the layers of governance. The prior activity developed a preliminary view, but we need to declare an official version. Again, there is not a single formula, and successful DG requires an understanding of why this is the case.

- **Stewardship is multidimensional.** A common error is to declare an individual as the steward of a subject or content area (e.g., "Bob in marketing is now the czar for customer data"). However, stewardship is **not** an individual role. The context and manner in which data is used will make a huge difference in the required style and intensity of stewardship. Figure 11-1 illustrates how a single subject—in this case—could easily have two or more parties officially accountable for

Stewardship is a function of context, business model, and relevance of content area

		Data Usage Category	
		Data as an Event or Transaction, e.g., enroll a new Member, sell to a new Customer, or repair machinery	**Data as a Domain, i.e., use information ABOUT the domain**
Sample Data Context	External Visibility e.g., Compliance to regulators	Data is gathered legally	Data is accessed legally	A
	Cross Functional Visibility - Use across multiple departments and functions	Transaction must be accurate	Data used by many areas needs to be accurate	B
	Departmental Visibility - Use to accomplish localized goals	Data needs to be useful for departmental use	Data with departmental visibility needs to be blocked from other areas	C

FIGURE 11-1

Example of Stewardship as Multidimensional.

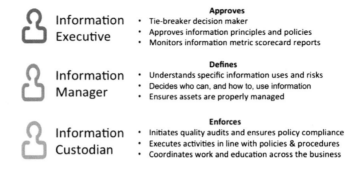

FIGURE 11-2

Multi-layered Stewardship Model.

some aspect of customer data. Row A shows customers in an external context. Rows B and C show two different internal views of customer data. We based this figure on a client example where a single subject area had not only multiple stewards, but also required a *customer stewardship committee.*

- **Accountability needs to stand out.** Stewardship can be considered a function, so in essence anyone who uses or touches data in any way can be viewed as a steward. However, this certainly misses the whole accountability concept. Unless you want to solely state that stewardship equals accountability, you are going to need to call out who is accountable. In my experience, the best DG frameworks declare everyone stewards and then have separate titles for layers of accountability and responsibility. This is one of those items that may not line up with other processes for deploying data governance.

Before we delve into the details, take time to review Figure 11-2. It shows a very simple representation of a DG framework in which the word stewardship is not mentioned. Figure 11-3 illustrates how one

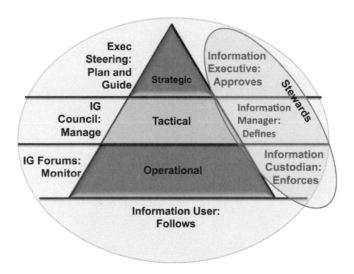

FIGURE 11-3

Sample Data Governance Framework.

organization connected the concept to its DG framework. Note that not only is there a clear distinction of accountability, but there is also a universal concept of stewardship. You need the concept of stewardship, that of accountability and responsibility, formally designated. Stewardship is not a narrow definition and should be adjusted as your organization sees fit. This entire activity is designed to create the specific framework required by a specific organization.

OVERVIEW
Activity: Design DG Organization Framework

This activity adds the detail to the DG processes (i.e., the specifics of "who does what"). The "V" evolves more with specifics of who is required in the various DG processes. We evolve our V model by

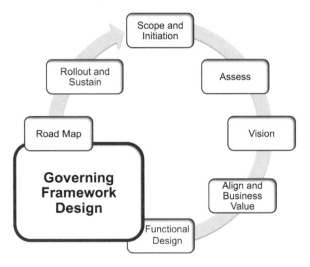

FIGURE 11-4

Process overview.

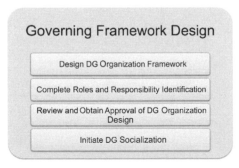

FIGURE 11-5

Activity Overview.

identifying lines of communication and authority. The results of this effort (a RACI chart) can be translated onto the V model. This activity can be time consuming if there is any debate or dissension regarding assignment of resources to stewards or other forms of accountability and responsibility.

The main technique here is the traditional RACI technique. RACI, of course, stands for Responsible, Accountable, Consult, and Inform.

*   *Responsible*—Group(s) or individual that performs or executes the work
*   *Accountable*—Group that ensures the work is done and, of course, bears accountability
*   *Consult*—Group whose input is required before the work is done
*   *Inform*—Group to whom work is reported

Each function or process is examined—this usually means a discussion concerning each process. Typically, an elapsed time of two weeks is the average duration for the RACI development, but you will also need to accommodate the time required to develop the charters.

Activity Summary Table

Objective	Develop the operating structure for data governance.
Purpose	Apply a reasoned process to show the organization the most desirable framework for DG.
Inputs	Functional model for DG
Tasks	1. Develop DG RACI from functional design. 2. Determine levels of federation. 3. Identify layers of oversight based on RACI. 4. Determine organization model. 5. Propose federated DG structure. 6. Determine potential staffing. 7. Identify leadership at all levels. 8. Develop charters for main levels of DG organization.
Techniques	RACI analysis
Tools	Excel
Outputs	1. DG RACI 2. DG federation layers 3. Organization layers for DG 4. DG organization chart 5. DG federation model 6. DG organization staffing 7. DG leadership 8. DG Charters

FIGURE 11-6

Activity Summary Table.

Business Benefits and Ramifications

Business ramifications are high in this activity. You are creating the framework within which governance will work. While two weeks is the norm, there may be more time involved. It may take two weeks to do the first cut at the chart, but it may take another two to four weeks of walking it around to make sure you have support. Remember that there is a high potential for politics and resistance as the DG team gets closer to the reality of implementation.

Approach Considerations

Given the potential for the DG team getting its first real dose of resistance (usually in the form of the organization expressing concern that this is the correct thing to do), this should not be a set of linear tasks that are executed without external contributions. Every output from this activity requires continuous vetting with potential stakeholders. Every step requires sensitivity to culture and politics. This does not mean the DG team dumbs down what governance is supposed to accomplish. It means to be resolute and navigate through the first set of real barriers.

The functional design from the Functional Design phase is used as input to develop a RACI chart. This means scrutinizing all activities described as necessary to perform DG and IM. The DG team will need to take the initial cut at the DG framework and make them the columns in the RACI chart work product. There will be multiple passes at this work product and much debate. Most likely, there will be an issue or two arising from this process that will require steering committee or executive-level intervention.

One of the key design aspects that will use the results of the RACI is the identification of the style or nature of federation. Remember, the concept of federation (in the context of data governance) means how we blend and stratify the various governance entities or functions across the organization. It is a refinement of where the DG elements touch the organization, how standards will be applied across various layers and segments of an organization, and what layers of governance are required (i.e., local, regional, global, enterprise, or others).

For example, if accountability for a subject area is hard to nail down, then most likely it is used in a context that will require some sort of multilayered oversight. The main factors for how federation is established are:

- *Enterprise size*—If there are differences in brands, operating divisions, or business operating models that will require differing styles and intensities of DG, then some type of federation needs to be defined.
- *Geography*—Is your enterprise spread across different countries? If so, then you are almost guaranteed varying types of governance based on differences in customs and regulations.
- *Organization style*—An organization that is accustomed to rigid central control will tend to adapt easily to DG, *if* its leadership is engaged in the DG process. Decentralized organizations will require *very* specific definitions of what is centrally controlled and what is distributed.
- *Regulatory environment*—Obviously, an organization that is highly regulated will embrace the central control of assets more readily than one that is not.
- *IT portfolio condition*—This factor can work both ways. An older application portfolio can create a desire to build anew and accept new conditions of governance. This is most common when a company implements SAP, which brings a set of constraints that are mostly based around success factors. Modifying functionality in SAP is not a good idea—you accept it "vanilla." Sustaining the advantages of SAP integration after you "go live" also requires ongoing data governance. The configurability of SAP can allow users to run amok. It is not uncommon to find SAP master files as badly managed as the legacy files they replaced.[2] Conversely, a beloved embedded (or tolerated) legacy application can be a barrier. It can be considered either ungovernable or immune from any perception of disruption. Lastly, if you combine

---

[2]The author got into trouble years ago after writing an article describing SAP software as "instant legacy—just add money." SAP took great offense to this, but they missed the meaning. If you treat the SAP application data the same as you treated your old systems data, you get the same result: junk data. At an average cost of $35 million per project (author's data), that makes for very disappointed CEOs.

a geographically dispersed company with a diverse and eclectic blend of applications, any kind of federation on a central basis is going to be an architectural challenge.

- *Enterprise architecture*—This factor is difficult, because it cannot be changed very easily, if at all. This is because the symptoms of an eclectic application portfolio and inconsistent and unplanned enterprise architecture produce the same challenges that create the need for DG. There is an entire other book to be written on the role of enterprise architecture and information asset management. So, briefly, enterprise architecture (the blend of all of the elements of People, Process, and Technology), or EA, can really influence federation. An organization with no formal approach to managing the blend of People, Process, and Technology will need to be almost militant in defining some sort of central data governance. This is because the DG program, for right or wrong, will be taking up the slack due to poor technology governance. An organization with a decent or robust approach to EA can leverage the dickens out of its IT and technology governance and define very clear lines of federation.

- *Culture*—The cultural factor can be divided into two subtopics, maturity (we called it IMM, or information management maturity) and capacity to change.

  ○ *IMM*—If an organization is not mature in terms of its understanding of information usage or the handling of its information assets, then federation should lean to more rigor or centralization. Of course, the immaturity will have resulted in a lot of informal information assets scattered about.

  ○ *Capacity to change*—DG means change. Many types of organizations are unaccustomed to or in denial of the need for change. Older cultures or closely held companies typically have a lower capacity to change, while younger organizations may be more amenable (but not necessarily).

All of these factors must be blended to determine the type of federation required to carry the DG processes forward.

Federation, then, needs to be combined with the various layers of governance that will evolve from an analysis of the RACI chart. For example, if we determine that customer data needs to be governed centrally, but the applications that use customer data are scattered about the globe, the accountable and responsible parties will need to be identified with some consideration of the distribution of authority. Therefore, there will need to be a centralized flavor of customer DG as well as a distributed flavor, and a collaborative set of processes will be required to facilitate DG for the customer subject area.

Of course, the framework to manage the various striations of governance will need to consider the federation and layers of DG. Remember, the organization is a framework, not an independent organization chart, so you are weaving DG within the existing organization chart.

The blend of federation and layers of DG oversight produce the representation of the organization and federation, usually in the form of a hierarchy or network (see Figure 11-8 in the output samples below).

While assigning bodies to positions occurs in detail in the next activity, it is organizational in nature to start to think of names. At this point, a list of names is okay, but make sure you focus on the talents and skills required to convert or enhance individual roles.

Names to actually list (and contact) would be the leadership of the ongoing DG framework. They may be your current executive sponsors or DG team leaders. If not, then there will need to be some initial socialization of the DG framework and vision for these folks.

Lastly, and probably most overlooked, is the need to draft succinct charters for the various layers of the DG governing framework. An outline of a typical charter is in the appendices.

Sample Output

Figure 11-7 represents a sample of results from the RACI analysis. The shaded columns are data governance functions. The rest are IM functions.

Figure 11-8 shows a federation example of a multinational, multibrand company.

Tips for Success

The basic RACI exercise performed here needs to be focused and the right people need to be in the room. If there are SMEs required, please make sure they are scheduled in advance and not subject to interruptions. If the SME starts to say that they need to check with the boss to see if this is okay, then it is the wrong SME. Get their boss in the room. There will be significant discussion on many of the functions. Inevitably, you will start to evolve an "organizational" view of the operating framework. (Remember, the term "organization chart" is to be avoided.)

If review of the chart turns into a set of tedious tweaking sessions, think about presenting each column of the RACI as a general position description.

Lastly, you will be constantly reviewing what RACI means. It gets confusing. Be patient with the attendees. Again, smaller groups are more effective. Do not schedule more than an hour at a time and have multiple sessions, if necessary.

Since the DG team is very familiar with the required functions and processes, we advise the first pass at the RACI be filled in by the DG team. It is not a good idea to do this as a "blank sheet" exercise. Then, various participants can either approve or modify the RACI.

Activity: Complete Roles and Responsibility Identification

This activity addresses the placing of names (officially) with DG roles. The specific roles of the new DG participants will be defined, along with any type of administrative tasks.

It may be disappointing (or at minimum, boring), but when you alter responsibilities and activities, you need to tell people what they will be doing and make sure it is approved by the human capital functions in your business.

Some of the roles and faces you will need to define are:

- *Council*—Members of the primary monitoring and issue resolution body will need to understand their role. Individuals in this position must not be shy about making decisions. In larger organizations, this group will not be made up of the highest-level executives, but of staff that are well regarded by leadership.
- *Committee*—If there is an executive committee (i.e., without the heavy lifting required of the council), their advisory role will require appointing individuals who understand DG and IAM.
- *Forums*—These subunits that are topically focused require the same considerations as council and stewardship members. They are subsets of councils but must be willing to dig into a specific issue.
- *Accountable Stewards/Owners*—These appointees need to understand that they are information executives, and they must take the role seriously. They will be ensuring that IAM as a mindset actually starts to "stick." If the information area for which they are accountable goes awry, they must be the right person to accept accountability, push an issue up to a council, or take action with subordinates when policies require enforcement.
- *Non-accountable Stewards/Custodians/Owners*—The stewards or custodians who are responsible but not accountable also need to accept a role that requires them to point out standards

Management Phase	Basic Enterprise Information Management & Information Governance Functions	Enterprise Info Mgmt Functions	Exec Steering Committee	Data Governance Forums	Data Governance Council	Organization Change Management	Project IM Functions	Project Mgmt Office	Project Steering Bodies
Plan	Align applications and project with business	C					A		
	Share and educate business area and projects on IM and DG policy and direction	A,R			C	I	I	I	I
	Plan principles, policies, standards, and controls for enterprise governance			R	A		R		
Define	Identify gaps and refine enterprise IM road map and environment	A					R,I		
	Identify gaps and refine enterprise IM roles, processes, and metrics	A					R,I		
	Identify gaps and refine enterprise IM principles, policies, standards, and controls	R		R	A		R		
	Define new principle, Policy, standard or control/Change to existing principle policy, standard, or control	R	A			I	C		
	Define enterprise BI and reporting metrics	A					R		
	Define processes to identify certified information sources	A			I		R		
	Identify certified sources of information	A			I		R		
	Define enterprise IM and DG organizations	A					R		
	Acquire new tools	C,R					R		A
	Approve enterprise IM principles, policies, standards, and controls	I	A	I,C	R	I	C	I,C	
	Define enterprise IM organization change strategy					A	R		
Manage	Manage information architecture, incl. data models, canonical models, rules & definitions, metadata	A,R					R		
	Manage information portfolio (actual files, data bases, content, data stores for ACME)	R					A		
	Follow existing principle, policy, standard, or control	R	A				I,R		
	Develop project documentation	C	I	R			R	A	
	Maintain inventory of certified information sources	A					R,C		
	Support and facilitate custodians	C			A		R		
	Ensure sustainable application data quality	A					R	A	
	Support and use enterprise IM and DG technology (Repositories, models, DQ tools)	C	A	C,I	R		C	I,C	A
	Manage and resolve DG and IM issues	R		R	A		I	R	
	Enforce enterprise IM principles, policies, standards, and controls	R	A	R	R		R	I	
Sustain	Ensure enterprise DG program is followed	I	I,C						
	Execute culture change management methodology tasks					A			
	Measure people performance to enterprise DG and IM goals					A			
	Measure progress towards enterprise change goals					A			
	Execute communications plan	C				R			A
	Execute training and education plan	C				R			A

RACI

FIGURE 11-7

Sample RACI.

AU5

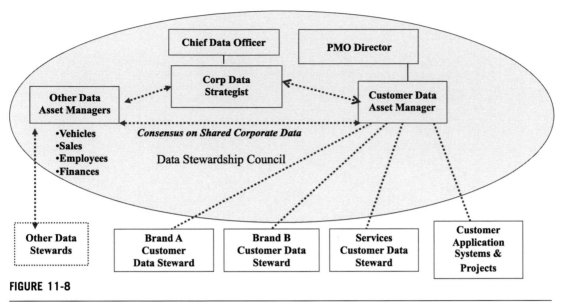

FIGURE 11-8

Sample Federated Data Governance Framework.

violations. Often these same personnel are participating in information management and development. They are at the bottom of the V.

This activity also requires that the assignments of recommended staff be presented and approved.

Activity Summary Table

Objective	Develop an approved list of accountable and responsible DG participants.
Purpose	Identify the core participants in the IAM process.
Inputs	The DG framework and the initial list of participants
Tasks	1. Define data stewards' roles and responsibilities. 2. Develop data steward/accountability identification approach. 3. Coordinate with HR and identified data steward(s) to revise data steward(s) performance goals and objectives. 4. Identify data governance oversight body(s). a. Identify council, forum, and committee members. b. Identify specific contact points and protocol.
Techniques	Organizational development, political skills
Tools	Word, Excel
Outputs	1. Stewards/owner roles and responsibilities 2. Accountability definition for DG 3. Revised performance objectives for stewards 4. Data governance oversight framework

FIGURE 11-9

Activity Summary Table.

Business Benefits and Ramifications

This activity prepares the organization for the initial "bump" or learning curve that gets DG started. You will now know who is affected in terms of new job responsibilities. You also will get another indication of how serious the organization is, simply because the individuals who will be the best in the DG roles are most likely in high demand.

Some ramifications will appear that may be new to the DG team. For example, HR may give the DG team a blank stare. Several times, we have taken the new responsibilities documentation to HR areas only to discover it has been a long time since new roles have been presented from another business area. While HR staff appreciates the need to manage people and have useful job descriptions, they do not do it very often and they do not understand DG.

- *Boundary problems*—The DG team may be accused of overstepping its charter by recommending organizational actions. This is something that can be avoided by early and frequent managing of expectations.
- *Political considerations*—Inevitably, some areas of an organization will have more power and influence than others. The DG team will need to figure out the political situation and either work with the more powerful areas as allies or get executive assistance to counter any pushback.
- *Incentives*—Corporate incentives are often used to move organizations toward better DG. HR will need to approve these, and they may even be useful in identifying programs that can provide a stimulus to DG acceptance.

Approach Considerations

This activity will occur in parallel with the presentation and approval of the DG framework. In very large and politically charged organizations, you will most likely identify personnel "as you go." That is, you will identify the DG personnel required for a particular portion of the information assets, such as the MDM project or the data warehouse. This activity will be revisited often as DG expands or personnel change.

Sample Output

Figure 11-10 shows a nice representation of various levels of authority and roles to go with names.

Tips for Success

Two useful hints stand out for this activity:

1. *Don't be afraid of some horse-trading.* That is, if you want a certain individual to be a steward, look for opportunities to provide backfill for them. If a politically powerful area wants to dominate the councils, then request they become full-bore sponsors and take on accountability.
2. *Now is the time to consider some incentives.* If accountability means holding a manager to particular data quality targets, then work with HR to tie the DQ metrics into their compensation.

In Chapter 5, we mentioned that this is more than just names on boxes. Some of the obstacles you may encounter and the useful responses to them are:

- *Perceived political threats from some getting "power" over data*—Show how everyone is subject to DG, not just particular areas.

Proposed Data Governance Operating Staff	
Information Executives	Approves • Tie-breaker decision maker • Approves information principles and policies • Monitors information metric scorecard reports
Names	....
Information Managers	Defines • Understands specific information uses and risks • Decides who can and how to use information • Ensures assets are properly managed
Names	....
Information Custodians	Enforces • Initiates quality audits and ensures policy compliance • Executes activities in line with policies and procedures • Coordinates work and education across the business
Names	....

FIGURE 11-10

Sample Data Governance Operating Staff List.

- *Human capital (or HR) concerns on changing job descriptions*—Convene a meeting between your executive sponsor and the head of HR. This is a core business issue requiring executive input.
- *Fear that adding additional responsibilities will damage current productivity*—There is a learning curve, so offering to backfill will help. Also, reinforce that the "extra time" is not permanent.

The one singular hint that the reader should take away is *never* accept a DG resource that is someone who is willingly offered and is known to be a poor performer. Do not accept stewards who are people that cannot get anything else done. Even if they would make good stewards, they will not have the required respect from their peers. You do not want the DG program to be a dumping ground for unwanted staff.

The last important tip is to not short change what it takes to be in a custodial or stewardship position. Being in a middle management position does not qualify an individual. Essential skills for anyone embracing a stewardship role are:

- An understanding of organization needs and culture
- A commitment to organization success
- A desire to learn how to improve their organization

Activity: Review and Obtain Approval of DG Framework Design

Once the RACI exercise, roles, and names are identified, the obvious step is to present the list of proposed players and functionality. Review and approval of the DG framework and participants is more than one presentation to management. Typically, there will be some back and forth regarding roles and the availability of higher-level resources.

You will need to explain roles, impacts, and "days in the life" (again). You will not get all of the stewards and other ideal personnel you want. There will be some back and forth, and there will be gaps between presentation and approval. The approval levels for these types of agendas are busy managers who may only meet once a month.

Activity Summary Table

Objective	Obtain approval of the DG framework and initial topics.
Purpose	Gain understanding and acceptance of how DG will actually work.
Inputs	Lists of candidates and DG framework
Tasks	1. Review and obtain approval of data stewards identification approach with leadership. 2. Develop data tewards identification template. 3. Identify data steward identification subject areas and prioritize them (e.g., customer). 4. Identify stewards and owners. 5. Obtain approval of stewards and owners.
Techniques	Facilitation, politics
Tools	PowerPoint
Outputs	1. Approval to acquire stewards 2. Steward template 3. Steward content oversight areas 4. List of stewards and owners 5. Approval of stewards and owners

FIGURE 11-11

Activity Summary Table.

Business Benefits and Ramifications

Management gets to see the desired span and impact of DG. This is yet another step in continuing to develop the understanding that DG is not a long-term addition to work, but a change in work. This activity also triggers the beginning of building out the DG framework and making it operational.

Approach Considerations

Be prepared with some simple examples of what and how the proposed DG stewards and custodians will operate, as well as the time commitment of training and long-term activity.

Sample Output

A list of stewards is a fairly simple concept, but the prioritized subject areas can be interesting. Conceptually, you need to present something akin to what is shown in Figure 11-12.

The DG framework will need some sort of guidance as to what is most important. The result will be fewer meetings if a prioritization scheme of relative importance of data areas is recognized.

Tips for Success

Plan to execute portions of this activity in parallel with others. It is likely that you will get conditional approval of the individuals who will be operating the DG framework. Then there will be changes or reconsiderations. We have never done any DG effort where this step did not take more time than we budgeted.

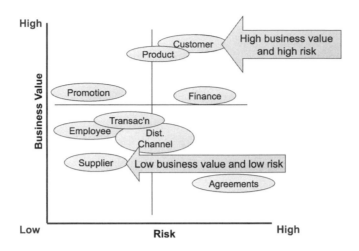

FIGURE 11-12

Subject Area Prioritization.

Activity: Initiate DG Socialization

Socialization is just that—start to be social about the new DG framework (it will be called an organization anyway) and meet and greet the new participants one at a time. This is the beginning of
orientation. If there is an associated MDM effort, you may already have a communications plan in
place, and this step will be an event in that plan. Otherwise, this is an activity to set and manage
expectations.

Activity Summary Table

Objective	Raise awareness of the new DG framework and operating model.
Purpose	Establish expectations and initial orientation with the new DG "organization."
Inputs	The DG framework and appointees
Tasks	1. Conduct data steward orientation. 2. Review IM/DG principles with councils and stewards.
Techniques	Facilitation
Tools	PowerPoint
Outputs	1. Completed orientation 2. Principle review session

FIGURE 11-13

Activity Summary Table.

Business Benefits and Ramifications

It is important to understand that you are still marketing. Most of the new participants in DG will not be
clear on what it is they have to do or even why they are doing it. This is a critical step in changing that.
The benefits of a casual socialization and "road show" will be to get everyone's thinking pointed in the
same direction.

Approach Considerations

Prepare a standard road show (i.e., a PowerPoint deck) and plan on many one-on-one sessions. Do not have one massive overview session and call this task complete. Gather individual impressions and factor those into your future presentations and orientation sessions.

Sample Output

See the appendices for some sample DG orientation material.

Tips for Success

If you are the leader of a DG effort, you should be the one to handle this chore. If you are not the lead, take the DG leader with you. If you can get a senior executive to kick this off, so much the better.

SUMMARY

Designing how the DG program is going to operate is no doubt a key step, but it is important to realize that you are not designing an organization in the sense of a separate department or functional area. You are really putting functionality into place within the existing organizational hierarchy. Granted, there is an implied hierarchy being defined here, but it is really a communications framework.

The tasks in this step can be done in parallel with or wrapped around the other activities required to initiate a DG function. However, make sure you take the definition of required functionality seriously and apply a diligent process to appointing the most effective group of people who will support and sustain the processes required to enact data governance.

Road map

Revolutions always come around again. That's why they're called revolutions.
—**Terry Pratchett**

The "Road Map" for DG is the penultimate work product for the DG program. That is, aside from the operating program itself, it is the most important output from the DG team's deployment efforts. It also forms the foundation for the sustainability of DG.

Almost any organization that has used automation for information processing has tried to do something formal to manage that information. We have said several times that the management of information already happens in organizations, but it just happens poorly. The road map process, therefore, must not only produce the list of events required to deploy DG, it must also provide an outline for success and sustainability.

Sustainability means acting to ensure that the right processes are in place by which the DG organizational framework will *continue* to perform the governance function. Core to this requirement is the overlooked fact that the organization *accepts* the governance of data—that the function be managed, its results be monitored and measured, and the obstacles that so often cause DG programs to falter or fail are overcome. In our experience, very few organizations think ahead about what needs to happen one or two years down the road.

Measuring change adoption and managing the required behavior changes are only a few pieces of the puzzle. Other critical components include developing and measuring the metrics that reinforce DG's value, having clear principles and policies documented and in place, and verifying that the organization has the resources required to support DG after it is rolled out.

You will need to put in place a formal *organizational change management* (OCM) program to drive the required behavior changes needed to sustain DG in your organization. The formality and discipline inherent in data governance is new and different for many organizations—and difference means *change*. Change requires that people adjust their behaviors to the new way of doing things, and changing behavior is no easy task—just ask those of us who make (and break) those New Year's resolutions every year! It won't happen just because you say it will or believe it's the right thing to do. People naturally resist change because they are afraid of it; afraid it will be hard, or they will fail in the new world, or lose something—power, competence, or influence—to name a few. You will have to overcome that resistance in order for DG to be successful and adopted by the organization. That formal OCM program, with the right executive sponsor, is critical to helping you accomplish that.

Organizational change management is a well-known discipline within the realm of *organizational effectiveness*. It can be thought of in three basic steps:

1. *Planning*—Assessing the need for change and developing the approach and detailed plan to manage change.

2. *Doing*—Executing the OCM plan to help people transition from the "old" state of work to the new.

3. *Sustaining*—Implementing the mechanisms and structures to ensure there is no reversion back to the old ways!

The "Road Map" phase contains the Planning and Doing aspects of OCM. The rest of the OCM tasks occur in the Sustaining phase, which is covered in Chapter 13. Yes, the activity of doing OCM starts now. Even while preparing the steps for deploying the actual program, there needs to be formal planned activity to ensure sustainability.

SUCCESS FACTOR

Observation

Unfortunately, OCM is a discipline that is rarely effectively deployed in organizations, particularly around DG and information management. Executives tend to think of it as "squishy" or "soft"; far from it, as the hard dollar costs (seldom tracked, by the way) of poorly managed change in an organization are significant. If you want to realize any benefits from your DG implementation, you MUST have an OCM program to drive the required behavior changes. Otherwise, you are wasting your investment in DG now because it won't stick, *period*. Think about it—is this really the first time your organization has tried DG? It's a "pay me now or pay me later" scenario.

OVERVIEW

Activity: Integrate DG with Other Efforts

Remember that you need to govern something, so this activity specifies the projects and programs DG will support and oversee. There may be a temptation to skip this step if a particular program has initiated DG, such as MDM. However, experience has shown that the devil is often in the details. For example, a large ERP effort may require many types of DG oversight. Reality sets in when the DG team sees that the process to embed DG in the new ERP-driven effort may require more resources than are available. The worst thing that can happen is to overwhelm a deadline-driven effort with activity that seems to be interfering. The most common areas to resist DG are always in the applications or

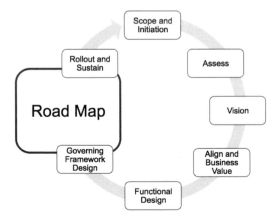

FIGURE 12-1

Process Overview.

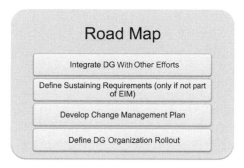

FIGURE 12-2

Activity Overview.

project-delivery areas. Therefore, the DG team needs to choose an activity where DG can assist the project in achieving its goals and not appear to be interfering. This may seem like "giving up" on enterprise DG, but it is not. Rather, this is a practical implementation strategy.

The integration with other efforts means getting embedded into other project plans, not observing. Your DG team will need to sit down at the table with the "lucky candidates."

Activity Summary Table

Objective	Identify initial projects or programs to be governed.
Purpose	Ensure the projects or programs are visibly governed and show the value of DG.
Inputs	DG function, RACI, projects planned or in process
Tasks	1. Identify projects and stakeholders subject to standards and governance. 2. Refine governance bodies and committees (if part of EIM). 3. Refine DG charters (if part of EIM). 4. Confirm stewardship and ownership model, if necessary. 5. Define the rollout of DG to support the EIM road map or other identified projects.
Techniques	Project planning
Tools	Microsoft Project
Outputs	1. List of projects and stakeholders subject to DG 2. Enhanced EIM oversight 3. Adjusted EIM/DG charters 4. Reviewed DG rollout with stewards and owners 5. EIM/DG rollout road map 6. DG rollout schedule

FIGURE 12-3

Activity Summary Table.

Business Benefits and Ramifications

The obvious benefit is the initial engagement of more stakeholders. There is an indication that DG is real (and hopefully there is visible sufficient support), and projects or programs will at least be open to the offer of assistance.

Of course, this is also a point where any potential resistance (which is guaranteed to happen) will become very evident. The OCM material developed in this activity will need to be brought to bear.

Approach Considerations

The projects that DG interacts with need to be visible but, if possible, not politically charged. It goes without saying that a project where careers are at stake is not going to be open to external governance. Many times, however, we see that DG is built into these high-visibility efforts, and it is a matter of leverage and coordination as opposed to additional oversight. Large SAP or other ERP efforts frequently have a DG program built in by the systems integrator that has been hired. In fact, your best friend may be the integrator who is overseeing a large program or project. Most large integrators (e.g., Accenture, Deloitte, etc.) bring DG, in some form, to every program they run.

If you have an EIM program and DG is being initiated within a formal EIM office, make sure you keep EIM leadership informed and adjust the various DG area charters to ensure the selected project and programs can fit into the charter for DG.

Each project or program selected will require identification of the accountable and responsible parties for DG (i.e., the stewards and custodians). They should get a good review session on why they were picked, and you can start to make sure they are amenable to the training and communications plans.

Lastly, develop the road map by showing the affected projects as well as the various DG efforts.

Sample Output

See Figure 12-12 below for a sample of how a program interacts with DG. Here, Figure 12-4 shows a typical road map that intertwines governed projects with the DG rollout.

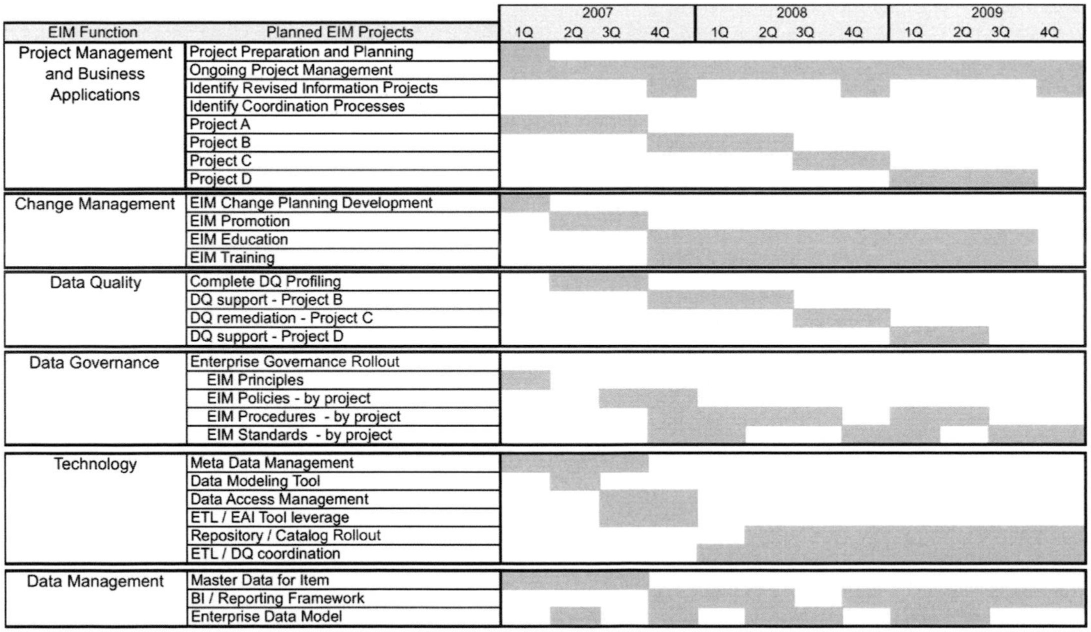

FIGURE 12-4

Typical EIM Road Map with Data Governance.

Tips for Success

Whatever the type of project or interaction you determine at this point, build it *into* project plans. Again, glance ahead to Figure 12-12 later in this chapter. Rather than hazy Gantt charts where you guess and approximate, set some measureable objectives.

Always emphasize that DG is there to help. It will not hurt to remind stakeholders you are looking for the "net zero" or minimal impact. This is not anything new—it is different.

Activity: Define Sustaining Requirements

At this point in the development of the DG road map, the team may have some idea of the extent of changes required to implement and sustain DG, especially if the change capacity and IMM assessments have already been done. It will be important at this stage to identify what needs to be put in place in order to maintain data governance for the long term. Being able to maintain DG requires that your OCM plan be attuned to the organization's culture. The work done during this activity to identify the sustaining requirements provides insight into how those cultural elements need to be addressed.

Although at this point we may have some idea of the extent of the change, we will need to be sure we have developed a specific analysis of the change impact on the stakeholder groups. The sustaining requirements are developed based on the analysis of all affected parties. What usually comes from the analysis are the following needs for the sustaining phase:

- Communication plans
- Education and training plans (by type of stakeholder and degree of impact)
- Sponsorship expectations and guidelines
- Individual coaching plans for executives to enable them to effectively support required changes
- A resistance management plan and tactics
- Process and policy alignment plans
- Organizational realignment plans for structure, roles

All of these elements together form the basis for the change management plan described later in this chapter.

Activity Summary Table

Objective	Identify the elements that must be addressed in the OCM plan if data governance is to be sustainable in the organization for the long term.
Purpose	Ensure all aspects of sustaining DG have been considered and will be addressed as part of an OCM plan.
Inputs	Change capacity assessment, stakeholder analysis, IMM assessment (if available)
Tasks	1. Review/perform stakeholder analysis (or perform in parallel). 2. Review other IM assessments. 3. Execute change capacity assessment (if not already done). 4. Identify change management resources required.

FIGURE 12-5

Activity Summary Table.

	5.	Cross reference touchpoints, change capacity, and stakeholder analysis.
	6.	Incorporate IMM results into the change capacity analysis.
	7.	Perform stakeholder analysis (if necessary). a. Identify DG stakeholders. b. Perform SWOT analysis (all stakeholders). c. Complete stakeholder analysis. d. Review with DG leadership. e. Assess levels of commitment for key stakeholders. f. Review results of stakeholder analysis with leadership (DG steering or sponsors). g. Determine action plan to address improving levels of stakeholder commitment.
	8.	Conduct an initial leadership alignment assessment.
	9.	Define nature, scope, and size of change.
	10.	Identify metrics and reporting requirements for sustaining DG.
	11.	Identify executive DG sponsor. a. Describe sponsor(s) experience and ability to lead change.
	12.	Develop plan to engage sponsors (if required).
	13.	Define training requirements.
	14.	Define communications requirements.
	15.	Prepare statement of change readiness.
	16.	Complete requirements to sustain DG.
Techniques		Assessment via interviews for leadership alignment Assessment via survey, if required OCM assistance from HR
Tools		Change capacity assessment survey Stakeholder analysis guide
Outputs	1.	DG sustaining requirements a. Stakeholder analysis b. Leadership assessment c. Metrics and reporting requirements
	2.	Ongoing DG program sponsor (not deployment sponsor)
	3.	Approved OCM strategy

FIGURE 12-5

(Continued)

Business Benefits and Ramifications

It has been said previously, but it is worth saying again to reinforce the idea: The *root cause* of the failure of data governance or any other related EIM-type program is the failure to recognize that organizational changes *must* be proactively managed. If you do not manage the movement from the current state of organizational behavior around data governance (scattered, inconsistent, or nonexistent) to the desired future state, you will fail. This is *not* squishy psychology or human resources stuff.

Approach Considerations

There are many change management processes available. All contain basically the same elements and all are effective when deployed properly. Adopt an approach that:

• Focuses on engagement and managing resistance

- Follows best practices and provides some metrics for consideration
- Offers sample tools for planning, assessment, and support of stakeholders and sponsors

The right sponsor for data governance is an essential OCM "best practice" that must be addressed early on.[1] Without a sponsor who has the political capital and backbone to drive the required changes, your chances of success are slim. Also, in most organizations IT does not have the credibility to sponsor something like DG. Go after a business executive and keep pushing until you get the right one.

Stakeholder analysis should be done considering all those who are impacted, to what degree, and what their likely reaction(s) will be. It will be important to understand how people will react so you can develop methods or approaches to address their resistance or engage their support.

Open, honest, and frequent communication is absolutely critical, and it is not through a list of required PowerPoint slides. Various stakeholder groups will require different and differing levels of communication and opportunities to provide feedback. Communication *must be two-way*. Only if you know what people are thinking or how they are reacting will you be able to "course correct" your plans and address the issues.

Managing resistance is essential. It is out there and cannot be ignored or it will undermine all your efforts, guaranteed. There will be varying levels of resistance, from openly hostile to passive. The important thing is to understand why people are resisting and to try to address it. Answering "What's in it for me?" (WIIFM) is an important OCM principle. It helps people connect to what is happening and move through their resistance to support.

If you have been doing this for a while, you have become accustomed to resistance in all of its forms. However, as someone who may be new, please bear this in mind: Many of the behaviors that DG deems risky (e.g., departmental databases with mission-critical spreadsheets copied to USB drives, etc.) are viewed as necessary and acceptable. Keep a positive outlook, identify available incentives, and provide education on the benefits and rationale for doing DG. Engage people in the process as much as possible. Keep negative responses as a tool, but deploy them only after trying the positive.

Sample Output

Due to size limitations, the appendices contain examples and templates of the following outputs:

- Stakeholder Analysis Grid
- Change Capacity Assessment
- Leadership Alignment Assessment
- Metrics for Sustaining DG

Tips for Success

The DG team would benefit greatly from the help of an organizational development (OD) specialist to help define the sustaining requirements and the change management plan. Many HR organizations have a unit of these professionals to help with change efforts. Make use of them if you have such a group in your organization.

Picking the right sponsor for DG (i.e., from the business) is essential. Per the Prosci Best Practices surveys since 2003, the right sponsor has been the number one success factor for any change effort. That person has the influence and political power to make things happen; get him or her engaged very early on.

---

[1]Prosci , "Best Practices in Change Management" Prosci, Loveland CO, 2012.

Activity: Develop the Change Management Plan

Earlier in the chapter, we discussed the development of the requirements, the "what will it take," for data governance to be sustainable. Once those requirements have been identified, then the detailed planning for managing the DG program changes can begin. A comprehensive plan and effective execution of the tasks (discussed in Chapter 13) outlined in the plan are the means by which you will build awareness, understanding, and acceptance of data governance for the organization.

Activity Summary Table

Objective	Identify the tasks and timelines required to implement and sustain a data governance process/function for the organization.
Purpose	Ensure there is a structured process, measures, and monitoring for integrating data governance into the culture of the organization.
Inputs	Sustaining requirements, stakeholder analysis, the DG roadmap, change capacity assessment

Tasks	1. Define conditions for sustainability success.
	2. Define and design capture of sustaining metrics.
	3. Identify OCM team members.
	4. Identify specific types of resistance (overt, passive, etc.).
	   a. Develop responses to resistance.
	   b. Develop resistance-management plan.
	   c. Review and approve resistance-management plan.
	5. Define and align staff performance goals and reward structures to new accountabilities.
	6. Develop the sustainability checklist for data governance.
	7. Develop the organizational alignment action plans.
	8. Identify and design change measures.
	9. Define feedback and monitoring approach.
	10. Develop staff transition approach (use HR as needed).
	11. Develop communication and training plans.
	   a. Develop DG communications plan.
	     – Identify audiences.
	     – Create messages and branding.
	     – Identify vehicles for communications.
	     – Define timing, frequencies, and delivery means.
	     – Review and approve communications plan.
	   b. Develop DG training plan.
	     – Identify audiences.
	     – Identify levels and extent of training: orient, educate, train.
	     – Identify vehicles for training.
	     – Define timing, frequencies, and delivery means.
	     – Review and approve training plan.

FIGURE 12-6

Activity Summary Table.

Techniques	Assessment via interviews for organizational alignment action plans
Tools	OCM planning template Communication plan template Training plan template Organizational alignment action-planning template DG sustainability checklist template
Outputs	1. Detailed OCM task plan and timeline 2. OCM team 3. Communications plan 4. Training plan

FIGURE 12-6

(Continued)

Business Benefits and Ramifications

Developing the set of tasks to make sure DG is sustained provides a level of proactive management for what it takes to get those critical behavior changes to stick. As we said earlier, many in the organization view things like individual departments with mission-critical spreadsheets as perfectly acceptable, but DG is viewed as a roadblock to getting things done. Therefore, the goal with a good change management plan is to make sure that those types of perspectives are addressed and overcome. Then rapid adoption will occur, along with the potential for earlier benefit realization and minimal churn while the organization adapts to its new state. Do not underestimate the damage and cost of poorly managed change. It might not show up on the balance sheet, but it is there and it can be a huge number nonetheless.

Approach Considerations

When building your communication plan, think about bringing people up a "change curve" from basic awareness through understanding to acceptance and commitment (see Figure 12-7).

It takes time and repeated reinforcement to get people through this curve. Consider all of your audiences, the degree of impact to them, the key messages you want to deliver (and who should deliver them), sequencing, timing, and media. Generally, the "big picture" stuff should come from the executive level while changes to day-to-day process and procedure are best delivered from the direct management or supervisory level. Also, plan to collect feedback on how well your messages are getting through. Remember that communication is *two-way*; you have to listen as well as deliver information and then demonstrate that feedback has been heard and acted upon.

When rolling out a data governance program, it is essential to be specific about what is changing so that those impacted understand precisely what to start, stop, or continue to do. Inability or unwillingness to provide clarity in this area causes people to become frustrated and confused, and will either elongate the adoption curve or sabotage your program entirely. Since data governance is new to your organization (assuming this is the first time you've tried it), you will need a full-fledged education and training program to ensure that people understand and have the skill sets to be effective in their (sometimes new) roles. Make sure your program is comprehensive, moving from the general to the specific and from the rationale and business case for DG to the specific skills or knowledge needed. While only a few people may need the specific information, the entire organization (and your implementation) will benefit from the "big picture" stuff.

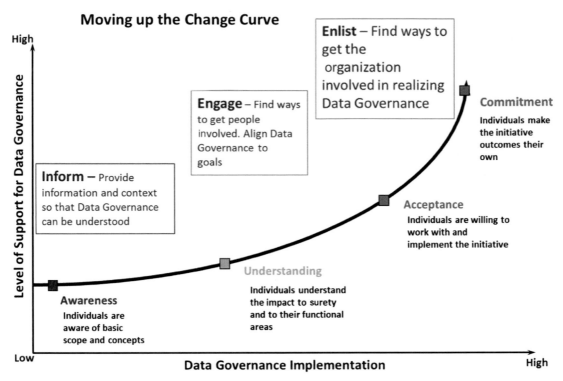

FIGURE 12-7

Change Curve.

Metrics and measurement are critical components of your change management approach. By this time, some measurement has already occurred in the form of the change capacity assessment and the stakeholder analysis. In addition, there needs to be concrete and specific data that reflects whether or not the change management program is achieving its objectives, including whether messages are being heard and training is effective. In general, you want the program to:

- *Measure achievement of initiative goals and objectives*—This is generally stated in the business case (see the section on DG metrics and monitoring).
- *Determine effectiveness of communication*—Test how well key messages are getting across to the organization.
- *Determine effectiveness of education/training*—Assess if the education has provided the target audience with the skills they need to be successful in the new environment and target areas where additional skill building may be required.
- *Measure speed of change adoption*—Examine the speed of adoption and intensity of resistance to any new principles and policies.

Sample Output

Templates for the following are in the appendices, due to size limitations:

- Communication plan template
- Training plan template

Tips for Success

As we said earlier, data governance generates a lot of resistance, and you cannot afford to ignore it. Resistance usually occurs across a continuum, from visible support and advocacy to overt hostility. Either end of the spectrum is easy to spot, but it is the passive resisters to worry about because they do not speak up and are very hard to spot. Make sure your plan contains the tasks and the time to understand and address all the types of resistance you will encounter. Your DG program will definitely benefit from the time spent.

Also, make sure your CM plan gets integrated into the overall DG roadmap effort. These tasks do not stand alone, and it is essential that they be coordinated with the overall effort.

Activity: Define DG Organization Rollout

It is obvious that you should not announce to everyone, "DG is here!" and then wait for DG to happen. Very often, it is too easy to develop a rollout strategy that does just that. No matter what good intentions are held, the rollout process for DG can very easily be perceived as force-feeding the organization. Remember, you need to govern something and it is perfectly fine to implement in small pieces, by project, or by program. This does not mean you have *separate* DG efforts for every program. You will need to coordinate among the projects to ensure the enterprise aspect of DG. The rollout of the DG framework entails a little bit of planning.

One key aspect of a rollout strategy is to get the governance structure busy doing some kind of DG activity. Too often, the stakeholders are sent to training and then told to wait for the first opportunity to govern. This activity, therefore, not only defines the incremental events that deploy DG, but also specifies what is happening in these events, as well as fine-tuning the structure to match the rollout approach.

Activity Summary Table

Objective	Define an incremental process to deploy DG.
Purpose	Ensure DG is absorbed into the organization in digestible portions.
Inputs	DG operating framework
Tasks	1. Develop DG management requirements. 2. Revise DG charter/mission, if necessary. 3. Develop/refine DG organization positions. 4. Identify immediate governing tasks. 5. Define DG rollout schedule road map.
Techniques	Project planning and coordination
Tools	Excel, project management
Outputs	1. Day-to-day DG management 2. Revised DG charters 3. Revised DG organization 4. DG rollout plan 5. Road map

FIGURE 12-8

Activity Summary Table.

Business Benefits and Ramifications

Success and sustainability for DG will require early visibility. This accomplishes two things:

- The DG participants gain valuable experience and the organization is exposed to DG.
- The early efforts in governing result in feedback that will indicate any required adjustments to training, staff, or the operating model of DG.

Approach Considerations

You can engineer the managing activity for DG, but until it is deployed you can never be sure it is ideal. Defining the management aspects of ongoing DG and specifying some immediate activity goes a long way toward a more refined and sustainable DG process.

You can also adjust other aspects of the DG operating framework as well as the charters as you start to see the operational details unfold and you define the initial DG tasks.

Sample Output

Figure 12-9 shows a sample of how we coordinated a series of short-term activities in conjunction with larger projects and the overall rollout of DG. Please note, some of the activities in this figure reflect change management tasks as well as targeted governance activity.

Tips for Success

Take a deliverables-based approach to this task. Even though you are rolling out a sustainable program, you still want to have the team work toward discrete work products and develop artifacts. It is easier for

Farfel Data Governance Rollout

January-12	February-12	March-12	April-12
Stand Up Corporate Stewardship			
Initial training - Data Governance Council (DGC)	Report of Capacity to adapt all aspects of IM and DG	Deployed DG / IM Rollout	DG / IM / EA Gap and Framework Direction
Intial Training - Custodians and Stewards	Preliminary Organizational Change Management Requirements	Refinements to DG / IM Organization	Deployed DG / IM Rollout
Stakeholder Assessment	DG Operational Training Requirements - How to act; new process & behavior change	DG Sustaining Checkpoint	Refinements to DG / IM Organization
Commmunications Requirements	Approved DG Principles and Policies	Final DG / IM Stand up Measurement and Feedback plan	DGC Meeting
Training Requirements	DG Organization offical kickoff	Enterprise reference data approach	Custodian / Steward Meeting
Approved Functional DG / IM Model & Charters	Final Change Management Requirements	Define modifications to SDLC / AGILE methods reflecting DG	Enterprise reference data approach
Finalized list corporate stewards and custodians	Final DG / IM Stand up Communications Plan	Enterprise metrics catalog reviewed	Enterprise metrics catalog reviewed
Rationalized Farfel DG Principles and Policies	Final DG / IM Stand up Training Plan	Modifications to SDLC / AGILE methods reflecting DG	Execute DG Organization Change Management
Custodian / Steward Initial tasks *	Final DG / IM Resistance Management Plan	Enterprise data model - enhanced	DG Tools and Process rollout
Rationalized Farfel DG Principles and Policies			
First group orientation for stewards and custodians			
DGC initial tasks	**DGC initial tasks**		
Address initial issues to test elevation process	Review ERP / DG Integration RACI		
ERP Project Interface consistency	Review ERP Issue log		
Item / Inventory definition issues			
SharePoint management	**Steward Custodian Initial tasks**		
Review IM and DG functions (the "V")	Attend Stewardship and Custodian Education		
Attend Stewardship and Custodian Education (walk the talk)	Address initial issues to test elevation process		
	Data Warehouse enhancement		
	Use of enterprise data model		
ERP Program Support			
DG integration	ERP DG RACI Deployed	ERP data flow / interface support	ERP / DG Organization Change Integration Plan
ERP DG interaction RACI	ERP portion enterprise data model	ERP metrics and BIR catalog	ERP / DGC Leadership Coordination meeting
ERP / DG Stakeholder Analysis	Verified list of ERP Stewards and Custodians	ERP Function and Service support (FD)	
ERP Subject Area Definitions and DG Scope	ERP data flow / interface support	ERP DQ standards	
Laser Portion Enterprise Model	ERP DQ standards	ERP MDM Standards	
ERP metrics and BIR catalog	ERP MDM Standards		
ERP DQ standards			
ERP MDM Standards			

FIGURE 12-9

Sample Data Governance Roll Out.

personnel new to DG to work toward a specific product. They will assimilate their knowledge by doing these and will mature more rapidly toward DG concepts.

Since this is the first set of tasks where the DG deployment group, the stewards, and the governed projects intersect, it may be useful to have some checkpoint meetings established. This is a good way to capture feedback and detect resistance without allowing it to ferment.

SUMMARY

There needs to be a conscious effort to maintain "sustaining" data governance. Otherwise, DG will fall into the same traps as all previous data management efforts. That is why the discipline of organization change management is key. However, the DG stakeholders also need to start right away. It is most likely a mortal blow to DG to train various groups to do something and then have nothing to do.

This activity is the first real interaction with the actual areas subject to DG. One concept that cannot be integrated into a tasks list or sample work products is the need to observe the actions and interaction of the DG team, stakeholders, and governed parties. To be very clear, somewhere along the way there will be eye-rolling, misunderstandings, or unreached expectations. There must be a keen awareness of what is going on behind the scenes and a sensitivity to what is really happening versus what is desired to happen.

Rollout and sustain

13

Too many people were working on the mind without paying sufficient attention to the heart.
—**Kotter and Cohen**

This chapter covers the phase of operating the DG program. It probably bears repeating that this is not the last phase of a linear process, but is instead the final step in a life cycle. It is also never ending. Like data governance itself, the Rollout and Sustain phase of the program represents the day-to-day activities.

The format of this chapter will also change, since discreet tasks are not as prominent here. Some sections will use the format we have used in Chapters 6–12. Others will appear differently, because there are no special techniques or deliverables to consider other than ones any competent professional would already know. Others will be a discussion or presentation of scenarios that represent the operational aspect of DG.

This phase represents a series of transitions. There are the transitions required of the organization to treat data as an asset, for real. There is the transition of the project to be governed and having project plans altered. There is also the transition of the DG effort itself. The DG deployment team needs to transition to an operating model. This means stepping out of the "project" mentality and triggering the operating framework.

Regardless of format, there are a series of very important pointers, tips, and techniques in the next few pages. Should your DG program reach this point (sadly, hardly any actually get enough traction the first few tries), you need to understand that while striving for socializing and embedding DG as a behavior where all of the personnel in your organization manage information as an asset on an instinctive level, you need to climb a maturity curve. Climbing this curve requires a conscious and proactive effort.

All of the activities in this phase occur in parallel. This chapter presents all of the "stuff" that needs to happen in an organized fashion. We could just have easily made one huge task list, but that is hard to read.

OVERVIEW

Activity: DG Organization Rollout

During this activity, the DG team not only follows the road map and deploys data governance, it also transitions from being the voice of DG to becoming part of the operating framework. In many

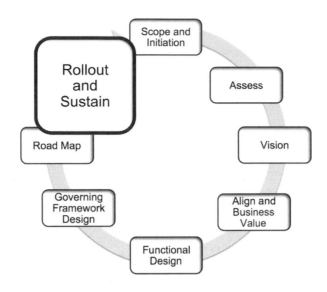

FIGURE 13-1

Process Overview.

FIGURE 13-2

Activity Overview.

organizations, especially large ones, there needs to be some sort of central body that is the data governance focal point. Hopefully, this is part of the framework that was defined. Even in the largest of organizations, this can be one person or a few people who act as "über" stewards. This ongoing body can be virtual or it can report to a functional department. Either way, its role is to make sure the DG program is operating as defined.

Activity Summary Table

Objective	Operate the DG program in a sustainable manner.
Purpose	Move from DG design to DG operation.
Inputs	All prior materials related to DG

Tasks	1. Complete new DG team identification/socialization.
	2. Socialize DG program and area to IT and compliance.
	   a. Socialize new DG managers.
	   b. Review DG charter(s).
	   c. Present charters and DG principles to new staff.
	3. Present sustaining activities and stakeholder analysis to DG staff.
	4. Orient executive team to DG organization (if not done in sustaining activity).
	5. Schedule DG team, committees, and executives for their orientation, training, or education.
	6. Align DG team functions with road-map projects.
	7. Ensure estimates are understood and project management practices are in place.
	8. Roll out initial DG functions.
	   a. Kick off initial stewards and projects.
	   b. Kick off DG organization.
	   c. Present initial road shows.
	   d. Publish guidelines and principles.
	   e. Implement DG policies/procedures, orientation, and training.
	   f. Publish and implement SDLC integration documentation.
	   g. Develop and conduct DG audit processes training.
	   h. Initiate DG audit processes.
	   i. Identify and define additional rollout activity for the sustaining phase.
	9. Implement DG program metrics.
	10. Implement tools and technology.
	11. Implement DG operations.
	   a. Promote and interact with change management.
	   b. Perform and review audits and service levels.
	   c. Interact with governing bodies.
	   d. Perform operations and functions of the DG framework—Data Governance committees and council.

Outputs	1. Verified DG team socialized 2. Understanding of the DG team role to constituents 3. An operational and effective DG organization 4. DG charter 5. Oriented staff 6. Oriented executive team 7. Training and orientation 8. Relocation 9. Job descriptions 10. DG managing projects 11. DG program kickoff 12. DG road shows 13. DG principles and policies 14. DG training 15. SDLC changes 16. DG audit processes training 17. DG audits processes in place 18. Additional activity as required 19. DG metrics definitions 20. DG/sustaining metrics comparison 21. Metrics presentation 22. Metrics collection mechanism 23. A set of metrics that are deployed and being used to report on the effectiveness of DG/IAM 24. DG tools 25. Operationalize DG

FIGURE 13-3

Activity Summary Table.

Business Benefits and Ramifications

There may be a sense of "too much too fast" in this activity. However, these are a series of events that need to happen, and the scheduling of these can be up to you and your organization.

Approach Considerations

Judging by the activity summary table (Figure 13-3), this is an enormous portion of DG, but the reality is that these are not all one-time tasks. They represent the high points in starting to operate DG. Most of the preparation work has been done prior to this. Remember, we have a very long list of functions and processes as well. Ideally, we should list all of the possible functions of IM and DG here! (They are in the appendices.)

Most of the time, you will need to be very creative in the definition and collection mechanisms of DG metrics. We understand that much of the data you would like to use may not exist, so you will have to utilize surveys or develop metrics based on the success of information solutions and business results (e.g., gross income per knowledge worker).

Sample Output

Since you are running DG, there are many kinds of work products you will need to show. The most significant example is that of the metrics to be reported. Figure 13-4 shows a list of metrics that can be reported on data governance performance. This is the same list shown in *Making EIM Work for Business* (Morgan Kaufmann, 2010), but it is modified slightly to be more specific to DG. We have arranged the metrics by how they are used. We also list how they are collected, provide a more detailed explanation (if required), and add remarks on deploying (if required). All of these metrics have been field-tested. In many cases, we collect the data and develop metrics even if the enterprise is hesitant to develop measures to assess the management of information assets.

DG Metrics Master List

In addition to designing metrics, there is a great deal of socialization required. Do not hesitate to present the same material over and over and over again. It takes a lot of repetition (research says at least six times, but it is probably more like ten) for people to get what you are trying to communicate, especially if it represents change. An outline of what is mandatory in socialization is shown next.

HELPFUL HINT

We have a few rules of thumb we apply regarding socialization and training. These are our own.

1. Many people will not "get it" right away. There are many concepts in information management (do you mean data governance?) that seem foreign (mostly because they have been incorrectly presented, but that is where we are). The DG implementers need to respect that and be patient.
2. Use language that is relevant to your audience. No one will be impressed by your display of EIM jargon.
3. Use relevant examples and stories from your organization as examples. Present DG in the context they understand. They need to see how they fit into the future governed world before they start to change.

DG Metrics	Definition	Collection
Measure Effectiveness of Data Quality Programs		
Counts of data occurrences that are in error	Report number of instances a specific field is stored incorrectly	Tool or programmed routine
Percentages of accuracy	Numerical values are not correct, but are within some percentage	Tool or programmed routine
Financial impact of critical, albeit incorrect data elements		
Specific samples of fields in error and the financial errors contained (e.g., location inventory missing returns)	Fields where error created financial impact to organization	
Total premium at risk is $$$$$ because NN% of policies contain bad information		Tool or programmed routine
Percentage of e-mails with "at risk" comments or that contain potentially damaging information		Collected
Cost of bad catalog entries and poor content management due to lost online orders or returned product		Collected
Lost funding for government entities or contractors		Collected
Loss of customer confidence due to errors		Collected
Loss of customers due to errors		Collected
Data quality profile results—percentage of completion, accuracy, relevance	Predefined algorithms that organize data and content errors by categories	Tool or programmed routine
Annual data quality index	The year-over-year delta of data quality metrics and profile results combined as an index	Tool or programmed routine
Measure Effectiveness of Data Governance Functions		
Counts of content by life-cycle stages (e.g., transactional, operational, decisional)	A content inventory of data or documents at various stages along the organization's information life cycle	Programmed routine
Document and data life-cycle times	The length of time content stays at one level of usage (e.g., an event or transaction), before it moves to another level of usage (e.g., managerial reporting); is content available when it needs to be, is it deleted when no longer of benefit	Programmed routine
Information inventory change	Delta of actual information content inventory against maintained directory of content	Programmed routine
"Hits" or click counts on web-based tools	Report of counts of access to repositories, metadata, DNA tools, data governance sites, collaborative sights, BI portals, or tools	Programmed routine
Application deployment to DG approvals ratio	Comparison or projects moved into production with projects data governance has provided oversight	Collected
DG approval and understanding	Feedback results from surveys of parties impacted by DG	Collected
Usage of standard elements of DG	Determines if standard elements and components of DG are being used, such as reference codes, master data	Programmed routine
Percentage of major data subjects that are "certified"	Sources or subject areas that are governed, reviewed, and agreed upon as sources of truth (e.g., number of customers stored in a customer master database and certified as accurate)	Collected

FIGURE 13-4

Sample Metrics for Data Governance.

Measure Legal/Compliance Risks Related to Content		
Potential penalties per subject area	Total penalties possible related to a subject area, such as Customer	Calculated
Loss of market/shareholder confidence	Estimate of reduction in equity if data causes loss of market confidence	Calculated
Litigation fees over time for data/document regulatory noncompliance	Possible fees to defend organization against data-related claims	Calculated
Cost per downtime event due to data quality (or other data related issue)	Financial impact of data issues cause operations to cease	Calculated
Legal fees to defend privacy issues	Possible fees to defend organization against data related claims	Calculated
The new ROI (risk of incarceration) and cost to enterprise	"What if" vision assuming penalties and prosecution	Calculated
Measure Financial Risks Related to Content		
Credit exposure	Possible loss in credit portfolio due to data issues	Calculated
Liquidity	Possible reduction in liquid assets	Calculated
Operational costs	Possible increase in operational costs	Calculated
Call out specific shifts in reserves, retained earnings, good will	Possible changes based on data and content issues	Calculated
Equity/market value reduction	Possible reduction in equity if data causes loss of market confidence	Calculated
Measure Contribution of DG to Business Goals		
Operating income for year divided by number of "Knowledge workers" (A knowledge worker is defined as someone who uses information to make decisions and take actions that cause the fulfillment of objectives, reads information)	Change in income divided by staff using data and content at touch points or analysis	Calculated
Relative value by subject area	Weighted score of subject area value based on perceptions of accuracy, relevance, data quality, and timeliness	Calculated
Measure DG Program Performance		
Incentives and performance	Counts of activities or artifacts related to DG performance	
Total count/amount of data governance or data quality incentive rewards		Calculated
Attendance at orientation and training		Collected
Issues presented to steering committees		Collected
Performance reviews done with DG targets included		Collected
Job descriptions revised with IAM accountability included		Collected
Performance targets achieved related to IAM		Calculated
Usage	Counts of use of data and content resources	
Number of users and access to single sources of truth		Collected
Reduction in departmental Access databases and spreadsheets		Collected
Business intelligence use by user logon ID to track who is doing what		Collected
Measure Efficiency of DG		
Total cost of IT/party (customer, member, etc.)	Enterprise IT budget divided by total occurrences of a subject area	Calculated
DG/compliance divided by total income	Annual cost of data governance and corporate compliance over income	Calculated
DG/compliance vs. risk reserves/premiums	Annual cost of data governance and corporate compliance over corporate risk numbers, either reserves or corporate insurance premiums	Calculated

FIGURE 13-4

(*Continued*)

Tips for Success

These are really success factors. You need to continue:

1. Visible and sincere sponsorship
2. Business alignment
3. Enterprise scope, local attention

You also need to continue to reinforce that DG is there to help versus only enforce. DG is the mechanism to ensure information asset management and, after the initial bump, it will (hopefully) be built into day-to-day work.

Activity: Execute Change Management Plan

This activity is where the rubber finally meets the road in terms of moving the organization toward DG. You have done all of your OCM assessing and planning, data governance is being implemented, and the tasks in this activity are running in parallel with the rollout of DG. This is the execution phase of the change management plan.

Every DG team will hear the same issues, and your change management plan execution will need to address those. Here in Figure 13-5 they are summarized, with the nasty language removed.

Perceived Issue	DG Response
You are slowing down my critical project.	The DG team needs to prepare metrics to prove no impact.
Why can't I call (insert name here) and get a file downloaded like I used to?	The DG team needs to design education to convey the need to adhere to IAM policies.
We don't need more rules. We are doing it the way we always have, since IT is never right.	The DG team needs to build responses to resistance through human resources or other channels. There need to be incentives to follow the new policies and accountabilities built into individual performance objectives.
How much is this costing us anyway?	The DG team will need to indicate that the net zero investment will add value.

FIGURE 13-5

Responses to Issues.

Activity Summary Table

Objective	To successfully accomplish the tasks previously defined in the change management plan
Purpose	Ensure that the organization understands and is prepared to accept the changes required for successful data governance.
Inputs	Change management plan—include communication plan, training plan, resistance management plan, staff transition plan, feedback collection and analysis approach, organizational alignment action plans, change metrics

FIGURE 13-6

Activity Summary Table.

Tasks	1. Communication plan.
	  a. Refine materials for training, orientation, road shows, etc.
	  b. Communicate short-term wins.
	2. Training development and delivery.
	  a. Refine materials for training.
	  b. Prepare logistics, sequencing, and scheduling.
	3. Staff transition to new roles (if required).
	4. Feedback collection and analysis of results.
	5. Perform final leadership alignment assessment.
	6. Monitor and manage resistance.
	7. Manage implementation of DG sustainability checklist.
	8. Develop additional advocates, if necessary.
	9. Execute organizational alignment action plans.
	10. Measure adoption.
	  a. Communicate status and measurements of progress frequently to leadership.
	  b. Identify issues and develop action plans to address them aggressively.
	11. Implement new accountabilities and performance goals.

Techniques	Interviews (leadership assessment, sustainability checklist), surveys to determine levels of adoption and issues to address, training delivery options (face-to-face, webinar, electronic tutorial), various communication media (meeting, website, e-mail)
Tools	Leadership alignment assessment template, feedback collection surveys
Outputs	Data governance program successfully adopted

FIGURE 13-6

(Continued)

Business Benefits and Ramifications

Your organization has probably spent a fair amount of money and time thus far in developing your data governance function. Effective and consistent execution of your OCM plan as it is rolled out helps ensure that the investment is not wasted.

Approach Considerations

At the risk of being repetitive, our opening quote from Kotter and Cohen is intended to reinforce an essential reality facing any change program: There is a tendency in business to ignore the fact that changes bring about that dreaded word, *emotion*. There is no getting away from it. Any change, no matter how small, creates an emotional reaction in people that *cannot* be avoided. You can minimize its impact with a good plan and strong execution, but you cannot make it go away. So be aware of that as you roll out your data governance program. Like we have said, it requires behavior changes, and those changes will generate an emotional reaction in the people impacted. So remind yourself of these success factors as you execute your OCM plan in support of data governance:

- Get the *right sponsor* in place. We said that in Chapter 12 and we are saying it again. It is absolutely imperative.

- Appreciate that *frequent and open communication* is important. Often companies will hide information out of fear of employee reactions in the mistaken idea that what people don't know won't hurt them, and change will then be easier to accomplish. All this is does is create ungodly rumors and organizational churn.
- Appreciate that there is a *psychology* to change. Understanding how people react is essential to structuring your DG initiative to deal with it.
- Be absolutely *clear and specific* about what is changing and what that will mean in terms of required behavior changes. People cannot change behavior if they don't know what they're supposed to change.
- Don't forget to *realign* those performance objectives and accountabilities. Change won't happen unless people are held accountable for required behavior changes.

Monitoring the adoption of the changes is a significant activity during your OCM plan execution. Consider starting even before the rollout to make sure that the appropriate levels of communication and training have occurred, and that those impacted feel as ready to go forward as they can at this point. It is very normal to find issues as a result of this analysis; prioritize them and put action plans together to address those essential to moving forward. Continue your assessments at regular intervals (consider 30, 60, 90, and even 120 days after rollout), and address the issues you find. You should see a steady increase in adoption and be able to determine when continued follow-up is no longer required.

Sample Output

We have placed a template for pre- and post-rollout surveys in the appendices.

Tips for Success

At this point, you may be wondering why so much time has been spent on dealing with the organization's likely reactions to the changes data governance will bring. Frankly, you can deal splendidly with all the situational aspects of rolling out a DG program, but if you don't deal with that dreaded word *emotion* and have an equally splendid OCM plan to go with it, you won't have much of a program to roll out. Why? Because you will have been sabotaged at every turn by those who do not see the need for it or who are threatened by it. So spend the time and the resources to deploy a strong OCM program in support of data governance. You will have a much happier outcome.

Activity: DG Project Management

This activity is performed for each effort that is being governed. During the first few months after the DG program goes "live," this activity serves to make sure that DG projects are managed, sustaining activities take place, education and training occur on schedule, and issues are dealt with. As time goes on, this activity will monitor the functions of DG. Remember, while there will be startup considerations, the sustaining phase is permanent.

Given that there is a large amount of basic material on program management available from many sources, this activity section will focus *only* on DG-specific activity and tasks.

Activity Summary Table

Objective	Start to govern selected projects or programs.
Purpose	Begin the organization's movement to information asset management.
Inputs	Projects and programs identified for DG, all prior deliverables as needed
Tasks	1. Orient major project steering bodies. 2. Align DG project management activities with existing IT practices. 3. Identify project templates. 4. Identify DG project estimating tools. 5. Identify DG tracking and accounting procedures for IT. 6. Forecast DG project resources. 7. Utilize modified SDLC. 8. Interact with enterprise PMO (if one exists).
Outputs	1. Awareness of ongoing operation of DG 2. DG/IT practice aligned 3. DG project templates 4. DG estimating 5. DG tracking 6. DG resources 7. DG enhanced work products 8. PMO DG interaction

FIGURE 13-7

Activity Summary Table.

Business Benefits and Ramifications

The meaning and impact of DG becomes fully evident at this point. The change management activity needs to parallel these tasks, as the need for communication, training, and resistance management are paramount.

Approach Considerations

This activity is in parallel with all of the other activities in this phase. Perhaps the biggest consideration to address is whether there is a PMO in place at your organization. The PMO is a tremendous vehicle to insert DG tasks into ongoing programs. It is easier to sell, monitor, and prove value. We are assuming an effective PMO, since many organizations have PMOs in name only.

For each program or project, the DG implementers need to prepare the nature, extent, and style of governance. For example, a business intelligence effort may focus governance on using the correct data terms and tools. An MDM project will require oversight of data quality and business process changes in addition to data standards.

Activity: Confirm Effectiveness and Operation of DG Organization

Any endeavor requires verification that it is actually working. Regardless of the amount of planning, DG will almost certainly require adjustments in processes, intensity, or structure. This set of tasks is grouped together to present the various areas to be assessed as data governance is operating.

Activity Summary Table

Objective	Confirm DG is working.
Purpose	Identify any course corrections, if needed.

Tasks	1. Evaluate organization structure.
	2. Confirm effectiveness of jobs/people.
	3. Confirm effectiveness of DG framework and processes.
	4. Verify policies/procedures.
	5. Review incentives.
	6. Confirm effectiveness of DG.
	   a. Monitor and report sustaining metrics.
	   b. Execute measurement surveys (if designed).
	   c. Hold focus groups/interviews for feedback.
	   d. Execute change integration checklist.
	   e. Change integration/adoption assessment.
	   f. Realign impacted policies/practices and procedures.
	   g. Revise staff performance objectives and reward structures.

Outputs	1. Verified DG organization
	2. Verified role transitions
	3. Verified operating framework
	4. Verified policies
	5. Verified incentives
	6. Revised incentives for DG
	7. Effectiveness reports
	   a. DG scorecard
	   b. DG surveys
	   c. DG focus group feedback
	   d. DG sustaining checklist
	   e. Change adoption assessment
	   f. Realigned DG policies

FIGURE 13-8

Activity Summary Table.

Business Benefits and Ramifications

DG support for EIM projects and programs will have many deliverables, outcomes, and interactions. This is where the business absorbs and makes the managing of information assets a part of any other business paradigm. DG will provide the additional discipline that is required. To be effective is to have all of the supported efforts leverage common information and content areas, and share common systems components. Note—I said *will*, not *should*. DG is part of EIM. EIM is the formal program to do information asset management. Even if it is being done in smaller slices via an MDM project or data warehouse, you are doing EIM. Therefore, you are measuring the EIM effort's performance. You also need to monitor the effectiveness of the change management efforts.

Approach Considerations

This activity is a collection of verifications and checkpoints. The key to all of the tasks will be how you gather data that is believable, and then place it into the measurement and reporting formats you have designed.

Tips for Success

The various programs or projects based on EIM subdisciplines must always make sure they are reporting progress and success. The value of IAM has to be reported continuously until it is woven into and accepted by the culture. Reporting early successes and progress is essential to gaining acceptance. Everyone wants to be part of a success story. You may have the best DG program in world, but if you don't tell anyone, it won't go anywhere. Do not underestimate the value of "tooting your own horn."

SUMMARY

The essence of the Rollout and Sustain activity is the execution of change management and DG management, and making sure both are working properly. "Changes of any sort—even though they may be justified in economic or technological terms—finally succeed or fail on the basis of whether the people affected *do things differently*."[1]

The change management tasks address the emotional element of adopting discipline that has been nonexistent. "More than any other single finding, we discovered in this … project that people changed less because of facts or data that shifted their thinking than because compelling experiences changed their feelings. This emotional component was always present in the most successful change stories and was usually missing in the least successful. Too many people were working on the mind without paying sufficient attention to the heart."[2]

DG needs to be applied to various programs and projects. This means integrating DG with these efforts. A PMO is very helpful as the vehicle for DG. If none exists, then the DG council(s) needs to make sure that individual efforts are using data governance oversight.

Lastly, the various programs and projects being governed need to be monitored for the effectiveness of the DG processes. Frequent collection of metrics and successes of the EIM-related projects are essential.

---

[1]William Bridges, *Managing Transitions* (Cambridge, MA: Perseus Books Group), 2003.
[2]John P. Kotter and Dan S. Cohen, *The Heart of Change: Real-Life Stories of How People Change Their Organizations* (Boston: Harvard Business School Publishing, 2002), Kindle edition.

Data governance artifacts and tools

I am not one of those who in expressing opinions confine themselves to facts.
—**Mark Twain**

All you need in this life is ignorance and confidence; then success is sure.
—**Mark Twain**

This short chapter concerns itself with some of the more mechanical and discrete elements of data governance. If you understand DG as a program, and implement it as such, sooner or later you are going to find yourself up to your hips in documents and files representing the multitude of artifacts being governed. Thus, it will be necessary to administer the governance program.

Talk to a corporate controller or a manager of documents in any large organization. The tracking and maintenance of policies, rules, manuals, websites, and so on can be overwhelming and requires some formal administration. After a short time, your DG program will be maintaining its own artifacts but will also start to deal with the artifacts of all of the information management efforts. The best examples of this are policies. In most organizations, you cannot swing the proverbial dead cat without hitting a policy (and some of them are even followed!). In our experience, the potential for administrative issues can threaten the vitality of your DG effort.

During the research for this book, the author sat with a few vendors regarding the direction of their DG administration tools. The research revealed a lot of good ideas, but not a lot of cohesive or consistent terminology or approaches. That is a problem, since the one great constant request of the varied consumers of information management tools and technologies has been some constancy across products and vendors of standard definitions of policies, principles, rules, etc. So presenting products and product features is confusing and impossible to keep up to date in a book like this. Therefore, we are presenting a basic framework for what you need to track, and how to determine what the mechanisms are to do the tracking. You may use some or all of the terms presented next. Think of this chapter as a checklist for what you may want to manage your DG artifacts and how to do it.

The content of this chapter is based *solely* on the experience of our DG practice. We are confident in what is being said, but it is presented through our lens. We use our terms and definitions of DG concepts, so review Chapter 2 if you need to at this point. The reader may also see a strong similarity between the DG components to be administered and key information management artifacts. This is no coincidence, as part of the role of DG is to govern the use and management of information management artifacts.

What Should Be Tracked?

There is a hierarchy, or taxonomy, of business elements and artifacts that DG will need to consider, track, create, or administer. There are also elements that DG will specify regarding tracking and use. In other words, both sides of the "V" have documents, policies, standards, and such that will require administration.

Business Elements

The categories of business elements to be tracked are:

Business alignment—The business alignment elements are made up of documents and files that express business direction, performance, and measurement. These elements must be monitored by DG because they are the direct component of business alignment. As we have said often, ensuring business alignment to IAM is a crucial activity for DG. These include:

- Strategy
- Goal
- Objective
- Plan
- Information levers

Business process—Process elements are everything that has to do with events and actions that do something with data. If you have a process modeling tool, for example, the artifacts from this tool would be addressed in this area. From a DG standpoint, process elements must be reviewed to ensure the controls are documented, as well as the key regulatory or compliance processes. Other processes, like events or communications, may require DG when the content for an external communication needs to be reviewed.

- Event
- Meeting
- Communication
- Training
- Process
- Workflow
- Life cycle
- Methodology
- Function

Policy—Policy elements have to do with artifacts that codify or document desired or required behavior. Obviously, DG will need access to these and, better yet, track them. A prime example is governance of documents, where there are legal, risk-based, and practical policies, which are often in conflict with each other. For example, everyone wants to keep those memos "just in case," while corporate counsel says to get rid of them as soon as possible. We include Principles in this category because policies stem from principles.

- Principles
- Policies

- Standards
- Controls
- Rule
- Regulation

Organization—This element covers the various roles and organization charts. DG will need awareness of this to manage who stakeholders and decision makers are. Granted, this is not an element you would need to place in an expensive tool. A spreadsheet would probably suffice with most organizations, but larger organizations may require a database of some sort, or use of the organizational entities in an enterprise modeling tool.

- Level
- Role (RACI)
- Location
- Assignment
- Community
- Department
- Team
- Roster
- Stakeholder
  - Type
    - Steward
    - Custodian

Business information requirements—This element must be traceable by DG. This is because it is critical to ensuring business alignment. In addition, one area where organizations go awry in the information realm is the poor identification and tracking of requirements. A critical function of DG is to monitor and review the development of EIM requirements:

- Metric or measurement
- List or domain
- Event
- Subject

Artifacts—Artifacts are documents or anything else that is stored permanently for subsequent use or review.

- Manuals
- Charters
- Presentations
- Work
- Project deliverables
- e-mail
- Policy—written versions
- Principles—written versions
- Publications

- Website
- Models
- Work products from all EIM projects

Data—Knowing where data is is important. So this element is not talking about the actual occurrences of real data, but rather where it is and what it means. The term metadata is used as well; however, we do not like that term any more due to overuse and distortion by vendors. This element represents all of the "data" required to be used by and to operate the DG program.

- Metrics
- Model
- Standards
- Dictionary
  - Definitions
- Metadata
- Digital processes
  - Scripts
  - Programs
- Blog
- Wiki
- Files
- BIR
- File
- Location

Technology—It is also good to track the technology that can use and affect data. This element represents the information about technology used to manage information assets.

- Product
- Hardware
- Software
- User

Thoughts on Tools

Since there is no one tool that can be used to track all of the elements scrutinized by a DG program, you need to think carefully about how you will track the various types of artifacts and automate them as efficiently as you can.

You need to be cautious about throwing up myriad Excel spreadsheets, since these can become unmanageable. The best approach is to use as many tools in the information management realm as possible—that is, the modeling tools, the enterprise architecture tools, and various catalogs and productivity tools.

SharePoint is an excellent option for linking and tracking myriad objects, but *only if designed and used efficiently.* Using SharePoint as a dumping ground for artifacts is useless and costly. Using Wikis as an internal entry point is being done as of this writing with great success in many organizations.

Whatever the technology, try and use a central entry point. This is where SharePoint or a Wiki are beneficial. At its core, data governance is a program that sits on top of a defined set of rules and workflows. (This is yet another reminder that DG is not special; it is just another business function with the same operational requirements.)

In data governance, technology is a challenge in developing workflow and document management. Taking out lists of elements and creating an internal taxonomy for DG is an ideal approach.

Workflows that you may want to wrap around your tools, or evaluate tools on, are core DG events. Tracking all of the items in taxonomy is ideal. For example:

- Exemption requests
- Changes to standards
- DG issue resolution; unresolved items

These are all DG processes that can be adapted to workflow and document management.

A few other technology components that can help DG are chat forums, data control products, and policy management tools.

Chat forums are useful as outlets for questions and advice while capturing crucial feedback on feelings about DG. Data control products have been around for years and offer excellent facilities to enter and observe the execution of rules. Policy management tools have also been around and offer a set of tools for DG stakeholders.

Summary

The bottom line for DG technology is that you will be striving to assemble a set of technologies. Many vendors, as of the writing of this book, are moving into the area of pure DG administration. Some are entering from the IM realm, others from the document management realm. Regardless, you will need to assemble a toolbox of capabilities. Create your own internal taxonomy (which can be woven into a taxonomy tool) and connect the taxonomy via a single entry point to your other tools. Again, traditional places to store artifacts, like SharePoint and Excel, are useful, but only if managed and, well—duh—governed.

Final remarks

The final words of this book will, and should, be a summary on the deployment of data governance. But before we recap the preceding chapters, it's important to reinforce that implementing more discipline in regard to data, information, or content is not really an option.

As this book was being finished, the author started another information management–related project for a new client—with one of the requested deliverables being "data governance." It was asked for in a shopping list given to the consulting team by the CIO, who was soliciting the consulting firms. To be precise, the request was to "deliver recommendations on ETL, MDM, BI, and data governance." The blast of acronyms was our first warning sign.

Since we were very familiar with their industry, and given that data governance was mentioned, we prepared our approach based on an assessment of the current maturity and business alignment. It was obvious from the beginning that this was going to be a hard project. To make a long story short, this effort, as of this writing, is fraught with risk. The CIO basically said, "I know the answer, you just need to give me a list of vendors." When we mentioned that data governance didn't fall into that type of recommendation, we were told to just make recommendations if data governance was "necessary" and to propose some standards.

The friction between this company's business and IT area goes back decades. The CIO absolutely feels he knows what the answer is, and wants a rubber-stamped report. The designated sponsor can't stand IT or consultants and says we should spend the few weeks of the assessment "doing reports they need." Do you think data governance would be front-of-mind in this scenario?

But the reason this company is in the mess it is in (and it is a huge mess, with many details being left out of this narrative) is simply because it has had no discipline or governance. The very thing it is deemphasizing is the reason they need expensive outside help to fix things. There is a lot of education to be done.

They do not understand that data governance is not part of a list of features. It is the underpinnings of all of the possible solutions to use data better. So let's revisit some of the critical items presented in this book.

CONCEPTS

Information asset management (IAM)—We spent some time to make sure the reader understands that "information as an asset" is not just a metaphor or brand for the information management program. It means applying the same serious rigor that is applied to other "hard" assets. If you say you need data governance, you are acknowledging belief in IAM. This gives you the right mindset.

The relationship of data governance to information management—We introduced the concept of the "V" in this book. Data governance (DG) is the oversight and standardization component of enterprise information management. DG sets the rules and processes. Information management carries out the defined processes. It's important to keep the governing and managing of data separate. This leverages the concept of separation of duties. Your go-to analogy is that DG is to IM as accounting standards are to finance.

E for Enterprise—Data governance should never be considered as a project feature. It is an enterprise program. The context of all DG discussions needs to be from an enterprise view. The rollout is iterative, and each deployment is different. But the ultimate goal must be a level of enterprise-level adoption.

Data governance is a business program—DG is *never* an IT program. It exists to provide the roles, rules, and controls for the data assets. It must be applied across the board to everyone in the organization.

Evolution vs. Revolution—You need to learn how to govern. From the executive councils down to the operational activity, you must realize that behavior changes and education moves from the top to the bottom.

Data governance means change—Top-to-bottom behavior changes require formal management via an organizational change management program (OCM). This is not really an option. Pursuing DG means you are not satisfied with what is going on. Something has to be different. Different equals change. So why not manage the change to the benefit of all the stakeholders? Formal OCM has been around for a long time. Allow OCM to work for your own DG effort.

THE VALUE OF DATA GOVERNANCE

At this point in time, the value of DG is either perceived as a traditional return on investment (a la a project) or as a program that is required for the success of other programs or processes. This situation makes the statement of value for DG difficult. You can place the operation of DG into a model where a hard ROI is generated. But that is not a long-term number. The generation of a longer-term value requires the acceptance of DG as a program, and so the team must sell this to management.

With this in mind, the DG deployment team must create a business case and overcome these obstacles. If not, there will be no foundation for measuring success. A strong sponsor is important, but you must have the means to prove to the sponsor that it is working.

The team needs to examine business opportunities and look for every opportunity to educate management on the importance of managing information as an asset. This will also address any long-term animosity between the business and IT.

THE CRITICAL SUCCESS FACTORS

For some reason, three critical success factors are important to people. So here are the three most important success factors (out of many that we have covered).

1. DG needs to be set up to disappear—not vanish or stop, but to melt into the fabric of the organization. The DG "organization" is not a stand-alone department. Everyone must do governance once it is adopted.

2. If you do not manage the organization's behavior changes, you will not get DG to stick. DG requires culture change management.
3. DG, even if started as a stand-alone concept, must be tied to an initiative. It is the best way to get visibility, try out policy, and designate targeted areas for training and orientation.

That sums up much of what we have discussed in the prior pages. We promised a lot of details on the basics. There is plenty of data on things that have gone wrong due to lack of data governance.

The knowledge presented here must be applied all the time. We are currently doing it with the client mentioned at the beginning of this chapter. Will the client drop their historically typical behavior? We hope so. We will recommend some significant changes to the protocols they currently use to manage IT projects and information access. They will have to adopt principles and policies that address their longstanding abuse of operational data, and they will need to wean themselves off of their spreadsheets and Access databases. Data governance must be more than just a bullet point on a slide for them. Whether or not they have the determination to actually change these things remains to be seen. Hopefully, you have learned enough from this book to help your own organization be successful with data governance.

Appendix 1

Phase	Activity	Tasks	Outputs/ Subtasks	Subtask Outputs
Scope (Initiation)	Identify business unit(s) - organizations subject to DG	List business units/ divisions that may be subject to DG	Business area candidates for DG	
		Identify key divisions in business units	Divisional candidates for DG	
		Understand significant strategies and initiatives	High-level business strategies driving DG	
		Determine if divisional differences merit different DG	Scope drivers of DG	
		Develop list of organizational units in scope of DG	DG program scope	
	Propose scope and initial plan to define and deploy DG	Define DG specific tasks	DG tasks	
		Define known constraints within proposed scope	Known constraints (e.g., market, time, regulations)	
		Define required assessments	Required assessment tasks	
		Define standard startup tasks	Standard enterprise program startup tasks (if any)	
	Develop DG rollout team structure	Identify DG team and key stakeholders	DG team and stakeholder list	
		Identify DG steering body	DG steering body names	
		Perform SWOT analysis on participants	DG participant SWOT analysis	
		Obtain team and steering body approvals and commitments	Approved DG participants	
	Approve scope and constraints	Review scope with proposed steering body	Proposed DG scope	
		Adjust based on feedback	Feedback adjustments	
		Develop final statement of DG scope	Final DG scope statement	

(Continued)

Phase	Activity	Tasks	Outputs/ Subtasks	Subtask Outputs
Assessment	Information maturity	Determine scope of survey instrument	Survey audience/ areas	
		Select or develop a maturity scale	Survey maturity scale	
		Identify all participants by name and group	Survey participants	
		Orient respondents on importance and anonymity	Survey orientation	
		Agree on survey delivery (online, written, group focus)	Survey delivery method	
		Review and modify maturity template	Approved survey contents	
		Produce final form for delivery	Final survey	
		Deploy survey instrument	Survey available	
		Monitor online survey OR	Managed survey data collected	
		Distribute and monitor written version OR	Managed survey data collected	
		Prepare and deliver focus session(s)	Managed survey data collected	
		Collect and evaluate data	Survey database	
		Derive maturity score based on selected scale	Proposed IMM score	
		Collect existing standards, procedures, and policies for information management, info, resource utilization, prioritization, and controls, and map to IMM scale	Mapped IMM to current state - gap analysis	
		Prepare findings for presentation	IMM survey presentation	
	Change capacity	Determine the formality of the assessment. That is an informal structured meeting format, or a formal survey instrument.	Change capacity survey format	

Phase	Activity	Tasks	Outputs/ Subtasks	Subtask Outputs
		Determine the target audience	Change capacity audience	
		Define the survey population or interviewees	Survey audience/ areas	
		Define the approach structured meeting, written or online	Survey approach	
		Administer the survey or execute meetings	Administered survey	
		Analyze and summarize findings	Survey database	
		Determine if additional investigation is required	List of business leaders requiring verification of support	
		Leadership alignment	Interviewed key individuals	
		Leadership commitment	Interviewed key individuals	
		Determine what will be reported now vs. sent to the DG team to use during subsequent phases	"Need to know" findings	
		Prepare Change Capacity Report	Change Capacity Report	
	Collaborative readiness	Determine the assessment's scope. Does it include:	Collaborative readiness assessment scope	
		Websites and content		
		Documents and sharing		
		Seeking and identifying existing communities of practice or interest		
		Workflow		
		Collaborative products		
		Contemporary facilities like Instant messaging, Texting, Twitter or Facebook		

(Continued)

Phase	Activity	Tasks	Outputs/ Subtasks	Subtask Outputs
		Determine scope of survey instrument	Survey scope	
		Determine assessment approach interviews, document review, or survey, or combination	Collaborative Readiness Assess Approach	
		Collect existing standards, procedures, and policies for document sharing, workflow, internal wikis, blogs, etc. for review	Assessment Source Material	
		Collect inventory of SharePoint, notes, or other workshare facilities	Assessment Source Material	
		Identify all participants by name and group if necessary	Collaborative Readiness Survey participants	
		Orient respondents on importance and anonymity	Orientation for respondents	
		Identify interview of focus group participants if necessary	Focus group names	
		Produce final form for delivery	Final Collaborative Survey instrument	
		Deploy survey instrument	Executed Survey	
		Monitor online survey OR	Executed Survey	
		Distribute and monitor written version OR	Executed Survey	
		Prepare and deliver focus session(s)	Executed Survey	
		Collect and evaluate data from surveys, documents, and meetings	Collaborative Readiness Survey database	
		Develop collaborative readiness statement based on predetermined scale	Collaborative Readiness "score"	
		Prepare findings for presentation	Collaborative Readiness Report	

Phase	Activity	Tasks	Outputs/ Subtasks	Subtask Outputs
Vision	Define DG for your organization	Define IAM for enterprise (if not defined elsewhere)	Definition of DG / IAM philosophy — Draft brief impact and considerations document	
		List possible DG measures	Initial list of DG metrics	
		Develop DG Mission and Value Statement	DG Mission and Value Statement	
		Present and refine Mission and Vision Statement	Refined Mission and Vision Statement	
		Obtain approval for Mission and Vision Statement	Approved DG Mission and Vision Statement	
		Develop straw person DG definition	Notional definition of DG	
		Build DG elevator speech	DG elevator speech	
	Draft preliminary DG requirements	Gather levers or stated goals and strategies and examine required content to enable them	Business goals affected by DG	
		Gather existing artifacts, such as data or process models or DQ surveys	Data artifacts affecting DG	
		Examine backlogs of report requests, website updates, and requisitions for external data, data issues, anecdotal requests for DG	Direct and indirect requests for DG	
		Identify obvious targets for improved quality or those that would benefit from external scrutiny	Data quality opportunities for DG	
		Examine significant business events and activities for content affecting risk such as safety, regulated products, rate filings, etc.	Risk areas benefitting from DG	

Phase	Activity	Tasks	Outputs/ Subtasks	Subtask Outputs
	Develop future representation of DG	Identify single page abstract of DG vision	DG Vision Statement	
		Identify notional DG touchpoints	DG business value proposition	
		Develop "day-in-the-life" picture	Day-in-the-life slide	
Alignment and Business Value	Leverage existing EIM (or other) business case	Review business documents, earlier findings	Business goals and objectives, findings from earlier activity	
		Confirm future relevance of goals and objectives to DG	Confirmed business goals relevant to DG	
		Confirm measures of goals and objectives	Metrics for confirming business goals	
		Clarify possible DG role in achieving business goals	DG roles in achieving business goals	
		Ensure each goal or objective is measurable	Confirmed metrics	
	Align business needs and data governance (if no source of business alignment)	Gather/verify collected business goals and objectives	Organization goals and objectives	
		Develop a list of known business challenges, problems, and potential opportunities	Categorized business goals etc. into opportunities, challenges, problems	
		Turn challenges and opportunities into business directions	Business opportunities	
		Ensure each goal or objective is measureable	Confirmed objectives and business metrics	
		Convert levers, goals, and strategies to data requirements	Enterprise data requirements	
		Gather metrics, indicators, and other BIRs	Consolidated metrics and BIR list	

Phase	Activity	Tasks	Outputs/ Subtasks	Subtask Outputs
		Identify industry metrics (if not done yet)	Standard or industry metrics	
		Map DG opportunities to BIRs and metrics to verify model relevance	BIR / metrics to data model cross-reference	
		Optional - Map measures to source systems where DQ may be a concern	Metrics / BIRs to data quality issues cross-reference	
		Connect BIRs to data issues	Enterprise DG touchpoints	
		Build data usage / value worksheets if required	Usage value / info lever worksheets	
		Determine the business context to present benefits for DG	Enterprise value context	
		Schedule facilitated session with business leaders or subject matter experts	Business discovery session schedule	
		Capture business benefit results in the session, or refine results after presenting them	Discovery session results	
		Confirm future relevance of goals and objectives to DG	Confirmed business goals relevant to DG	
		Confirm measures of goals and objectives	Metrics for confirming business goals	
		Clarify possible DG role in achieving business goals	DG roles in achieving business goals	
	Identify the business value of data governance	Connect data issues with business needs	List of data issues cross-referenced with related business needs	
		Align DG opportunities with business benefits	DG opportuties to address issues affecting business needs	
		Identify potential cash flows from business goals	Business cashflow from affected business issues	

(Continued)

Phase	Activity	Tasks	Outputs/ Subtasks	Subtask Outputs
		Extract opportunities for using content and data		
		Identify touchpoints where new managed content or data will touched, or be leveraged, to improve business	Possible value points for new processes	
		Isolate the processes that create value or achieve the goal related to the originating action	Detailed actions in business processes achieving results through managed information	
		Apply the various financial benefits and the costs to whatever benefit model is in use	Financial benefit model for DG	
		Create Value Statements of interaction of data and business goals	DG Value Statement	
		Publish results to the DG team and/or steering committee	DG Value presentation	
		Align business data needs with DG benefits (Show connection between business goal, required information, and data governance activity)	DG business value	
Functional Design	Determine core information principles	Use seed principles	Initial list of information principles	
		Apply GAIP	Verification of principles to GAIP	
		Align with existing enterprise principles and policies	Adjusted and rationalized principles	
		Add rationale and implications for each principle	Draft enterprise information principles	
		Submit and approve principles to DG steering body	Approved information principles	

Phase	Activity	Tasks	Outputs/ Subtasks	Subtask Outputs
	Determine baseline data governance policies and processes to support business	Draft initial policies from principles rationale	Draft DG policies	
		Identify DG processes		
		Identify processes to sustain key business measures or metrics model	Metrics and BIR management processes	
		Gather existing policies related to information management	Existing IM policies	
		Identify processes to support standards, controls, and policies	Standards and controls for management processes	
		Identify processes to support master data & ERP projects	MDM & ERP DG processes	
		Define/support regulatory drivers	Regulatory DG processes	
		Identify any planning or management functions	DG planning and management processes	
		Identify requirements and processes for enterprise data model standards and procedures		
		Identify requirements and processes for reference and code policies/procedures	Reference and code DG processes	
		Identify processes to administer policies and standards	DG administration processes	
		Ensure processes and policies are not in conflict	Policy/process cross-reference	

(Continued)

Phase	Activity	Tasks	Outputs/ Subtasks	Subtask Outputs
		Optional: Work with Finance and Compliance and perform a pro-forma "Information Risk Forecast"	Information Risk Forecast	
		Identify gaps in current state of Data management	Processes to close current DG deficiencies	
		Specify adequate controls	Data controls	
		Specify privacy and security concerns	Privacy/Security controls	
		Specify compliance and regulatory concerns	Compliance and regulatory DG processes	
		Specify key DG process flows	Define issue resolution process	DG issue resolution flow
			Define process for DG policy and standards changes	Policy and standards maintenance flow
			Define DG and project interaction	Project DG flow
			Develop new organization performance objectives	DG performance objectives for business areas
		Identify other DG detail processes	Identify changes to SDLC processes	SDLC change requirements
			Design DG process details, deliverables, and documentation for SDLC integration touchpoints	SDLC changes
			Develop revised process/policy alignment plan (Review/update existing policies and processes related to data governance and EIM)	Revised polices affected by governance
≈	Identify/refine IM functions and Processes	Specify/identify IM processes	Revised IM processes (not DG)	
		Separate IM functionality from DG	Separate lists of IM and DG functionality	

Phase	Activity	Tasks	Outputs/ Subtasks	Subtask Outputs
	Identify preliminary accountability and ownership model	Examine processes requiring DG accountability	Accountability processes	
		Identify business area touch points with DG functions	DG touchpoints	
		Define preliminary DG operating layers	Preliminary view of DG operating layers	
	Present EIM DG functional model to business leadership	Prepare DG functional presentation	DG functional presentation	
		Gain acceptance of data governance processes in principle	Approved function list	
Governing Framework Design	Design DG operating framework	Develop DG RACI from functional design	DG RACI	
		Determine levels of federation	DG federation layers	
		Propose federated DG structure	DG federation model	
		Identify layers of oversight based on RACI	Organization layers for DG	
		Determine organization model	DG framework "organization" chart	
		Determine potential staffing	DG organization staffing	
		Identify leadership of all levels	DG leadership	
		Develop charters for main levels of DG organization	DG charters	
	Complete roles and responsibility identification	Define Data Stewards' roles & responsibilities	Stewards/owner roles and responsibilities	
		Develop Data Steward/ accountability identification approach	Accountability definition for DG	
		Coordinate with HR and identified Data Steward(s) to revise Data Steward(s) performance goals and objectives	Revised performance objectives for stewards	

(Continued)

Phase	Activity	Tasks	Outputs/ Subtasks	Subtask Outputs
		Identify data governance oversight body(s)	Data governance oversight framework	
		Council, forum, and committee members		
		Identify specific contact points and protocol		
	Review and obtain approval of DG organization design	Review and obtain approval of Data Stewards identification approach with leadership	Approval to acquire stewards	
		Develop Data Stewards identification template	Steward template	
		Identify Data Steward identification subject areas and prioritize them (e.g., Customer)	Steward content oversight areas	
		Identify stewards and owners	List of stewards and owners	
		Obtain approval of stewards and owners	Approved stewards and owners	
	Initiate DG socialization	Conduct Data Stewards' orientation	Completed orientation	
		Review IM/DG principles with councils and stewards	Principle review session	
Road Map	Integrate DG with other efforts	Identify projects and stakeholders subject to standards and governance	List of projects and stakeholders subject to DG	
		Refine governance bodies and committees (if part of EIM)	Enhanced EIM oversight	
		Refine DG charters (if part of EIM)	Adjusted EIM/DG charters	
		Confirm stewardship and ownership model if necessary	Reviewed DG Rollout with Stewards and Owners	
		Define rollout of DG to support EIM Road Map or other identified projects	EIM/DG Rollout Road Map	
		Define DG rollout tasks and schedule	DG rollout schedule	

Phase	Activity	Tasks	Outputs/ Subtasks	Subtask Outputs
	Define sustaining requirements (only if not part of EIM)	Review/perform stakeholder analysis (or perform in parallel)	Stakeholder impact on sustainability	
		Review other IM assessments	Change readiness report	
		Execute change capacity assessment if not already done	Change readiness report	
		Identify change management resources required	List of resources for change management (team, facilities, tools)	
		Cross-reference touchpoints, readiness, and stakeholder analysis	Change management areas	
		Incorporate IMM results into the change capacity analysis	Maturity/change capacity targets	
		Perform stakeholder analysis (if necessary)	Identify DG stakeholders	DG stakeholders List
			Perform SWOT analysis (all stakeholders)	SWOT by DG stakeholder
			Complete stakeholder analysis	Summarized conclusions from SWOT
			Review with DG leadership	Reviewed SWOT findings
			Determine levels of commitment for key stakeholders	Classified stakeholders
			Review results of stakeholder analysis with leadership (DG steering or sponsors) _	Reviewed SWOT findings
			Determine action plan to address improving levels of stakeholder commitment	SWOT action plan (can be part of sustaining requirements)

(Continued)

Phase	Activity	Tasks	Outputs/ Subtasks	Subtask Outputs
		Conduct an initial leadership alignment assessment		
		Define nature and size of change	Sustainability scope and impact	
		Describe ability of sponsors to lead change	Sponsor ability report	
		Develop plan to engage sponsors (if required)	Sponsorship sustainability approach	
		Define training requirements	DG sustaining training requirements	
		Define communications requirements	DG communications requirements	
		Prepare statement of change readiness	Change readiness presentation	
		Complete requirements to sustain DG	DG change management and sustaining requirements	
	Develop the Change Management Plan	Define conditions for sustainability success	Sustainable DG criteria	
		Define and design capture of sustaining metrics	DG sustaining metrics	
		Identify OCM team members	DG Change Teams	
		Identify specific types of resistance	DG Resistance Profile	
		Develop responses to resistance	DG Resistance Responses	
		Develop resistance management plan	DG Resistance Remediation Plan	
		Review and approve resistance management plan	Approved response to DG resistance	
		Define and align staff performance goals and reward structures	WIIFM statements	
		Develop sustainability checklist	Sustainability Checklist	

Phase	Activity	Tasks	Outputs/ Subtasks	Subtask Outputs
		Identify and design change measures	DG change management success metrics	
		Develop staff transition approach (use HR if necessary)	Staff transition approach	
		Develop Communication and Training Plan (see below)	Communication and Training Plans	
		Develop DG Communications Plan	Identify audiences	DG communications audiences
			Create messages and branding	DG messages, branding
			Identify vehicles for communications	DG communications delivery mediums
			Define timing, frequencies, and delivery means	DG communications schedule
			Review and approval of Communications Plan	Approved DG Communications Plan
		Develop DG Training Plan	Identify audiences	DG training audiences
			Identify levels & extent of training: orient, educate, train	DG training syllabus
			Identify vehicles for training	DG training delivery methods
			Define timing, frequencies, and delivery means	DG training schedule
			Review and approval of Training Plan	Approved DG Training Plan
	Define DG operational rollout	Develop DG management requirements	Day-to-day DG management	
		Revise DG charter/ mission if necessary	Revised DG charters	

(Continued)

Phase	Activity	Tasks	Outputs/ Subtasks	Subtask Outputs
		Develop/refine DG organization positions	Revised DG organization	
		Identify immediate governing tasks	Near term governance activity	
		Define DG rollout schedule/ road map	Road Map	
Rollout and Sustain	DG operating rollout	Complete New DG team Identification/ socialization	Verified DG team socialized	
		Socialize DG program and area	Understanding of the DG team role to constituents	
		Socialize new DG managers	An operational, effective DG organization	
		Review DG charter(s)	DG charter	
		Present charters and DG principles to new staff and stakeholders	Oriented staff	
		Present sustaining activities and stakeholder analysis to DG staff	Oriented staff	
		Orient executive team to DG organization (if not done in Sustaining Activity)	Oriented executive team	
		Schedule DG team, committees, and executives for their orientation, training, or education	Training and orientation Relocation Job descriptions	
		Align DG team functions with Road Map projects	DG managing projects	
		Ensure estimates are understood and project management practices in place	DG managing projects	
		Roll out initial DG functions	Kick off initial stewards and projects	DG Program Kickoff
			Kick off DG organization	DG Program Kickoff

Phase	Activity	Tasks	Outputs/ Subtasks	Subtask Outputs
			Present initial road shows	DG Road Shows
			Publish guidelines and principles	DG principles and policies
			Implement DG policies/procedures orientation and training	DG training
			Publish and implement SDLC integration documentation	SDLC changes
			Develop and conduct DG audit processes training	DG audit processes training
			Initiate DG audit processes	DG audits processes in place
			Identify and define additional rollout activity for the sustaining phase	Additional activity as required
		Implement DG program metrics		DG metrics definitions
				DG/sustaining metrics comparison
				Metrics presentation
				Metrics collection mechanism
				A set of metrics that are deployed and being used to report on effectiveness of DG/IAM
		Implement tools and technology		DG tools
		DG operations	Promote and interact with change management	Operational DG
			Perform and review audits and service levels	Operational DG

(Continued)

Phase	Activity	Tasks	Outputs/ Subtasks	Subtask Outputs
			Interact with governing bodies, data governance committees, and councils	Operational DG
			Perform operations and functions of DG framework - data governance committees and councils	Operational DG
	Execute the Change Management Plan	Communication plan execution	Communication events	
		Training development and delivery	Training events	
		Transition staff to new roles (if required)	Transitioned staff	
		Feedback and analysis of results	DG sustaining feedback	
		Perform leadership alignment checkpoint	Leadership alignment update	
		Perform organizational impact analysis	Impact of DG on organization	
		Manage resistance	Remediated resistance	
		Manage implementation of DG checklist	DG checklist	
		Refine materials for training, orientation, road shows, etc.	Refined materials	
		Develop additional advocates if necessary	Revised sponsors	
		Communicate short-term wins	Short-term win communications	
		Communicate status and measurements of progress, often to leadership	DG Progress Scorecard	
		Address problem areas aggressively	Issues resolution log	

Phase	Activity	Tasks	Outputs/ Subtasks	Subtask Outputs
	DG Project Management	Orient major project steering bodies	Awareness of ongoing operation of DG	
		Align DG project management activity with existing IT practices	DG/IT practice aligned	
		Identify project templates	DG project templates	
		Identify DG project estimating tools	DG estimating	
		Identify DG tracking and accounting procedures for IT	DG tracking	
		Forecast DG project resources	DG resources	
		Utilize modified SDLC	DG enhanced work products	
		Interact with enterprise PMO (if one exists)	PMO DG interaction	
	Confirm operation and effectiveness of DG operations	Evaluate organization structure	Verified DG organization	
		Confirm effectiveness of jobs/people	Verified role transitions	
		Verify policies/ procedures	Verified policies	
		Review incentives	Verified incentives	
		Monitor and report sustaining metrics	DG Scorecard	
		Execute measurement surveys (if designed)	DG surveys	
		Hold focus groups/ interviews for feedback	DG focus group feedback	
		Execute change integration checklist	DG sustaining checklist	
		Change integration/ adoption assessment	Change adoption assessment	
		Realign impacted policies/practices and procedures	Realigned DG policies	
		Revise staff performance objectives and reward structures	Revised incentives for DG	

Appendix 2

The Change Capacity Assessment identified can classifies the types of issues the organization will have adapting to data governance.

#	Survey Questions	Strongly Disagree 1	Disagree 2	Neutral or Undecided 3	Agree 4	Strongly Agree 5
1	I understand the rational for, and the focus of, the upcoming changes					
2	Our senior leadership has communicated a clear and compelling reason for why change is critical to the organization's long-term success					
3	People in the organization feel they can speak candidly to anyone, even if their views are contrary to leadership's					
4	Previous changes in the organization have been well-managed (i.e., we have a good track record of managing change)					
5	I am confident that I will have the opportunity to express my opinions and make suggestions about upcoming changes					

(Continued)

197

#	Survey Questions	Strongly Disagree 1	Disagree 2	Neutral or Undecided 3	Agree 4	Strongly Agree 5
6	I am confident that my opinions and suggestions will be given fair consideration					
7	I am confident that barriers to success of the change will be identified quickly and addressed					
8	Our senior leadership is aligned and committed to making the changes that will best position us for success					
9	The way people think and act in my work unit will be compatible with the changes that are determined to be necessary					
10	Although we haven't yet identified the specific changes that will be implemented, I trust that the organization will provide me with the resources needed to be successful in the future					
11	People throughout the organization understand the implications of the change for their areas of responsibility and feel that the change is *urgently* needed					
12	I believe that by improving our business processes and technology, I will be able to make more valuable contributions to the organization in the future than I can today					

13	I am confident that I will receive honest and accurate information about the change initiative and its impact				
14	People throughout the organization feel that changes to our business processes are urgently needed				
15	The risk and issues associated with the change have been identified in advance and appropriate actions have been taken to reduce their impact				
16	I am confident in my own ability to successfully implement any required changes that are identified				
17	I am the type of person that naturally embraces work-related changes				
18	I would be willing to function as a change advocate, helping my co-workers and business partners to embrace and implement the necessary changes				
19	I believe that the organization will be even more successful in the future as a result of the changes				
20	Our people have the skills, interest, and commitment to support the upcoming change initiatives				

(Continued)

#	Survey Questions	Strongly Disagree	Disagree	Neutral or Undecided	Agree	Strongly Agree
		1	2	3	4	5
21	Communication regarding the changes is open, direct and regular					
22	Expected business results have been clearly identified up front targets set, and measures established					
	Open-ended questions					
23	What are the biggest challenges we face in making these changes?					
24	What have been the biggest contributors to the success or failure of other major change initiatives in which you have taken part?					
25	What are the organization's greatest strengths in addressing these kinds of changes?					
26	What are the best ways for us to provide support to you for the upcoming changes?					

The Information Maturity Assessment identifies how well the organization can manage and use information relative to externally defined stages.

#	Survey Questions	Strongly Disagree 1	Disagree 2	Neutral or Undecided 3	Agree 4	Strongly Agree 5
1	The enterprise has published principles on how we will view and handle data and information					
2	There are standards for how data is presented to all users					
3	There are policies for managing data that are published					
4	The data policies are understood and adhered to consistently					
5	There are rules for sharing and moving data in and out of the company					
6	There is a widespread understanding of the importance of data quality					
7	People are willing to be held accountable to a single standard of data quality					
8	Data controls are adequate enough so we trust all numbers and information that is published					
9	We can easily tie our need for information to specific business programs					
10	Our transaction systems have all the data we need to do reporting					
11	Data controls are adequate and we do not worry about regulatory issues due to data issues					
12	My department owns the data we use; that is, we are responsible for using it accurately and correctly					

(Continued)

#	Survey Questions	Strongly Disagree	Disagree	Neutral or Undecided	Agree	Strongly Agree
		1	2	3	4	5
13	The numbers my department reports to management are accurate					
14	The reports we produce sometimes disagree with similar reports produced in other areas					
15	The role of IT is to deliver data to me so I can analyze it and do all of my reports					
16	We use different people to do analytics than generate reports					
17	We have too many things to do to take time for data standards					
18	My company adapts quickly to changing business circumstances					
19	We are good at data analysis—very few decisions are "gut"					
20	We cannot finish anything					
21	My department has several data bases, spreadsheets or other data stores that we build and use to do reports					
22	I have the knowledge available to me to meet my department's goals					
23	If I have to I gather the data we need regardless of guidance from IT and standards					
24	My company operates on experience and gut feel					
25	Knowledge is freely shared between members of my group and others no matter what functional area they come from					
26	I understand the key indicators that measure my organization's performance					
27	My company recognizes trends that signal obstacles or opportunities for company performance					

28	I collect and analyze information related to my work						
29	I use data analysis to make changes in my work processes to improve performance						
30	There are standards within IT for describing data						
31	My department has to do its own data collection since IT cannot deliver in a timely fashion						
32	I have the knowledge available to me to help achieve company goals						

The Collaborative assessment identifies the ability of the organization to use facilities that promote cross-functional work. There may or may not be overlap in this and the Change Capacity Assessment. It depends on organization size and the scope of data governance.

#	Survey Questions	Strongly Disagree 1	Disagree 2	Neutral or Undecided 3	Agree 4	Strongly Agree 5
1	Do you feel that you can call, email or talk to a co-worker in another department about a process issue that affects both of you with some action being enabled by the conversation?					
2	Are your work processes inhibited by "siloed" functional areas and organizational hierarchies?					
3	Are your work processes inhibited by a lack of management communication?					
4	Are your work processes inhibited by leadership priorities?					
5	Do you understand other functional areas' work goals and objectives?					
6	Do you and your co-workers understand each other's work-related problems and difficulties?					
7	Can you and your co-workers change a process if it is not working effectively?					
8	Do you know what other functional areas are involved in your work processes?					
9	Do you feel that your organization adapts effectively to changing business circumstances?					
10	Do you think the organization believes sharing "Lessons Learned" with others helps improve performance?					

11	How freely is knowledge shared between the members of your group and team, no matter what functional area they come from?				
12	Do other work groups or teams from other functional areas have any responsibility that affects your work processes?				
13	Do other work groups communicate with you?				
14	Do you feel you can follow-up with other work groups regarding questions at any time you need clarification?				

Appendix 3
Data Governance Charters Template

INTRODUCTION

The charter is a critical document for a data governance program. It has several purposes:

1) Set out the operating framework
2) Document the purpose and objectives of the program
3) Identify the various components, such as councils or sponsors
4) Establish the level of authority the DG operating bodies will have
5) Identify the type of federation
6) Identify the names of participants

Consider that you may need a charter for each "layer" of your operating framework. A separate charter for sponsors, councils, and forums might be necessary in larger organizations.

The charter is a living document, and should adapt to the growth and changes in data governance as the program evolves. Below is a basic outline featuring important aspects of charter documents, along with an explanation of each section.

Background

State what brought about the DG program. An MDM effort? Or a general program (EIM) to better manage all data and information?

Purpose of the DG Charter

State the purpose of the charter. Is it emphasizing scope? Is there a DG Office that will oversee the program or is there an informal virtual operating framework? Is it describing all of the DG areas or one specific area? Describe the scope of the DG program.

Terminology

Very often a lot of new terms appear. Terms like MDM and data quality should be defined if they are key concepts integral to the DG program.

EIM Vision and Mission

If the DG program is a component of a general move towards enterprise information management, then make sure the Vision and Mission of the EIM program is described . Describe the context of DG within the EIM program.

Objectives

Describe the *specific* measurable objectives of the DG program. What are the standards to be achieved that prove DG is working?

Reporting and Metrics

Related to the objectives, what metrics are to be collected and reported?

Value Proposition

Describe how the organization will be improved by implementing data governance.

IG Operating Framework Summary

Describe the various arrangements and interactions of the organizational elements that will operate data governance. This means describing roles, responsibilities, and core processes.

Data Governance Council

One key area is the council that will essentially manage data governance. Describe the following key characteristics:

○ Touch points – Where will the council touch the organization?
○ Structure – Is it a formal hierarchy, a virtual body, a dedicated area (rarely)?
○ DG Council's Vision for Information Management – Describe how is the council supposed to view the formal management of information assets. This includes their:
  1. Roles
  2. Processes/Tasks
  3. Responsibilities
  4. Representation
  5. Sub Teams

DG Office

There is usually a small coordinating body, usually virtual in nature, that acts as the permanent first point of contact for data governance. Even in the largest companies it is only a few people.

DG Forums

Describe the forums, or the operating groups, that report to the council. This will be made up of stewards and custodians as well as personnel preforming information management duties. Also describe their vision for information management.

1. Roles
2. Processes/Tasks
3. Responsibilities

4. Representation
5. Sub Teams

DG Executive(s) or Sponsor

There needs to be a sponsoring role. Describe this as you do the other roles, but make sure you also specify clearly the responsibility aspect before anything else. Sponsors have a tendency to fade away.

1. Responsibilities
2. Roles
3. Processes/Tasks

Logistics

This section describes how the data governance framework will execute its core operations.

1. Meetings
2. Voting
3. Communication

Authority

This section contains a clear statement as to the extent the data governance operating bodies can carry out the enforcement of standards. This section must be vetted by upper management and sponsorship and receive explicit approval.

Website

Describe the internal website(s) that contains information regaring DG, such as principles, policies, memberships, mission, visions, etc.

Document History

The charter is a living document. It needs to be flexible and easy to read. As such it will go through many changes.
    Amendments

Appendix 4

Data Governance Orientation and ongoing knowledge transfer template

Three LEVELS of Knowledge Transfer for Data Governance		
1 - Orientation	Understand vision, concepts, and value proposition so one can act and be visibly in support of change or activity	Master the WHY
2 - Education	Ensure that the desired activity or change takes place from accountability and the managerial view, what, why	Master the WHY and WHAT
3 - Training	Ensure action takes place from view of those responsible for execution, "feet on the ground"	Master the WHY, WHAT, and HOW

Level	Topic	Section Name (useful to create reusable decks)	Data Governance Council Orientation Template
Orientation	**Enterprise Information Asset Management**	Concepts of IAM	Concepts of IAM, Terms and Definitions
			General Vision of What IAM Looks Like
			Typical Mission, Vision, and Value Statements
			Ramification and Impact of IAM
			EIM Solutions Overview - MDM, BI, DQ, DG
Education	**Organization EIM Orientation**	Organization EIM Program Overview	Concepts of Organization for EIM
			Organization Vision for EIM
			Organization EIM Value Proposition
Orientation	**Data Governance**	DG Concepts	Definitions, Value, and Concepts
			Value of DG

(Continued)

Level	Topic	Section Name (useful to create reusable decks)	Data Governance Council Orientation Template
		DG Framework Requirements	Principles and Policies
			Best Practices
			Intro to Organization Framework for DG
			Intro to Organization Principles and Policies
Training	Enterprise Data Governance and Oversight	DG Orientation	Organization IG Framework (ITLC, IGC, CCC)
			EDG Value and Vision
			Intro to the V
		EIM Principles Orientation	EIM Principles Detail
	Organization Management	EIM & EDG Organization Overview	Organization IG Framework (leadership, sponsors, councils, forums)
	Enterprise Data Governance and Oversight	EIM Principles In Action	Organization Principles in Action
			Organization Policies Detail
		DG Operation	Organization DG Critical Processes (Issues, Policy Change, etc.)
			Organization DG Metrics
			Moving up and down the "V"
			Organization DG Road Map
	Sustaining Management	Organization Sustaining Requirements for EIM/ Organization EIM Overview	Organization EIM Change Management Overview
			EIM Culture Change Process
			EIM Maturity
			EIM EDG SWOT
			EDG Risk Areas
			OCM Resistance approaches
Ongoing Topics for Clarification	Ongoing Orientation	Concepts of IAM	Concepts of IAM, Terms and Definitions
			General Vision of What IAM Looks Like
			Typical Mission, Vision, and Value Statements
			Ramification and Impact of IAM
			EIM Solutions Overview - MDM, BI, DQ, DG
	Data Governance Value	Periodic Updates on the Value-add of DG	Key Metrics Reporting
			DG Brand and Meaning
			Changes in Business Alignment
	Data Governance Compliance	Periodic Review of the Enforcement and Effectiveness of Policy	Policy Rollout
			Process Effectiveness
			Issue Resolution

Level	Topic	Section Name (useful to create reusable decks)	Data Governance Council Orientation Template
	Organization Change Management	Progress of Organizational Change	Job Changes
			Incentive Progress
			Adjustments to Incentives
			OCM Metrics
			Ongoing Surveys for OCM

Appendix 5

	Information Management/Data Governance Functions	IM	DG	OCM
	This is a generic starter list of functions. Don't confuse these with the deployment tasks.			
Plan	Align data architecture with the enterprise business strategy.	x		
	Establish priorities for information projects.	x		
	Understand the goal for enterprise applications.	x		
	Understand the business model.	x		
	Develop a privacy policy for data collection use.	x	x	
	Align the information architecture with the enterprise business strategy (revise scenarios, levers).	x		
	Identify an approach to data governance.		x	
	Identify areas requiring governance.		x	
	Identify legal compliance areas.		x	
	Clarify the nature of the changes data governance will have.		x	
	Identify the key stakeholder groups and how they will be impacted: new skills, different behaviors, etc.	x	x	x
	Identify champions and sponsor(s).		x	x
	Understand the information management culture in which the change will occur.	x	x	x
	Classify resistance points.	x	x	x
	Develop a change management approach.			x
	Assess information maturity.	x		
	Assess the ability to change.			x
	Fund data and information solutions applications.	x		
	Establish the data technology infrastructure.	x		
Define	Establish data principles, policies, and standards.		x	
	Define data meaning and business rules.		x	
	Establish communications mechanism(s).		x	x
	Conduct promotion/information sessions.			x
	Confirm enterprise architecture principles with information principles.	x	x	

(Continued)

215

Information Management/Data Governance Functions	IM	DG	OCM
Develop concepts for designing interfaces to new applications to ensure the gradual expansion of data management.	x		
Plan the education program (usually for middle management and up).			x
Plan training (usually for middle management and below).			x
Define the process for metrics: performance, process, financial – maintenance.	x		
Develop processes for enterprise information content and delivery (data models).	x		
Develop and establish the enterprise metadata management environment.	x		
Define IM usage metrics to determine the effectiveness of IM.	x		
Develop application code management requirements for reusability and consistency.	x	x	
Define enterprise master data management (policies, design, processes).	x	x	
Identify and define enterprise metadata management requirements.	x	x	
Identify corporate hierarchies and maintenance processes.	x	x	
Create and maintain the IM Implementation Plan (road map).	x		
Determine IM technology requirements and establish a direction for IM technologies.	x		
Establish the Data Stewardship Council.		x	
Establish the Data Quality program.	x		
Define steward and owner dimensions, DG organization.		x	
Define IM roles and responsibilities.	x		
Consider the change management road map.			x
Prepare a detailed change management plan, with an emphasis on rewards, resistance, and measurement.			x
Define the IM organization structure.	x		
Determine the required education, training, and skill sets required to ensure success.			x
Acquire and maintain the appropriate skill sets to support IM.	x		x
Establish data access and data control guidelines and requirements.		x	
Design and maintain a metadata layer.	x	x	

	Information Management/Data Governance Functions	IM	DG	OCM
	Mediate and resolve conflicts pertaining to data.		x	
	Define business requirements for information systems.	x		
Manage	Enforce data principles, policies, and standards.		x	
	Manage data architecture, models, and definitions.	x		
	Manage the portfolio of information systems.	x		
	Refine the data governance rollout strategy and metrics.		x	
	Refine the information architecture rollout strategy and metrics.	x		
	Establish the Enterprise Information Architecture Governance Repository.		x	
	Periodically establish priorities for IS projects; consider value drivers and the roles of process and applications areas.	x		
	Validate IM alignment with business and strategic planning.	x		
	Track industry trends in enterprise data management and determine how to best leverage them in the IM architecture.	x		
	Integrate the change management plan with the overall project plan.		x	x
	Execute the change management plan in conjunction with the DG rollout.			x
	Develop processes for information management.	x		
	Manage the data technical infrastructure.	x		
Operate	Ensure data quality and integration (by subject).	x		
	Secure data.	x	x	
	Implement business processes and systems for data privacy.	x	x	
	Facilitate BI/ODS/DW design and maintenance (includes providing architecture and implementation).	x		
	Execute processes to support the data privacy policy.	x	x	
	Execute processes to support data access.	x	x	
	Execute processes to support data controls.	x	x	
	Implement regular metrics and the measurement of DG implementation.		x	

(*Continued*)

	Information Management/Data Governance Functions	IM	DG	OCM
	Realign policies/practices and procedures to clearly support the new IM and DG vision, not contradict it.	x	x	
	Develop Customer/Vendor/other Subject Area hierarchies.	x		
	Assess data quality (IS systems planning, implementation, and cycle production).	x		
	Determine the security requirements of enterprise data (including privacy and access).		x	
	Enforce the use of integrated and managed data.		x	
	Mediate and resolve conflicts pertaining to data.		x	
	Ensure business requirements are reflected in information requirements.	x		
	Create and maintain a logical enterprise data model, including mappings and aliases.	x		
	Define data and business rules.	x		
	Create and maintain project logical data models, including mappings and aliases.	x		
	Maintain modifications to Annual Strategy Planning, Strategy Execution, Solutions Delivery, and Project Portfolio Management.	x		
	Maintain policies for data collection and use (includes privacy, control, and data access).		x	
	Maintain business scenarios/use cases within process models.	x		
	Maintain metrics: performance, process, and financial.	x		
	Enforce enterprise master data management (policies, design, processes).		x	
	Facilitate physical data models (technical database design).	x		
	Evaluate and select the IM technology.	x		
	Install and maintain the IM technology.	x		
	Monitor and tune the IM technology.	x		
	Identify and resolve any IM technology problems.	x		
	Maintain and manage the business rules repository.	x		
	Maintain an accurate inventory of enterprise data management resources in all its forms in a CMDB (Configuration Management Database).	x		

	Information Management/Data Governance Functions	IM	DG	OCM
	Enforce data principles, policies, and standards.		x	
	Manage the portfolio of information systems (applications and infrastructure components).	x		
	Maintain the metadata layer.	x		
	Develop and support application systems.	x		
	Design and maintain the metadata layer.	x		
Sustain	Enable the appropriate access to data.	x		
	Use data for analysis and data mining.	x		
	Provide guidance, education, and assistance in the support of data access.	x		x
	Update staff performance objectives and reward structures to reflect new accountabilities and compliance to new rules.			x
	New roles/responsibilities must be clearly defined and communicated, and the staff must be trained in new skills where needed.			x
	Continuous improvement mindset — take lessons learned and use them to improve.			x
	Visible and vocal leadership support.			x
	Provide guidance, education, and assistance in support of data usage.	x		
	Oversee data integration and transformation.	x		
	Maintain IM Portal Content.	x		
	Roll out the education program.			x
	Conduct training.			x
	Maintain the alignment of IM across all organizations.	x		
	Monitor and ensure that data usage adheres to privacy and regulatory requirements.		x	
	Ensure the design of interfaces to new applications to make certain of the gradual expansion of data management.	x		
	Create and maintain a logical enterprise data model for third-party applications, including mappings and aliases.	x		
	Apply the retention policy as described.		x	
	Execute an ongoing survey of cultural temperament.			x
	Adjust change management as required.			x
	Promote collaborative communities and communities of interest.	x		
	Sell/promote information sharing.			x

Appendix 6

Stakeholder Analysis

What is a stakeholder?	What is their role?	How will they react?	What will be their primary concerns?	What do we need from them?	How should we work with them?
A stakeholder is any organization or person that:	Identify each stakeholder's role or roles. Will this stakeholder:	How will the results of the effort be likely to impact the stakeholder? Will this stakeholder benefit or be adversely affected?	What are the primary concerns of this stakeholder?	What do we need from this stakeholder?	Given what we know, how should we work with this stakeholder?
✔ Can influence the change	✔ Need to approve resources and/or decide whether the change can proceed (thus acting as a sponsor or gatekeeper)?	Given the likely impact and prior behavior, how is this stakeholder likely to react?	✔ What do they need or expect from the change?	✔ Approval/ resources	✔ How will we prepare them for the change?
✔ Is affected by the change			✔ What might influence whether they are supportive of the change?	✔ Visible support/ public endorsement	✔ How will we communicate with them?
✔ Stakeholders can be:	✔ Need to change as a result of the effort (a target)?	✔ Vocal, visible support?	✔ What will this stakeholder need to feel informed, involved, prepared, or validated during the change?	✔ Access to them	✔ How will we address their needs/concerns?
✔ Individuals	✔ Need to implement changes or convince others to change (an agent)?	✔ Cooperative, quiet?		✔ Access to people on their team	✔ Do we need to learn more about their needs, concerns, or likely reaction?
✔ Senior leaders		✔ On the fence?	✔ What are the "red flags" or hot buttons for this stakeholder?	✔ Lack of interference with or blocking of the effort	
✔ Groups of employees such as IT or division managers	✔ React to or judge the success of the effort?	✔ Say ok but be obstructive or complain behind the scenes?		✔ Information	✔ Should they be part of the change team directly or indirectly involved (be a representative on the team, solicit input, or provide regular feedback)?
✔ Committees	✔ Need to be an advocate of the effort (a champion)?	✔ Express concerns vocally?		✔ Task completion	
✔ Customers				✔ Flexibility	
✔ Government or other regulatory agencies	✔ Perform work that can influence the success of the effort (a resource)?			✔ Change in behavior	
✔ Brokers/agents					

Appendix 7

Leadership Alignment Assessment

Question	Purpose
What do you think the ultimate contribution of data governance will be for your organization?	Measures alignment around the data governance vision, the organization's goals, and the true purpose of the anticipated changes.
What do you see as the major issues in successfully implementing data governance? What can be done to address them?	Provides perspective on what's critical to successful implementation (specific actions, issues, or processes). Measures alignment around what needs to be done now to improve the chances of success.
Is data governance an incremental or transformational change for the organization?	Measures alignment around perceptions of data governance impact on the organization and the need for change leadership behavior from the leadership team.
What do you think are the best ways to encourage positive reception of data governance by key stakeholder groups inside and outside of the organization?	Measures alignment around the most effective approaches to the stakeholder. Stakeholder groups could include branches, home office functions, service centers, IT departments, producers, customers, and others.
What is your definition of success for data governance?	Determines alignment among the organization's leaders as to what success with data governance means. A common definition of success drives common actions and behaviors.
Who's accountable for delivering on data governance results?	Measures alignment around roles and responsibilities, and who is ultimately responsible.
What do you think your role is as a leader in making data governance a success?	Measures alignment around leadership accountability and where authority for decisions will be situated.
What are your biggest concerns about the changes that data governance will drive? How would you address those concerns?	Provides some insight into what the concerns are among the organization's leadership. Measures the degree of alignment about areas of concern.
What other periods of significant change have you experienced in your time with the organization?	Gauges the change leadership has experienced and the skill level of the organization's leadership overall. Provides insight into the organization's history with change and methods that have been effective or ineffective.

Appendix 8

Communications Plan

A Communications Plan should be developed early in the life of the project to ensure that communication needs are identified and plans are established to meet those needs. The Communications Plan identifies who needs information, what information they need, the frequency and vehicles for communication, and the parties responsible for providing, consolidating, and disseminating the information. By providing a structured plan, we ensure that each stakeholder gets what he or she needs when they need it.

Event	Target Audience	Purpose & Objective	Timing, Frequency, & Location	Description and Vehicles	Responsibilities – Sender, Creator	Feedback Mechanism
Provide the name of the communication	Detail the recipients of the information	Provide the purpose of the communication	Provide frequency of communication (e.g., one-time, every Friday at 10 am in conference room a), date, and, if appropriate, a location.	Describe the communication in terms of contents, format, delivery medium	List who is responsible for creating the communication as well as who is responsible for providing input	Describe the means to explain how the communications mechanism is working
Executive Steering Committee Meetings	Executive Steering Committee	Update committee members on project status Approve EIM projects/initiatives Set direction for EIM and EIM	Monthly	Meetings, status reports	Executive Sponsor	Immediate discussion and comments captured in meeting minutes
Data Governance Council Meetings	Working Steering Committee	Update committee members on project status Resolve issues Confirm direction	Monthly	Meetings, status reports	Data Governance Council	Comments captured in meeting minutes
Data Management Committee Meetings	Committee Members	Allow the team to address issues relating to the quality of data and other data issues Provide direction and decision-making at the stall level Forum for escalating issues to DGC	As Needed	Meetings	Committee Lead	Immediate discussion and comments captured in meeting minutes

(Continued)

Event	Target Audience	Purpose & Objective	Timing, Frequency, & Location	Description and Vehicles	Responsibilities — Sender, Creator	Feedback Mechanism
Executive Cascade	EIM SC DGC	Key points, action items, and to-do's for cascading key EIM Project messages down to their organizations	Monthly	Email or SP	Director, EIM	Event Feedback Form
Executive Toolkit	EIM SC DGC	Slides, scorecards, other files, and to-do's for cascading EIM Project messages down to their organization	Monthly	Email SP	Director, EIM	Event Feedback Form
EIM Project Team Meetings	Team Leads Project Manager Team Members	Review status Review issues Identify, analyze, and mitigate project risks	Weekly	Meetings or Conference call	Project Manager	Action items, decisions and status as captured in meeting minutes
OCM Meetings	Sustaining Mgmt Team Project Manager Sponsor	Review status of sustaining activities Identify issues and risks Fine-tune plan based on progress	Monthly (after Comm Plan and Education Plan are completed and accepted by Sponsor)	Meeting or conference call	SMT/OCM Lead	Action items, decisions, and status as captured in meeting minutes
"Did You Know"	All Stakeholders	Promote tidbits and new information about data quality and data governance The "hooks" — What's in it for me?	Weekly	Farfel web	EIM Team	Embed questions and opportunities to win prizes for those who visit the portal to review information
Monthly DG Update	Data Governance Committee	Where is DG in terms of status, progress, and maturity?	Monthly	Metrics and status report	DG Team, Data Management Committee	Review instances for completeness
Monthly EIM Update	All Stakeholders	What is complete and where is EIM with the transformation, maturity, and update of the DW Roadmap and DW projects?	Monthly	Newsletter — create list of EIM staff and key stakeholders	EIM Team	Review instances for completeness

Event	Target Audience	Purpose & Objective	Timing, Frequency, & Location	Description and Vehicles	Responsibilities — Sender, Creator	Feedback Mechanism
Data Steward Forums	Data Stewards	Allow the team to discuss tips and techniques for managing data quality Obtain direct input from forum lead on issues and concerns Information sharing	Quarterly	Meetings	Manager DQ	Action items, decisions, and status as captured in meeting minutes
Leave Behind	All employees	Keep IG/IM in front of mind	As needed	Mouse pad Brochure Mug	OCM Team	Review instances for completeness
Public Reminder	All employees	Keep IG/IM front of mind	As needed	Posters	DG Team, Data Management Committee	Review instances for completeness

Appendix 9

Training Plan Example

Track	Track	Topic	Unit	Class #			Module Name	Abstracts	Audience	Date
				Level	Unit	Level				
100	EIM Fundamentals	Enterprise Information Asset Management	n/a	100	001	1	Concepts of IAM	Concepts of IAM, General Vision, Mission Value Prop., & Ramifications of EIM, Definition of EIM solutions (MDM etc.)	Custodians, Stewards, Councils	
200	EDG Fundamentals	Information Governance	n/a	200	002	1	DG Concepts	Definitions, Value and Concepts	Custodians, Stewards, Councils	
				200	002	2	DG Framework Requirements for ACME	Principles and Policies; Best Practices, Intro to ACME DG Framework	Custodians, Stewards	
300	ACME EIM EDG Knowledge Transfer	ACME EIM Orientation	Basic Program Overview	300	101	1	ACME EIM Program Overview	Concepts of ACME EIM, ACME Vision, Value Prop. at EIM	Custodians, Stewards, Councils	
		Enterprise Data Governance and	Data Governance Processes, Organizations	300	102	1	DG Orientation	ACME DG Framework, Incl. Principles, Value and	Custodians, Stewards, Councils	
		Oversight	EIM Guiding Principles, Supporting Policies				EIM Principles Orientation	Vision, The "V"	Custodians, Stewards, DGC	

(continued)

Track	Track	Topic	Unit	Class # Level	Class # Unit	Class # Level	Module Name	Abstracts	Audience	Date
			Data Governance Processes, Organizations	300	102	2	DG Operation	ACME DG Road Map, Policies and Measurements	Custodians, Stewards, DGC	
			EIM Guiding Principles, Supporting Policies				EIM Principles In Action	Framework, Critical Process Review, The "V"	Custodians, Stewards, DGC	
		Organization Management	Enterprise Information Architecture and Management Organization	300	116	1	ACME EIM/ ACME EDG Organization Overview	Concepts, Role Names of EIM and EDG Organizations	DGC, Stewards	
		Sustaining Management	Initial Organizational Change Management	300	117	1	ACME Sustaining Requirements for EIM/ACME EIM Overview	ACME EIM Change Management Overview, Process, Maturity, SWOT, Risk Areas, Resistance Management Approaches	DGC	
		ACME EIM Road Map	ACME EIM Business Case/ Alignment	300	125	1	ACME EIM Road Map Orientation	ACME Road Map Overview, Maturity Levels, Metrics, Success Criteria	DGC, Stewards	
			ACME EIM Success Measures							
			Recommended Support/ Application Projects				ACME EIM Projects	EIM Project Overview	DGC, Stewards	
			Incremental Phased Rollout Timeline				ACME EIM Project Update			

Appendix 10

Post-rollout Checklist

	Yes	To Some Degree	No
Are leaders acting as sponsors for and supportive of the new environment?			
Is the staff excited about the changes that are coming?			
Is there a safe outlet for feedback (such as reactions, concerns, and comments) for everyone?			
Is there adequate support for people to do their jobs effectively?			
Do people have time to do their jobs effectively?			
Does the organization have the skills/ competencies to get the job done?			
Has the organization been trained in the new skills/competencies they require?			
Have competencies and capabilities been built effectively so that objectives are met and results are achieved?			
Are there comparisons of progress against metrics and targets?			
Have new performance measurement and reward systems been implemented?			
Are we tracking performance that achieves results?			
Do we publically recognize individuals who demonstrate desired behaviors so that objectives are met and results are achieved?			
Do we acquire and place talent in a way that ensures objectives are met and results are achieved?			
Is the organization structure appropriate for the future state?			
Does our organization structure ensure that objectives are met and that results are achieved?			

Index

Note: Page numbers with "f" denote figures; "t" tables; "b" boxes

Related Titles from Morgan Kaufmann

Master Data Management
David Loshin
ISBN: 9780123742254

The Practitioner's Guide to Data Quality Improvement
David Loshin
ISBN: 9780123737175

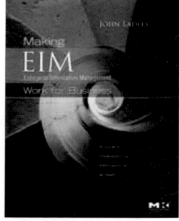

Making Enterprise Information Management (EIM) Work for Business
A Guide to Understanding Information as an Asset
John Ladley
ISBN: 9780123756954

Data Architecture from Zen to Reality
Charles D. Tupper
ISBN: 9780123851260

Data Mining, Third Edition
Concepts and Techniques
Jiawei Han, Micheline Kamber, and Jian Pei
ISBN: 9780123814791

Data Mining, Third Edition
Practical Machine Learning Tools and Techniques
Ian H. Witten, Eibe Frank, and Mark A. Hall
ISBN: 9780123748560

mkp.com

Made in the USA
Lexington, KY
06 May 2018